ED KENNEDY'S WAR

From Our Own Correspondent
JOHN MAXWELL HAMILTON, SERIES EDITOR

Illuminating the development of foreign news gathering at a time when it has never been more important, "From Our Own Correspondent" is a series of books that features forgotten works and unpublished memoirs by pioneering foreign correspondents. Series editor John Maxwell Hamilton, once a foreign correspondent himself, is the founding dean of the Manship School of Mass Communication at Louisiana State University and currently the executive vice chancellor and provost of LSU.

ED KENNEDY'S WAR: V-E DAY, CENSORSHIP, & THE ASSOCIATED PRESS

Edited, with a Prologue and Epilogue, by
JULIA KENNEDY COCHRAN

With an Introduction by
TOM CURLEY and
JOHN MAXWELL HAMILTON

LOUISIANA STATE UNIVERSITY PRESS
BATON ROUGE

Published by Louisiana State University Press
Copyright © 2012 by Julia Kennedy Cochran and Louisiana State University Press
All rights reserved
Manufactured in the United States of America
First printing

DESIGNER: Michelle A. Neustrom
TYPEFACE: Chaparral Pro
PRINTER: McNaughton & Gunn, Inc.
BINDER: Acme Bookbinding

LIBRARY OF CONGRESS CATALOGING-IN-PUBLICATION DATA

Kennedy, Ed, 1905–1963.
  Ed Kennedy's war : V-E Day, censorship, and the Associated Press / Ed Kennedy ; edited, with a prologue and epilogue, by Julia Kennedy Cochran ; with an introduction by Tom Curley and John Maxwell
Hamilton.
      p. cm. — (From our own correspondent)
  Includes bibliographical references.
  ISBN 978-0-8071-4525-8 (cloth : alk. paper) — ISBN 978-0-8071-4526-5 (pdf) — ISBN 978-0-8071-
4527-2 (epub) — ISBN 978-0-8071-4528-9 (mobi) 1. Kennedy, Ed, 1905–1963. 2. World War, 1939–
1945—Press coverage. 3. World War, 1939–1945—Censorship. 4. World War, 1939–1945—Personal
narratives, American. 5. V-E Day, 1945. 6. Government and the press—United States—History—20th
century. 7. War correspondents—United States—Biography. 8. Associated Press—Biography.
9. Associated Press—History—20th century. I. Cochran, Julia Kennedy, 1947– II. Title.
  D799.U6K46 2012
  070.4'4994053092—dc23

                                                                                                2011043189

Contents

Illustrations follow page 100

Introduction

TOM CURLEY AND JOHN MAXWELL HAMILTON

AT 3:24 P.M., MAY 7, 1945, THE PHONE RANG IN THE LONDON
bureau of the Associated Press.[1] The newsroom, as later described, was
filled with cigarette smoke and anticipation. Hitler and Mussolini were
dead. The Russians were in Berlin. German forces had surrendered in
Baldham, Breslau, the Netherlands, and elsewhere. Allied forces occupied
Flensburg, on the Danish border, where the caretaker Reich Government
was now located. Allied heads of state were writing victory speeches,
their staffs planning celebrations. But when would the war officially end?

Now, with the ringing phone, the answer came. "This is Paris calling,"
said a faint voice over a military line. Lewis Hawkins could not recognize
the caller's voice. He asked for verification. Edward Kennedy, the head of
the Paris bureau, got on the phone.

"This is Ed Kennedy, Lew. Germany has surrendered unconditionally.
That's surrendered unconditionally. That's official. Make the date Reims,
France, and get it out."

The London staff took dictation until the connection, which faded in
and out, went dead in the middle of a quote from German general Alfred
Jodl, chief of operations staff in the German High Command, who had
signed the surrender document at Reims. Kennedy had sent about three
hundred words.

"Well," said Kennedy to his staff after hanging up the phone, "now let's
see what happens."[2]

Within minutes, the AP had the story out on the wires. Radio stations across the United States interrupted programming to announce
the news. Newspapers flooded the streets with extra editions. Kennedy's

byline appeared under a highly unusual four-line headline spread across the front page of the *New York Times*.

This should have been a moment of triumph for the AP war reporter. But it was not, as explained by a press report the next day:

> Edward Kennedy, chief of The Associated Press Western Front staff, who scored the news beat—acclaimed by editors throughout the United States as one of the greatest in newspaper history—was indefinitely suspended from all further dispatching facilities by Supreme Headquarters in Paris.[3]

What had Kennedy done wrong? He and sixteen other reporters had been allowed to witness the middle-of-the-night German surrender to General Dwight D. Eisenhower at his Reims headquarters on the condition of holding the story until given the green light. Then, on the afternoon of May 7, when the correspondents were back in Paris, a German radio broadcast from Flensburg announced the "unconditional capitulation of all fighting troops." Kennedy, who suspected Allied forces had authorized the broadcast, considered the embargo voided and told a senior Army censor he no longer felt obliged to uphold the agreement. Using a military phone connection to London that was not subject to censorship, Kennedy broke the story. British censors, having no brief for handling surrender stories and, in any case, dealing with a story from abroad where other censors had responsibility, raised no objections.

The lifting of Kennedy's credentials was only the beginning of his troubles. Furious and embarrassed at being beaten, fellow correspondents the next day gathered at the Hotel Scribe, where Allied press operations were centralized, and voted 54–2 to condemn him for "the most disgraceful, deliberate and unethical double-cross in the history of journalism."[4] On May 10, midday New York time, the president of the AP board, Robert McLean of the *Philadelphia Bulletin*, came forth with a statement saying the AP "profoundly" regretted the story. Kent Cooper, the general manager of the AP, recalled Kennedy.* When the correspondent's ship landed in New York on June 4, Kennedy told the group of journalists who interviewed him that he had done nothing wrong. "I

---

*Today the head of the AP board carries the title of chairman, not president; the chief executive officer (known as the general manager until 1985) is the president and CEO.

would do it again. The war was over; there was no military security involved, and the people had the right to know."[5] At first put on indefinite suspension by Cooper, then quietly let go, his promising career with the Associated Press was over. Kennedy was forty years old.

The owner of the *Santa Barbara News-Press* in California, who thought Kennedy was in the right, hired him as the paper's managing editor.[6] Kennedy was struck by an automobile in 1963 and died five days later, age fifty-eight. This memoir of his career in the Associated Press foreign service has never been published.

* * *

By the end of World War II, Edward Kennedy had become one of the AP's most respected reporters in the field. His experience was so deep and varied that very few people—journalist, diplomat, soldier—could match him. Even with the massive improvements in communication and travel that have come since, he stands out.

Kennedy embraced international adventure at a young age. He headed to Paris in 1927 as a student, enjoying the heady atmosphere and staying until his wallet was empty. He returned four years later, living on meager wages working for the *Chicago Tribune*'s Paris newspaper, which along with the Paris *Herald* was an incubator of many of the century's greatest correspondents. Once back in the United States, he hitched up to the Associated Press, which became an express ticket back to Europe. After stints in AP bureaus in Pittsburgh and Washington, D.C., and an obligatory stop at the New York foreign desk, he arrived in Paris in September 1935 at the moment the League of Nations fumbled its and the world's future in failing to stand up to Fascist aggression.

Kennedy built his AP career country by country, battle by battle. He observed Fascists in Spain and Italy. He covered the ugliness of French colonial rule in northern Africa and Syria. He was posted in Cairo, then subject to English rule, and he was sent throughout Eastern Europe and the Balkans, torn seemingly forever by ethnic blood feuds. He observed inefficient and shaky regimes in these places—rulers who were not up to the jobs and who wouldn't hold them for long.

Kennedy was in Cairo when the United States entered the war in 1941. In the coming months he became responsible for all Middle Eastern and

North African war coverage. In 1944, he covered the Seventh Army's invasion of southern France and, with a few other reporters, a jeep, and a soldier as driver, headed north through Maquis territory. Task Force Kennedy, as they called themselves, had their credentials temporarily revoked when they reached Paris. Authorities were angry they had moved across command areas without authorization.[7]

Credentialing—and the access and support it provided—was a direct way of controlling correspondents. The journalists could not function if they were cut off from communications facilities or blocked from travel to the field with military units. Equally heavy-handed was censorship. Nothing was sent home that a censor did not approve. But more subtle ways to shape news were just as effective.

One technique was to encourage the kind of reporting that made Ernie Pyle famous. "Correspondents acquired the habit of giving in their dispatches the names, address, and favorite 'girl friends' of the G.I.'s to whom they talked," observed historian Joseph Mathews. "Public relations officers set up special units to see that a steady flow of accounts went to home-town papers about local boys."[8]

Shared danger with GIs and the need to find good stories that passed the censor also led correspondents to first-person reporting that the military abetted. True to its tradition of avoiding sensationalism, the *Christian Science Monitor* instructed its reporters not to "soup-it-up." Nevertheless it carried plenty of stories like this: "As I am writing this, with the shells of our artillery batteries rushing overhead. . . ."[9] When a correspondent with a Canadian newspaper, the *Montreal Standard,* took shrapnel in his buttocks, he burst out, "What a story! What a story!"[10] An Australian correspondent wrote a parody of such stories and sent it to his paper, the *Melbourne Herald.* His editors thought the account was the real thing and published it.

The AP, too, relished this kind of reporting. Correspondents Don Whitehead and Hal Boyle excelled at Pyle's hometown approach.[11] Kennedy himself wrote a stirring account of flying on a bomber over Greece in 1942. "For me, this is a special day," he reported:

A year and a half ago I was bombed from the Olympus line to Thermopylae, then to Piraeus, bombed again at sea, dive-bombed in Suda Bay and machine-gunned as I slept under olive trees in Crete. I finally arrived in Egypt with a brave but defeated Army so "bomb happy" I could hardly write the story.

I felt then we would return to Greece one day. But I never thought it would be like this—to be taken there by our own American planes, to be with Americans like these and to be on the giving instead of the taking end of a bombing. [12]

Editors and generals liked these stories because they resonated with readers at home. And, in fact, there was much to commend them. Here was news that gave a sense of what the war was like. Being at the front also was a way to support the troops. As Kennedy observes in this book, "The presence of correspondents had an effect on the morale of combat troops—it made them feel that they were not forgotten, that the people at home were following their every move." Even so, these small-bore stories did not come close to telling the whole story.

Kennedy found much of the censorship more amusing than threatening. In his memoir, he is philosophical about some of the sillier episodes. "This flood of written and vocal matter was, in the main, the Army's opinion of the Army. It was usually a high opinion." Or, "If you give a man a blue pencil and the authority of a censor, strange things happen to him." But censors crossed out much about the war that was important. Not one story on American atrocities was reported during World War II.[13] Grisly photos of dead Americans or traumatized troops were blocked. It was a struggle to report details of military blunders. This is why correspondents such as Kennedy were so important. While he could write about "our boys" in foxholes and thrilling first-person accounts of bombing missions, he constantly butted against news restrictions.

Kennedy did it all well. He was beloved by colleagues and respected by the people he covered. Rising in the ranks of the AP, he was entrusted with managing the huge and complicated logistics of covering massive military operations on the fly across an immense territory—the toughest role in journalism.

Kennedy was self-assured, a trait developed over many years of operating independently on significant assignments. At one point he said he had more scoops than any other war correspondent, not to brag but to point out that he didn't need another scoop to make a career or earn someone's respect. He published his story on the German surrender because he thought it the right thing to do.

* * *

What should the verdict on Kennedy's decision be? That of the AP management, which dismissed him? Or his own? Today, when the techniques to control and distort news have become increasingly sophisticated, this question has become poignantly relevant. Kennedy details his actions and reasoning in this memoir. Here we add historical context, new facts gleaned from the AP archives and declassified military files in the National Archives, and our own judgment.

Context is important, starting with this: A new president, Harry Truman, had recanted Franklin D. Roosevelt's pledge that the only censorship imposed by the United States would be to protect the safety of the fighting forces. Truman's decision to hold the Reims surrender story so the Russians could stage their own Berlin surrender ceremony was purely political. General Frank Allen, Eisenhower's chief public affairs officer, was clear about this in explaining the embargo to the correspondents in Reims. "General Eisenhower," he said, "is desirous of having the news announced immediately for its possible effect in saving lives, but his hands are tied at a high political level."[14]

Kennedy was a thoughtful, deeply serious reporter. His responsibilities weighed on him. AP executive Alan Gould described him as "intense and sometimes moody."[15] When he heard the German broadcast announcing the war was over, Kennedy didn't rush to print. But he was angry about the continuing embargo, and his frustrations, after so many months of dealing with censorship, spilled out. He tried protesting directly to the chief of Allied public relations, but General Allen was not available. He next went to Allen's aide, a lieutenant colonel, who recalled the conversation vividly when the military did an investigation later:

> Kennedy ranted to me to the effect that there was no security in the story and that it was being held for no good reason [sic] that he was going to "bust" it if he had to send every one of his men to the Swiss and Spanish

border. . . . He repeated something about being able to get the story out
without its going through censorship. . . . I advised Kennedy that the
position was unchanged and he left.[16]

Kennedy then retreated to the privacy of his room and thought over
the decision to publish for fifteen minutes. He concluded he had no
choice. This was the biggest story he had ever known. The formal surrender already had occurred more than twelve hours earlier. Given that
the story was out via radio broadcast from Flensburg, the embargo no
longer applied. Besides this, no one was put in harm's way as a result. On
the contrary, lives likely would be saved by a story that blared "Stop the
killing." That very day a German submarine sank two merchant vessels
off the coast of Scotland. The fighting continued in Czechoslovakia and
Yugoslavia. (When the Flensburg radio message came on May 7, German
authorities in Prague thought it an Allied propaganda ploy and continued
to fight.[17]) In making his decision to publish, Kennedy believed he stuck
to the rules.

Afterward Kennedy did not flinch. By 4:40 that afternoon, the military had suspended all filing facilities for the AP in the European theater
and launched an investigation. When one of the officers encountered him
later that day, he asked Kennedy how he had managed transmission. "It
is up to you to find out," Kennedy replied. He added, "Neither the Associated Press nor I recognize political censorship and this story to my
mind does not carry any military security. I will fight political censorship
whenever I find it."[18]

AP's ownership was less steadfast, less thoughtful. It made a kneejerk
response to repudiate him publicly to staunch an uproar. The uproar was
not from the government, which went silent after Kennedy broke the
story. Powerful AP board members were angered that their organizations
were beaten on the scoop. Others were frightened about possible adverse
public reaction. Of course, there was none. The public was jubilant at the
news. A message from Army chief of staff George Marshall on May 8
informed Eisenhower, "The Press here is almost unanimously taking the
line that Kennedy only reported to the people of the United States what
was true and what they had a right to know. In view of the attempt to
martyrize [sic] him, I suggest that you may wish to make a factual state-

ment from SHAEF."[19] SHAEF, the acronym for the Supreme Headquarters, Allied Expeditionary Forces, lifted the ban on the AP but kept it on Kennedy. Allen issued a statement with his side of the story.

Robert McLean took the first wrong step with his public apology for the Kennedy story on May 10. Although "Allen and his crew have the reputation of botching things up," he believed Kennedy had a duty to go along with the other correspondents and stick to the timed announcement, as he told Kent Cooper in a letter on May 23.[20] In a second letter that same day to the AP general manager, he added, "Just think of the howl that would have gone out against the Army and the Government if Kennedy had stuck by his [embargo] pledge. In the long run, no player is acclaimed when he wins by deliberately breaking the rules of the game. He is as a rule excluded from further competition, for after all, anyone can win that way—once."[21] He never saw it as the free-press issue that Kennedy did. The handsome, connected patrician McLean moved to fight politics with politics when he should have fought politics with journalistic principle.

Then there are Kent Cooper's actions. The day after Kennedy's story appeared, he cabled the reporter to say reaction was "nothing but favorable."[22] Cooper also that day demanded an explanation from General Eisenhower for suspending Kennedy.[23] But his support ebbed over the next days. In a message to Kennedy in Paris on May 9, he expressed "disappointment" that the newsman had not consulted with New York before sending the story.[24] The next day, the same day as McLean's apology, Cooper transmitted a message to Eisenhower that repudiated Kennedy at the same time he professed to be helping him:

> Please understand that my hope is that actions I shall take because of failure of Kennedy to warn us what he was doing in connection with unauthorized transmission of dispatch should bring no repeat no prejudice against Kennedy in connection with investigation your staff is making as respects his pledges and obligations to military authorities.[25]

This message from Cooper along with McLean's was included in the SHAEF investigation report on Kennedy, which recommended that Kennedy lose his accreditation but not undergo court martial. Reading over the file, one cannot help but think Cooper added to the weight of evidence against his man, as did unsolicited smarmy messages from disgruntled American news executives. This one was cabled from the European general manager of the United Press to Eisenhower:

> Your statement issued through general allen connection associated press violation announcement german surrender renders another great service to freedom of press and speech which you champion so ardently stop . . . your reaction properly reflects attitude all serious objective journalists because it justly places blame where it belongs.[26]

With limited communications, Kennedy was hampered in making his case, while General Allen and other military authorities could defend their actions and raise doubts. The statement by McLean, the AP's non-management board leader, made it more difficult for Cooper, the service's senior executive, to render the independent judgment he said he was intent on providing once Kennedy returned to AP headquarters.

Cooper's disappointment with Kennedy only grew while the newsman sailed toward New York. "I have no doubt," Cooper wrote to McLean on May 21, "that this terrible mess would not have occurred had Kennedy not taken advantage of the confidence of The Associated Press in him."[27] It did not help, as was noted years later in the AP Alumni newsletter, that McLean and few other board members "set up a hotline for members of the AP's executive committee. The effect was to tunnel under Cooper's promise against prejudgment."[28]

In internal memoranda and correspondence on Kennedy, Cooper decried censorship. "I do not want my decision in any way to be taken to mean that I approve of political censorship. I abhor it. Military authorities had no right whatever to impose it."[29] But his decision, like McLean's, was political. He wanted to prevent antagonism against AP from rising. Nor did he want to antagonize board members. Cooper wrote to McLean two weeks after the surrender story that membership interests came first. He said, "The writers and reporters do not work directly for the readers but are instruments of a very much larger all-inclusive entity, which is called The Associated Press, which has an obligation to the newspapers in their service to the public."[30]

Cooper's argument that he fired Kennedy because he wasn't consulted on the decision to send the story does not stand up. Kennedy had no way to consult with New York about the story. The Paris censor would not have allowed Kennedy to ask the home office for guidance. The telephone line between Paris and London faded in and out repeatedly before it died, so that avenue was not open for discussions. It took two days before Cooper and Kennedy could exchange cables. They had no ability to talk directly until June.

Other context also is important. The AP's editors had expected the story of the German surrender for hours. The German announcement of capitulation had been public for an hour. The delay and the fact that no one reported the surrender should have sounded alarm bells first on the control desk in London and eventually all the way to New York. New York held the flash for eight minutes, bolstering its authenticity by affixing Kennedy's byline to it. He was AP's go-to guy for credibility on what was believed to be the world's biggest story. There was no reason to hold the news.

Kennedy and his editors performed superbly. They delivered one of the most significant scoops in journalism history. They did four things right. A great correspondent was assigned to the story. He kept reporting even after the censors tried to shut him down. The London desk moved the news without hesitation. The correspondent and editors adhered to the wartime reporting rules as they knew them.

Finally, Kennedy wins the argument on a technicality. With the signing of a surrender treaty, there was no longer a war in Europe and not any excuse to submit to censors.

* * *

Cooper thought he handled the Kennedy case smartly because he kept it quiet. He reported to the board that he had ended Kennedy's AP career as "inconspicuously" as he could.[31]

It was easier to treat matters thus in those days. Reporters still feared for their jobs and dreaded a return to breadlines. No internet protest campaign was possible. Staff was anything but empowered to rally against the decision of an employer. This also was war, and the members of the press had grown comfortable with saluting. In stark contrast to Cooper, Kennedy took full responsibility. As he told reporters on his return to New York, he'd "do it again."

In every way, Kennedy was right. Cooper should have stood behind him even if it cost Cooper his job. It likely would not have. Cooper never faced up to the decision he had made. His handling of the issue in later years remained as fraught with awkward explanations and muddled reasoning as it had been originally.

In a book written after he retired from the AP, Cooper gave his side of story, relating a conversation with Kennedy after his return to New York. First, he told his correspondent, no journalist can disregard an agreement to withhold information "when he knows that those who imposed it still hold it to be in force."[32] Second, Kennedy had said upon his return that he "would do it again." "It thus became indelibly written into the record as your own conception of proper procedure," Cooper told Kennedy, "in spite of the fact that you knew President McLean, on behalf of The Associated Press, had publicly expressed regret for your action." Cooper's first point gave the government enormous, unwarranted power. The second revealed that McLean had, indeed, made it impossible for Cooper to act independently in deciding the Kennedy case. The book in which this story appeared bore the ironic title *The Right to Know: An Exposition of the Evils of News Suppression and Propaganda*.

Cooper's autobiography, written a few years later, sidestepped his Kennedy decision altogether. Cooper painstakingly reported on dinners he attended with famous people and even included a section on sacrifices of war correspondents. He made no mention of Kennedy, the man who did so much to enhance the AP's reputation during the war, except to note him in a perfunctory listing of former AP men who experienced success elsewhere—in Kennedy's case, as an executive at California newspapers.[33]

In yet another irony, it was Cooper's own vision of a more expansive news service that had led to a proliferation of AP jobs internationally— one of the jobs that opened for Edward Kennedy. Cooper worked his way up in the technology department of AP and was widely hailed as a visionary for breaking the old-world news agency monopolies abroad. As America flexed its power internationally, an American cooperative news agency at last went global. Furthermore, Cooper had on many other occasions championed press rights. His failure to stand behind the newsman who made a correct decision to file in the face of unreasonable news restrictions remains one of the worst moments in AP history.

Nor do Kennedy's fellow correspondents come off well in this story. They tabled a motion to censor General Allen and turned on Kennedy. Their vote of rebuke was one of envy and self-protection, not principle. It was made even worse by the fact that the vote recommended that the military suspend all AP correspondents' credentials, a recommendation that validated the idea that the military had broad license to control and punish journalists. A more honest verdict from Kennedy's peers came from United Press's Reynolds Packard, who was furious at being beaten on the surrender story. The hulking reporter stormed around the press quarters saying over and over, "Goddamn that Kennedy, wish it was me."[34]

One of the staunchest defenses of Kennedy came from A. J. Liebling, who had covered the war for the *New Yorker*. In his article, titled "The A.P. Surrender," he rehearsed various indignities imposed on war correspondents and decried the ease with which they went along with it all.

> The row can do a lot of good if it brings into the clear the whole disturbing question of military censorship imposed for political, personal, or merely capricious reasons and reveals the history of the prodigious amount of pure poodle-faking that has gone on under the name of Army Public Relations. . . . The habit of saying yes to people you don't respect is hard to break, which is one reason I think well of Edward Kennedy for breaking it. Also, I think that if any severe punishment is inflicted on the first journalist to disobey an unreasonable order, an era of conformity will set in that will end even the pretense of freedom of the press in any area where there is a brigadier general to agree with.[35]

Also in Kennedy's corner was Wes Gallagher, an equally tough AP front-line correspondent. Gallagher took over Kennedy's post in Paris. Shortly after arriving he told Eisenhower, "If I'd been Kennedy, I'd have done the same thing—except that I'd have telephoned you first."[36] When Ike said he would have clapped Gallagher in jail, the crusty newsman replied, "That wouldn't have stopped the story." Twenty years later, by which time Gallagher had ascended to Cooper's top job at the AP, he elaborated.

Once a story was released by one source, he wrote, "it was considered that the security had been breached and (the information) should be released immediately to all sources."[37]

The army, which initially treated Kennedy badly, later showed its enlightened side (with a little prodding from several legislators). It exonerated the newsman, clearing him to cover the military anytime, anywhere. Still the issue did not die, as Cooper hoped it would. In 1947, the trade publication *Editor & Publisher* published an editorial under the headline "Kennedy Cleared": "Now we know that the joint Allied announcement was just an excuse cooked up on the spot. Actually SHAEF had authorized the German radio station at Flensburg to break the story. . . . [Kennedy's] story will go down in the books as one of the greatest journalistic beats in history."[38]

Alarmed, Robert McLean wrote to Cooper: "I have every desire not to see the Kennedy matter reopened but I wonder if some word of caution ought not to be said privately to somebody in *Editor & Publisher*?"[39]

✻ ✻ ✻

This book matches the best memoirs by World War II combat reporters for quality of writing and telling detail, some of it gripping. And in one way it surpasses the others. Not only does Kennedy give his final, thoughtful explanation for what happened on May 7, 1945. In describing his struggles with censorship and bureaucratic red tape and stupidity over many months, not just on May 7, he provides the fullest first-person account we have of the difficulties World War II correspondents encountered every day trying to do their jobs.

Perhaps in some small way we bring posthumous recognition to an American hero and embrace—too belatedly—what McLean and Cooper and the AP board could not admit. Edward Kennedy was the embodiment of the highest aspirations of the Associated Press and American journalism.

NOTES

1. The details on the London newsroom atmosphere are in *New York Times*, May 8, 1945; Dwight Bentel, "Scene in AP Office When Story Arrived," *Editor & Publisher*, May 12,

1945, 60. For discussion of the various surrenders that took place in those last days, see Martin Gilbert, *The Second World War: A Complete History* (New York: Henry Holt, 1991), chapter 48.

2. John Hightower, *AP: The Chief Single Source of News* (unpublished manuscript, 1973, located in the Associated Press Corporate Archives, New York, hereafter APCA), chapter 18, 115.

3. *New York Times,* May 8, 1945.

4. Alan Gould, "Scoop & Woe: How an AP Staffer Gave Americans the News They Were Entitled to Have," *Cleartime,* April 1980, 2.

5. Hightower, *AP,* chapter 18, 120, APCA.

6. John Barbour and Wes Gallagher, *While the Smoke Is Still Rising* (unpublished manuscript, APCA), 306.

7. Hightower, *AP,* chapter 17, 83, APCA.

8. Joseph J. Mathews, *Reporting the Wars* (Minneapolis: University of Minnesota Press, 1957), 194.

9. Erwin Canham, *Commitment to Freedom: The Story of the* Christian Science Monitor (Boston: Houghton Mifflin, 1958), 303–305.

10. Quentin Reynolds, *By Quentin Reynolds* (New York: Pyramid, 1964), 279 (quote); Phillip Knightley, *The First Casualty: The War Correspondent as Hero and Myth-Maker from the Crimea to Kosovo* (Baltimore: Johns Hopkins University Press, 2002), 323–324.

11. On the same day that Kennedy reported the German surrender, Boyle's war reporting won a Pulitzer Prize.

12. Among the places this story appeared is the *Seattle Times,* October 8, 1942.

13. Michael S. Sweeney, *The Military and the Press: An Uneasy Truce* (Evanston, Ill.: Northwestern University Press, 2006), 104, 116.

14. See page 161 this volume.

15. Alan Gould, "Scoop & Woe," *Cleartime,* April 1980, 2.

16. Lieutenant Colonel Merrick, "Memorandum to Colonel Warden," May 7 1947, SHAEF Files, Record Group 331, Entry 1, Box 4, National Archives, College Park, Md. (hereafter NA).

17. Richard Bessel, *Germany 1945: From War to Peace* (New York: Harper Collins, 2009), 134.

18. Burrows Matthews, "Statement of Officer," May 8, 1945, SHAEF Files, Record Group 331, Entry 1, Box 4, NA.

19. Marshall to General Dwight D. Eisenhower, May 8, 1945, SHAEF Files, Record Group 331, Entry 1, Box 4, NA.

20. Robert McLean to Kent Cooper, May 23, 1945, APCA.

21. Robert McLean to Kent Cooper, May 23, 1945, APCA.

22. Kent Cooper cable to Kennedy, May 8, 1945, "Log on Kennedy Unconditional Surrender Story," APCA.

23. Kent Cooper, "Message to General Dwight D. Eisenhower, SHAEF, Paris," May 8, 1945, "Log on Kennedy Unconditional Surrender Story," APCA.

24. Kent Cooper, "Message to AP Paris," May 9, 1945, "Log on Kennedy Unconditional Surrender Story," APCA.

25. Kent Cooper to General Dwight D. Eisenhower, May 10, 1945, SHAEF Files, Record Group 331, Entry 1, Box 4, NA. Also found in "Log on Kennedy Unconditional Surrender Story," APCA.

26. Virgil Pinkley to General Dwight D. Eisenhower, SHAEF Files, Record Group 331, Entry 1, Box 4, NA. More credit goes to Roy Howard, who headed Scripps-Howard and had been burned in 1918 when he sent a false United Press report of an armistice. "The Associated Press has a well-earned reputation for public-spirited journalistic service," Howard wrote to President Truman on May 7. "It and all of its member papers should not be subjected, as was the United Press and its clientele in 1918, to the unfair inferences which are sure to result unless this suspension is immediately withdrawn." May 7, 1945, "Log on Kennedy Unconditional Surrender Story," APCA.

27. Kent Cooper to Robert McLean, May 21, 1947, APCA.

28. Ben Bassett, "A Biased Perspective," *Cleartime*, April 1980, 3.

29. Kent Cooper to the Board of Directors, June 7, 1945, APCA.

30. Kent Cooper to Robert McLean, May 21, 1945, APCA.

31. Kent Cooper to Robert McLean, July 14, 1947, APCA.

32. Kent Cooper, *The Right to Know: An Exposition of the Evils of News Suppression and Propaganda* (New York: Farrar, Straus, 1956), 232.

33. Kent Cooper, *Kent Cooper and The Associated Press* (New York: Random House, 1959), 237.

34. "Levit Had a Plan," *Cleartime*, April 1980, 4.

35. A. J. Liebling, "The A.P. Surrender," *The New Yorker*, May 19, 1945, 59–60.

36. Hightower, *AP*, chapter 4, 86–87, APCA.

37. Hightower, *AP*, chapter 18, 124, APCA.

38. "Kennedy Cleared," *Editor & Publisher*, July 12, 1947.

39. McLean to Cooper, July 12, 1947, APCA.

Prologue

JULIA KENNEDY COCHRAN

IN 1950 MY FATHER, EDWARD KENNEDY, COMPLETED THIS MEMOIR of his ten-year experience as a foreign correspondent in the Spanish Civil War and World War II. Five years earlier, his breaking the news of the German surrender had been hailed by some as "the scoop of the century" and denounced by others as "the greatest double-cross in the history of journalism." The affair has been cited as one of the greatest examples in history of governmental suppression of freedom of the press.

He was unable to get the memoir published during his lifetime. When he died in 1963 at age fifty-eight, I was sixteen. I inherited the manuscript, but I was too young at the time to fully understand it. My father had never spoken to me about his war experiences, so I had little knowledge of them. My mother attempted to explain his importance in journalistic history, saying, "Someday you'll understand what this is all about." She added, "Maybe you can publish the memoir eventually."

In addition to the manuscript, I also inherited my father's framed front page of the *New York Times* for May 8, 1945, with his bylined story. The headline reads: "The War in Europe Is Ended! Surrender Is Unconditional; V-E Will Be Proclaimed Today." The framed page had hung in his office as long as I could remember.

For more than forty years the manuscript was packed away. I graduated from college, became a journalist myself, married, had children, divorced, changed careers, and remarried. I moved from New York to Seattle and retired to Bend, Oregon. There I finally found time to devote to this project, which has given me a profound understanding of my father that I never had growing up.

Edward Kennedy had an unlikely background for a prominent journalist. He was born in 1905, the oldest of five children, to Michael and Julia Kennedy, Irish Americans who lived in a rambling, three-story frame house at 231 Albemarle Road in the Flatbush section of Brooklyn. Michael owned a small potato farm in Brooklyn but lost it during the Depression. Then he was employed on a series of Works Progress Administration projects for several years, but after the WPA was disbanded in the early 1940s he could not find a steady job. He was probably in his fifties by then, and employers had no use for a middle-aged man with few job skills. Julia, née Crimmins, came from a well-off Irish clan from Staten Island. Kennedy family members believe that the Crimmins family supported Michael and Julia during the war and afterwards.

Because of the Kennedys' modest circumstances, at age ten Ed began to work after school, delivering meat orders for the local butcher. He adored his mother, who encouraged him to read and excel in school, but he didn't get along with his father.

Ed's three sisters, Marie, Dorothy, and Emma, and his little brother, Jimmy, loved his marvelous sense of humor, which he frequently exhibited by playing pranks on them. None of the Kennedy children had a middle name, but Ed once told his sisters that he had a middle name that began with the letter *L*. This made his initials *ELK,* which he believed meant good luck because they spelled a word. However, he told one sister that his middle name was Lloyd, another that it was Llewellyn, and the third that it was Lewis. The sisters bickered for days over which middle name was his real one; and they demanded to know why their parents had not given them a middle name as well. Ed remained straight-faced as the rest of the family argued and shouted. Finally, his sisters cornered him, and he was forced to admit, with great glee, that he had made the whole thing up.

After graduating from high school, Ed wanted to go to college, but he could not afford the tuition. He took a job as a reporter for the *Syracuse Journal.* Yearning to see Europe, he saved enough money for ship passage, and in 1927 he sailed for Paris, where he studied French. When his money ran out, he returned to the United States. Over the next three years he took jobs at the *Newark Star-Eagle,* the *New York Sun,* and the *Washington*

Star. In 1931 he again scraped together funds for ship passage to France and worked in Paris briefly for the *Chicago Tribune.*

The soaring cathedrals and fine public buildings of Paris must have inspired him, because when he returned to the States he enrolled in the Carnegie Institute of Technology in Pittsburgh with the goal of earning a degree in architecture. But he soon ran out of tuition money, and so he sought another job as a journalist, joining the Associated Press in Pittsburgh. Recognizing his talent, the AP transferred him to the Washington, D.C., news bureau in 1932. In 1935 he landed an assignment to his favorite place, Paris. He sailed to Europe on the SS *Deutschland,* arriving in early fall, and that is where the manuscript begins.

Acknowledgments

THIS BOOK OWES ITS EXISTENCE TO MY LATE MOTHER, LYN CROST Stern, who saved Edward Kennedy's manuscript from oblivion. She was thoroughly familiar with it, having typed it for my father. After a short and stormy marriage, they divorced, and she remarried a few years later. When my father died in 1963, she searched his desk at his home in Monterey, California, to find the manuscript. Since I knew nothing about the manuscript at the time, it might have ended up in a trash can if she had not saved it. Although their marriage had failed, she had always believed that his story should be published.

I might never have started this project without the love, support, and encouragement of my husband, Ron Cochran. Growing up in a news-centric family—his father, also Ron Cochran, was the evening television news anchor at CBS in New York in the 1950s and the anchor for the ABC Evening News from 1962 to 1965—he appreciated the importance of my father's story and believed it could be published even when I doubted it.

And I might never have completed this project without the help and experience of Ellen Waterston, a Bend, Oregon, poet and author with several books to her credit. Mary Heather Noble, Helen Vandervort, and Linda Mack, members of my writers group, provided invaluable advice and constructive criticism and were my constant cheerleaders.

I wish to thank all the AP employees, present and former, who helped me with research on my father's career with the Associated Press. These include Tom Curley, president and CEO, who welcomed my endeavor (even though it may cast the AP in an unfavorable light) and graciously co-wrote the introduction. Valerie Komor, director of the AP Corporate Archives, arranged for me to peruse the archives for stories my father wrote and faithfully answered my many e-mails seeking further information. Also aiding me there were Sam Markham, assistant archivist, and Francesca Pitaro, processing archivist. Other AP folks who encouraged and helped me include Larry Heinzerling, former director of world services and deputy international editor (and son of Lynn Heinzerling, who worked for my father in Italy during the war); George Bria, former foreign correspondent who worked for my father briefly in Rome after the city was liberated from the Germans and Richard Pyle, former New York City bureau reporter and foreign correspondent.

I am especially grateful to John Maxwell Hamilton, Louisiana State University provost and executive vice chancellor, a big supporter of this project and co-author of the introduction. My special thanks to Alisa A. Plant, my editor at the Louisiana State University Press, who created a positive collaboration between us and pruned this memoir intelligently. And thanks to Mary Lee Eggart, who created a wonderful map of my father's travels during the war.

A particular bonus for me in writing this book was reconnecting with my cousin, Thurston Balfour, after many years. He filled me in on details about the Kennedy family and their home in Brooklyn. Many thanks to his daughter, Renee Balfour, for finding me through the Internet and putting us together.

I also wish to thank Joe Livernois, executive editor of the *Monterey County Herald,* and Debbie Foster, of the California Newspaper Publishers Association.

ED KENNEDY'S WAR

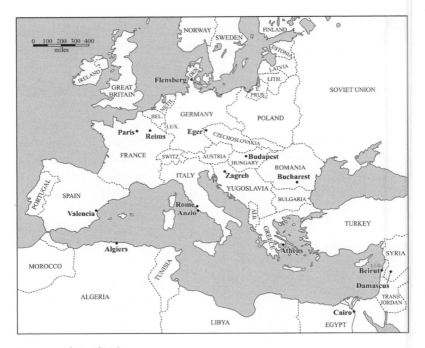

Europe and North Africa, ca. 1939

Chapter 1

PARIS

SEPTEMBER 3, 1935, WOULD SERVE AS WELL AS ANY DATE TO MARK the beginning of the prewar period, the start of the buildup for World War II. The postwar era ended in the middle twenties, when the last patch was put on the physical wreckage of World War I. An interlude of precious calm, highlighted by the Truce of Locarno, followed.[1] But the fabric of peace was too delicate to withstand the world depression which began in America in 1929, and from 1931 the European situation deteriorated. Nineteen thirty-three put Adolf Hitler in power, and in 1934 there were rumblings of what was to come. Treaties were repudiated and defiance was barked, but as yet there was no overt act to break the peace.

September 3 was not a day of great news, but it was the day I arrived in Paris to join the staff of the Associated Press there. I stepped out of the Gare St. Lazare onto streets bathed in feeble sunshine but still glistening from a shower. This is the time when postcard photographers must be busy in Paris, for the postcard makers like to show buildings in the sunlight with their reflections on wet pavements.

Paris was not new to me. I had lived there in 1927 as a student and again in 1931 as a member of the staff of the Paris edition of the *Chicago Tribune*. I had not found much time for study during my first visit, at least for study out of books. Nineteen twenty-seven was the best year France enjoyed between the two wars. Paris was bubbling over with exciting things, living was cheap, and I was twenty-one. But even in that happy

1. This is a reference to seven treaties negotiated and signed in Locarno, Switzerland, in October 1925, in which Great Britain, France, Belgium, Italy, and Germany agreed to a number of provisions intended to ensure peace in Europe. As a consequence of Locarno, Germany was admitted to the League of Nations. In 1936, however, Hitler declared the truce a dead letter and invaded the Rhineland.

year some older Frenchmen told me it was too bad I had not known Paris before the war—ah, in those days, Paris was really *quelque chose.*

My "student days" in Paris ended when my money ran out, a little ahead of time. I returned home and spent three years on the staffs of newspapers, on the *Newark Star-Eagle,* the *New York Sun,* and the *Washington Star.* Those were days of police blotters and murder trials, and I enjoyed them. A little startled to find myself a few hundred dollars to the good in 1931, I left abruptly for a second fling in France.

There were two havens for American newspapermen in Paris—the *Herald* and the *Tribune,* and the *Tribune* was the lesser haven. Their pay scales were low, the *Tribune's* lower than the *Herald's,* and their turnover was rapid; in the twenties almost anyone who could read English (and a few who couldn't) could land a job at one of them. But by 1931 the depression had hit France and especially the tourist business, and these papers were published mainly for American tourists. I made frequent and unsuccessful visits to both, and to all the American news bureaus. Before long, my money was gone and I was experiencing something new—hunger. It was not, of course, the long-term hunger that I was to see among others later but merely the sensation of walking about on an empty stomach and frequenting places where an invitation to dinner from a fellow American might be received. I did not confide my condition to anyone, but I was deeply impressed by the changed outlook on life which hunger brings. I had established uneasy credit for my room in a shabby hotel on the Île St. Louis, and I somehow ran into a meal almost every day. Finally, an American girl, sensing my situation, advanced me a loan, which lasted me until a job opened at the *Tribune.*

The Paris edition of the *Chicago Tribune* had been established during the war as a service to American soldiers. It remained in the field as a weak competitor of the *Herald,* founded well before the turn of the century by James Gordon Bennett, Jr., as the European edition of his *New York Herald.* The *Tribune's* circulation was a secret, but we guessed it to be about 20,000, partly free distribution by hotels to their American guests. It was published in a triangular agglomeration of buildings having floors at varying levels and with rooms and sections linked by a maze of hallways, stairways, and doorways. The layout had changed with the needs of tenants; here doorways were sealed, there new ones had been cut through. In the interior there was a courtyard. The labyrinth housed the plants of several newspapers using a common press at assigned hours, shops, wholesale and manufacturing establishments, apartments, and a girls' school.

The assortment of newspapermen that put out the *Tribune* was as strangely matched as its building. Half had never worked on a newspaper at home but drifted into newspaper work abroad. One, affectionately known as "Doc," gave treatments for gonorrhea. Another augmented his journalistic stipend by steering American tourists to selected brothels on a commission basis and got room and board at one of the establishments. And there were some whose conduct was as circumspect as it would have been in a small town in Iowa.

I received six hundred francs a week (then $24) from the *Tribune,* which was one-third of what I had earned at home. The paper could get all the American newspapermen it wanted at that wage; there was a never-ending supply of new arrivals who were glad to take any salary for the privilege of living and working in Paris. We were paid twice monthly, but one could draw advances against payday at a usurious interest rate. The interest, we were told, went to an employees' welfare fund, but we never heard of anyone who benefitted from it.

The *Tribune* had night and day staffs, operating quite separately. The day staff covered such news as was of special interest to Americans in Europe. The night staff, ensconced around a big table, converted cabled briefs of news from home and clippings from French newspapers into material for the paper. On writing a story, a man tossed it to his neighbor for copy-reading and a headline. This system of mutual copy-reading was a guarantee of tolerant treatment, for mutilation of the fine prose output of any man could bring a reprisal when he took over his copy-reader's copy. A maximum of liberty was permitted—encouraged, in fact—in the rewriting of cabled dispatches, necessarily brief because of the tolls. A man might be asked to render a ten-word bulletin from Washington into half a column. To do this he needed only to draw liberally on his background of the subject and perhaps supply a few suitable direct quotes. Usually the confected product turned out to be just about what happened. If not, there was seldom any complaint.

The two members of the *Tribune* staff whom I came to know best were Wilfred Barbour and Madison Kirby. Barbour's outlook was gloomy. The depression had come to stay, the days of Americans in Europe were over, the *Tribune* would fold, it was doubtful that Paris could support even one American paper. Changes in the international situation were to him simply different degrees of darkness. He saw no hope for Europe, little for America, and not very much for the human race. Four years later, as many of his glum predictions were coming true, Barbour was in Ethiopia as a member of the *Chicago Tribune*'s foreign staff. In quest of first-hand information, he went into a disease-ridden area which foreigners had been advised to avoid and died there of fever.

The *Tribune*'s editorial room was on the third floor, with two large windows looking out on the courtyard. The windows were separated by six feet of wall. Kirby had a trick of walking out one of the windows. He appeared to step into space. Anyone seeing the performance for the first time usually gasped and expected to hear him crash on the pavement below. But Kirby, with the agility of an acrobat, clung to a ledge, made his way along the outer wall to the other window and nonchalantly walked in. A few months after returning to America, I picked up a newspaper and read a short dispatch from Paris that Kirby had been killed in a fall from a third-story window. That was all it said, but I didn't need any details.

I had heard Kirby mention a French girlfriend whom he called Horse-face. Some five years after his death, I was talking to a girl in Paris. On learning that I was a newspaperman, she said, "I once knew an American journalist. Ah, what a marvelous fellow! His name was Madison Kirby."

I looked at her elongated visage and said, "Then you must be Horseface."

"Ah," she cried with delight. "So he told you about me. Oui, Orseface, c'est moi!"

* * *

The Paris to which I returned in 1935 was less gay than that of 1927 and more sober than that of 1931. The Associated Press office was on the fifth floor of a building on Rue Vivienne, off the Place de la Bourse. John Evans headed the staff. The other members were Richard G. Massock, Robert B. Parker, Charles Foltz, and Adelaide Kerr, who wrote about fashions. Henry Cassidy, later of Moscow fame, joined us about six months after my arrival. Evans was inclined to be fussy over trivialities, such as undotted i's and uncrossed t's. His theory was that if you taught a reporter to be careful and reliable in small matters, it would become a habit and he would be careful and reliable in big matters. I did not agree with him at the time—none of us did—but it probably was good training.

Not long after my arrival, there was a minor tragedy in the office. Moroney was fired. Moroney was an Englishman of considerable culture who had been with the Associated Press for thirty years. He could hardly be described as an alert and zealous reporter, since he harbored a deep conviction that all the worthwhile stories had already been written. Let any member of the staff get enthusiastic about something he was writing and Moroney would say: "I wrote the same thing in 1904. Sykes did a splendid job on it in 1911. I batted it out again in 1924. There's really nothing new in it, you know. If I were you, my boy, I'd forget the whole thing. It's been written already."

The staff worked around the clock. There was no key to the office; it had been lost years ago and nobody had missed it. The least desirable shift was the "early," when a man held the fort from midnight until 8:30 in the morning. Moroney liked these hours; they enabled him to get away from the turmoil of the day, to think without distractions. He would survey the situation through the thirty morning papers of Paris and invariably come to the conclusion that tension in Europe had lessened, that the outlook was brighter. He got that cheery note into his dispatch each morning for the early editions of afternoon papers in America.

By mid-morning, Evans, with our assistance, would usually have ferreted out some disturbing factor to provide a "new lead"—and justify a bigger headline—for the Paris story. This continued through the day, and by nightfall the war clouds again would be gathering in Europe, according to the Associated Press. European correspondents of the period frequently were denounced as warmongers and sometimes blamed for keeping the Continent disturbed. It is true that some irresponsible dispatches from Europe were published in America, but by and large the press accounts of happenings there merely reflected the jitters of a Continent torn by dissension and moving inevitably toward a new collision.

Moroney, at fifty-seven, had wearied of political crises and threats of war. His real interest was his little home in a sleepy village on the Marne, twenty miles east of Paris. He was awaiting retirement and had based all his plans on being eligible for a pension at sixty. But the Associated Press foreign staff had little use for a man who had lost interest in news, so Moroney had to go, and without a pension. I succeeded him on the "early" shift. I was the watchdog of American newspaper readers in the French capital during those hours, with a teletype at my side to alert them if anything untoward occurred. My main task was to pore through the morning papers, and the multiplicity of Paris newspapers being what it was, that alone was practically a day's work. The job gave me little opportunity to show what I could do as a reporter, but it gave me time to study the newspapers with care and learn what each stood for and what interest was behind it. It also enabled me to review the events of the preceding day and try to make a sound appraisal of the course of events.

* * *

Benito Mussolini's invasion of Ethiopia was the big news of the autumn of 1935. Here was the last chance of the League of Nations to save its system. A combined fleet of the League members placed before the Suez Canal could have stopped Mussolini, but it would have meant war, or so the British and French people thought. Who wanted to die for the Negus?[2] The pitiful military weakness of Italy which World War II disclosed makes Mussolini's bluff of 1935 all the grander. In the spring came Hitler's remilitarization of the Rhineland. As British statesmen distinguished finely and learnedly between an overt aggression and a mere violation of League law inside one's country, Parisians simply said the situation was bad but they didn't want to go to war about it.

An election took France further to the left than at any time since the Commune of Paris of 1871.[3] It put in power Léon Blum and his People's

2. The emperor of Ethiopia, Haile Selassie. Italian forces invaded Ethiopia in early October 1935, and Mussolini established a military occupation of the country in May 1936. Ethiopia regained its independence in 1941, during the Allies' East African campaign.

3. The Commune was a short-lived radical government that took over Paris in the wake of French defeat in the Franco-Prussian War and the collapse of the Second Empire in 1871. It was the bête noire of the European Right until the Bolshevik Revolution (1917).

Front, with an ambitious program of social reforms.[4] The Rightists applied themselves to an equally ambitious program of sabotage. The introduction of the forty-hour week in France was hailed as a big gain for the workers, but it was not adequately backed up by technological advances to permit reduction of working hours without impairing production. Across the frontier, German workers were putting in fifty-two hours a week. When the Spanish Civil War started in July 1936, the People's Front Regime showed itself no more capable of appreciating and facing the true situation of Europe than its predecessors.

It was evident even to so unqualified an observer as myself that something was very wrong with France. I suspected that the decay shown in the disintegration of the parliamentary system and in the lack of direction of intellectuals ran deep into the French people. Some French friends reassured me. "Oh, France is like that," they said. "It is better for us to have our Republic and our crises. They don't mean anything. We are a revolutionary people and we need frequent falls of the government to satisfy us. Even the sit-down strikes do not mean much. Just workers taking a rest. France, after all, is a rich country, almost self-supporting in food and with an empire to draw from. We can afford the luxury of a little turmoil. We'll pull through." France might have pulled through had France not been in Europe.

Life was pleasant in Paris in that period, at least for me and most of my acquaintances. In an attempt to improve my French, I placed an advertisement in *L'Intransigeant* offering to exchange French-English conversation. Most of the replies were serious, although there was one that said: "Je suis blonde, mince, and j'ai vingt-quartre ans. Je ne demand pas le marriage, Monsieur. . . ."[5] I made the acquaintance of several earnest young men and women of various classes in the venture and learned a little about the French people. I often found that the celebrated French thrift was mostly avarice and the equally celebrated French logic was sometimes nonsense, but there was a joy and ease and feeling of freedom in Paris which I have seldom encountered elsewhere. I have never had

4. Léon Blum (1872–1950), leader of the Socialist Party, served as prime minister of France three times.

5. "I am blond, thin, and twenty-four years old. I am not asking for marriage, Sir. . . ."

sympathy with Americans who said they loved France but disliked the French. France was what the French had made it.

* * *

The 1914–18 conflict was not war and revolution; it was only war. It left millions dead and impoverished a continent, but it had solved nothing. The European situation was basically the same as before we intervened, except that the sting of defeat and the imposition of terms which the vanquished felt unjust—and all the more unjust for our interference—left a deep resentment, a sense of frustration and hatred which were bound to lead to action as soon as circumstances permitted. To the conquered, escape from the terms of Versailles not only meant throwing off shackles—it meant honor and justice. In short, World War I did not lead to internationalism, but gave new stimulus to the nationalism which had been developing in Europe for more than a century. This nationalism was heady stuff, and democracy only increased its use. The greater the participation of the masses in world affairs, the more of it was drunk. It was as opposite and contradictory to any new era of internationalism as a gin binge is to teetotalism.

The Treaty of Versailles left Europe festering with sores.[6] The worst of these was the dispute over the Polish Corridor, and as it happened, Germany's eventual resort to arms to resolve this question was the immediate cause of World War II.[7] The Poles and Germans had fought over the territory for eight hundred years. Both had plausible historical and ethnic title to it. To the Germans, its cession to the Poles without even a plebiscite was as unconscionable as a Canadian corridor down the Hudson Valley to the sea would be to us. To the Poles, its return to Germany was viewed as we would view a return of California to Mexico. To the Germans, it was a barrier against their expansion eastward almost as un-

6. The Treaty of Versailles, signed in 1919, concluded World War I. It imposed harsh penalties on Germany, including the cession of much territory to France and massive reparation payments.

7. The Polish Corridor, given to Poland in the Treaty of Versailles, was a strip of land running between the German territories of Pomerania and East Prussia with an outlet to the Baltic Sea.

reasonable as the wall the French might have raised against the move of our pioneers westward had they retained the Louisiana Territory. To the Poles, its return meant not only the loss of a big part of their country's choicest land and the consignment of one-tenth of the Polish people to German slavery but the first step in a new partition of Poland.

Consider Transylvania, ceded to Rumania in the liquidation of the Austro-Hungarian Empire. This fertile region had no majority, but Rumanian, Hungarian, and German minorities. Under a system in which these peoples were primarily regarded—and regarded themselves—as human beings with a common interest in the welfare of their territory rather than as three separate peoples, permanent tranquility might be achieved. But such a system was not permitted to prevail between the two wars.

These and many other sores emphasize the basic insolubility of Europe's problems of the interbellum era. To the Poles, the idea of self-determination meant the Corridor. To the Germans, it also meant the Corridor. To the Hungarians, it meant their God-given right to the Realm of St. Stephen. And to a Transylvanian, what it meant depended on whether he was a German, Magyar, or Rumanian Transylvanian. So often the issue was not so much right versus wrong, but right versus right. The history of the period at least demonstrates that the ills of Europe cannot be cured by palliatives or makeshift medicine. The Germans of 1914 had a drastic treatment. Dr. Hitler showed up twenty years later with a remedy worse than the disease. Now the Russians have a plan. . . .

Unlovely as history may judge the period between the two wars, it had its beauty and its brilliance. Almost forgotten now is the shining skill with which French statesmen—notably Poincaré, Paul-Boncour, and Briand—reestablished the prestige and influence of their country in Europe.[8] The French virtually kidnapped the League of Nations, achieved an elaborate array of alliances, and imposed on Europe a peculiarly French system of *ordre*. France would have nothing of British experiments in the

8. Raymond Poincaré (1860–1934), president of France during World War I, negotiated the Treaty of Versailles for France. Augustin Alfred Joseph Paul-Boncour (1872–1972) was a French Socialist politician who opposed the formation of the Vichy government and urged the French to fight against Nazi Germany. Aristide Briand (1862–1932) was a pre–World War II French Socialist politician and a co-winner of the 1926 Nobel Peace Prize for his role as a lead negotiator in the Locarno Treaties.

direction of trusting Germany. They were cautious enough, but France was taking no chances at all.

Among the defects of Security House, the magnificent mansion that France built, was a foundation composed almost exclusively of fear of Germany. All French policy came out to the same thing: Don't let the Germans get on their feet. The French position was that of a boy who had been taking a trouncing from a bully much bigger and stronger than he. Some small boys, then a big boy, came to his aid. Among them, they knocked the bully out. And from that time on, France sat on the bully and stayed there, knowing that once up, the bully would get in a decisive sock before aid came.

The Boy France did not give sufficient attention to three factors: 1.) He was keeping the bully from his productive job and this was affecting the economy and convenience of the whole village; 2.) He was spending too much of his own time and energy in holding the bully down; and 3.) The fact that the bully was strong enough to outlast him on the ground and eventually to get up and hit him all the harder for having been held down so long. And yet, what else could the Boy France do? Get up and invite the bully to punch his nose?

Also forgotten, or almost so, is the acrimony over our attempts to collect the so-called war debts, which were not rightly war debts at all—we forgave those—but money we had shoveled out for the rehabilitation of Europe. By our standards we had a perfect moral right to demand repayment, and our own bitterness was based mainly on the fact that our righteousness was questioned. We saw the repayment of the debts as something unrelated to the collection of reparations by our former allies from Germany. But in the eyes of our former allies, Germany caused the war, Germany lost the war, and who should pay for it but Germany? It is not merely that they counted on squeezing out of Germany all they had to pay us; they resented having to pay us even in this manner. They suffered losses; why shouldn't they keep all they could get from Germany as recompense?

Had Germany been occupied in 1918 and had the withdrawal of troops been conditioned on payment of as stiff a sum as could be levied on the conquered country in a lump amount, it would have been collected. But the imposition of tribute for half a century, no matter how well justified, on a basis of damage done by the Germans and the costs of the war which they were accused of having provoked, was an invitation to trouble. The fact that the Weimar Republic was compelled to assume the reparations was almost a guarantee of its eventual replacement by a regime which would repudiate them. As it worked out, it was Americans who largely paid the bill, for our private investors began lending Germany large sums. These found their way into reparations payments, and the reparations money gave Britain, France, and other of our allies the cash with which to meet their debt payments to us.

Even this juggling of money from one pocket to the other did not solve the situation. The Germans saw the mounting American mortgage holdings on their industry as a new foreign incursion; American creditors worried over the safety of their investments and looked to their government to protect them; the French and British regarded reparations from Germany as their rightful due, but their debt payments to the United States as the exactions of a merciless Shylock.[9] President Herbert Hoover's attempt to ease the situation with a moratorium in 1931 ran smack into this web of conflict and engendered ill-will on almost all sides. But at least it had the merit of being the *coup de grâce* of the whole impossible situation.

* * *

Late in 1936, Great Britain was clutched by what Agency Havas discreetly called a *crise constitutionelle*. In other words, Mrs. Simpson had nabbed the King.[10] Edward was still on the throne, but events were moving swiftly, and excitement was running so high that his lady love had quit the country and come to France. She had left the train at Creil, before she got to Paris, and boarded a waiting automobile. After that, there was a blackout on her movements until late that night, when she was reported at Blois. I was assigned to chase her across France to her unknown destination. I had time to throw a toothbrush and a few shirts into a bag,

9. The usurious moneylender in Shakespeare's *Merchant of Venice*.
10. Edward VIII renounced the English throne in December 1936 to marry Wallis Simpson, an American socialite and divorcée. They were thereafter known as the Duke and Duchess of Windsor.

enough for the few days I thought I would be away. I hired a big car and driver in partnership with a British correspondent and started out. I did not get back to Paris for a year.

We never caught up with Mrs. Simpson; she had too good a start. But at least we had the satisfaction of arriving in Cannes, her destination as it turned out, not long after her. She secluded herself in the villa of Mr. and Mrs. Herman Rogers, American friends. Soon there were eighty British and American reporters and photographers in Cannes, described by the local paper as "les grands maîtres de journalism d'outre-mer et d'outre-manche."[11]

The assignment consisted of watching the villa and reporting Mrs. Simpson's movements. It was the nearest thing to keyhole reporting that I ever was asked to do by the Associated Press, and I did not like it. If I needed to know anything about the faking of newspaper stories, I learned it at Cannes; and the faking of our British colleagues, especially the sob sisters of the London tabloids, surpassed anything of the kind I had seen in America, in gall if not in imagination. Servants were bribed for any hint of what was going on inside the villa, and some of the information they supplied was worthy of the fertile brain of their fellow-citizen of the south of France, Tartarin of Tarascon.[12] There was a possibility that Mrs. Simpson might try to give the press the slip by departing during the night, so I hired a local worthy to stand guard outside the gate. After his first watch, he reported nothing had happened, except the woman's scream and those three shots he had heard fired about 3 a.m. On careful questioning, he admitted he might have been hearing things.

There was only one development at Cannes which might possibly be regarded as news, and that was the statement of Mrs. Simpson, on the eve of Edward's abdication, that if the affair was injuring the British State she would gladly "withdraw" from it. I happened to get this statement through to Paris first, thanks to the alertness of our permanent local correspondent and unexpectedly good telephone service. Congratulations came pouring in from New York as though the dispatch had been the announcement of the discovery of a new continent.

11. "The grand masters of journalism from overseas and across the Channel."
12. The lead character in an 1872 novel of the same name by the French author Alphonse Daudet.

As public interest in Mrs. Simpson's sojourn in Cannes dwindled and most of the correspondents were recalled by their papers, the lady decided she would make peace with the reporters. She received three of us for a pleasant chat in the garden. We told her we were sorry if we had annoyed her; we were only doing a job that we disliked. She said she understood.

Among the correspondents at Cannes was Luigi Barzini, Jr., of the *Corriere della Serra* of Milan. The interest of the Fascist press in the case was, of course, to exploit it as new evidence of the decadence of the British. Barzini had spent part of his boyhood in New York, where his father edited the Italian newspaper *Il Corriere d'America*. He proved an extremely clever Fascist propagandist; never having been in Italy, I swallowed most of what he told me.

"You Americans are inclined to judge Fascism on the single point of the suppression of freedom of the press," he said. "It is true that Mussolini does not permit criticism of the Regime in the popular newspapers. But before Fascism, most of our newspapers were corrupt and their inflammatory editorials did not represent honest criticism but merely what they were paid to say by some special interest. And the Italian people simply did not have the political maturity to see through them. All that has been suppressed. But for any qualified person, with honest motives, the greatest of freedom is permitted in criticizing the Government. They can express their views in weekly and monthly publications of a serious nature which are read by that part of the population which has the intelligence to understand it. The trouble is that Americans never see these publications." Nor did I ever see such publications when I went to Italy. I found the so-called intellectual weeklies and monthlies as full of Fascist propaganda as the daily press. The next time I saw Barzini was after the fall of Fascism. By then, of course, he was an outstanding anti-Fascist.

I spent Christmas in Cannes, and on New Year's Eve Pope Pius XI fell ill and was believed in danger of death. I was instructed to go to Rome to augment our staff there. "Ah, you Americans didn't get an American queen, so now you're trying to get an American Pope," said an Englishman as I checked out of the Grand Hotel. The Pope recovered, and after a stay of a few weeks in Rome, I was ordered to Valencia, wartime capital of Loyalist Spain.

Chapter 2

SPAIN

IT MAY HAVE BEEN THAT I MET ONLY PRO-FASCISTS IN PERPIGNAN, on the French side of the Pyrenees, but everyone I talked to told me to expect the worst in "Red Spain." I had intended to obtain a Spanish visa there but was advised that it would be better to enter the Loyalist side of Spain without one, for the Spanish consul in Perpignan was for Franco.[1] The civil war was six months old, and anti-Loyalist propaganda, promoted everywhere by Rightists, was at its height. I heard many stories of the killing of priests and nuns and the burning of churches. All Loyalist territory was a shambles, assassins were everywhere in Barcelona, and Madrid was worse. The mere wearing of a necktie would stamp me as a capitalist and might cost me my life. I could hardly believe there were any people so depraved as the tales indicated, but started out to see.

I had no trouble at the frontier; the passport officer was of anarchist leanings and didn't believe much in credentials. He simply took down my name and address and said he hoped I'd enjoy my visit. The train on the Spanish side moved at a snail's pace because of damage done to the line by bombings, and it was late at night when it pulled into Barcelona. There I saw my first blacked-out city and other ominous signs of war—hospitals and air-raid shelters. Outside the station, I observed one dim light two blocks away and walked toward it. It was a restaurant. After a meal, I told the waiter I had just arrived and was unfamiliar with the city; could he

1. The Spanish Civil War began with a military uprising in July 1936, and the insurgents soon came to control a large part of Spain. They were known as Nationalists; their opponents, supporters of the legitimate government of the Republic, were called Loyalists. The Nationalist victory in the spring of 1939 ushered in the lengthy dictatorship of Francisco Franco (d. 1975).

get me a room for the night? Yes, there was a comrade in the restaurant who could do that.

A misshapen man in a cap agreed to take me to a room. As I lugged my heavy suitcase, we turned into a side street, then an alley, all in darkness. We could not talk much; I knew only a few words of Spanish and no Catalan. Suddenly, the quiet was pierced by the shrill crow of a cock. The surprise of such a cry in the middle of a city was appalling. All the superstitions of my remote ancestors seemed to pour out of some recess of my brain. It was plain: this ugly little man was leading me to the end of an alley to shoot me down for the money and baggage I carried. A second before I had been wholly at ease; now I was gripped by an overwhelming fear. The situation seemed so hopeless that I simply resigned myself to an almost certain doom.

My guide stopped before a door and unlocked it. I followed him in, thinking now that the job was to be done indoors. He led me to a shabby room, turned on a light, and pointed out the toilet down the hall. Then he smiled, gave me the clenched-fist salute, and said, "Buenas noches, Camarada." I looked at him in the room's dim light; his was indeed an ugly face, but there was no evil in it. It was rather the face of the oppressed, of the eternal underdog. I said goodnight and thanked him, chagrined over my fear and mistrust and hoping he had not detected it.

The trip to Valencia was another long ride in a train filled with soldiers of the Republic, in uniform or semi-uniform. Some had their girlfriends along. The railroads, seized by workers in the first days of the war, were at that period operating under the supervision of the two big labor federations, Anarchists and Socialist-Communists. Trains departed at uncertain hours, made long intermediate stops, and eventually got to their destination. We pulled into Valencia at 3 a.m. My predecessor had left before my arrival, turning his files over to the American *chargé d'affaires.* Before starting to work, I wanted a fill-in on what had been happening in Valencia and what news had been sent out, but in attempting to get possession of the files, I ran into State Department bureaucracy at its crassest. Yes, they were Associated Press files and I represented the Associated Press, but could I prove that I personally had a right to them? Did I have a letter, a document, a piece of paper of any kind? I got what I wanted after a three-day siege.

Valencia was overcrowded, as one would expect of a provincial city turned capital. Its utilities were taxed beyond capacity, and the inadequacy of its sewage system offered a serious health threat to the swollen population. Its streets were thick with *milicianos*,[2] mostly garbed in dungarees and carrying their rifles, often rusty, strapped over their backs as though they were about to set out on a rabbit hunt. The unmilitary bearing of this citizens' army was a distress to Colonel Stephen O. Fuqua, the American military attaché. Like John Evans, Colonel Fuqua believed that if you teach a soldier to be meticulous about small matters, he will prove capable when called upon to handle big matters.

By the time of my arrival in Spain, the fronts which divided the two sides had become stabilized. Unlike our own civil war, this was a conflict of classes rather than regions, but the failure of Franco and his generals to overwhelm all Spain in their coup had resulted in a geographically artificial division. The workers had triumphed in the three highly industrialized cities of Madrid, Valencia, and Barcelona, and these roughly formed the points of the great triangle which was Loyalist territory. The Basque country on the Bay of Biscay, where democratic sentiment was always strong, held firmly against the Franco revolt though cut off from the main government area. Other Loyalist *îlots*, like Badajoz, near the Portuguese frontier, had not been strong enough to stand, and workers' resistance there had been ruthlessly crushed.

In November 1936 Franco had marched on Madrid against rapidly crumbling opposition. The government fled to Valencia, insurgent troops were at the gates of the capital, and the Loyalist cause looked lost. But the International Brigade, then largely French, had made a stand and halted Franco.[3] This was the Brigade's greatest day; the embattled volunteers from outside the country showed the demoralized Spanish Loyalists that the fight was not hopeless, that the enemy could be held.

---

2. Members of the Republican militias, usually organized by labor unions or political parties.

3. The International Brigade was a force of foreign nationals that fought in Spain on the side of the Loyalists. Although their total number has been estimated at more than 30,000, no more than 20,000 were active at any one point in the conflict. Most of them were individuals affiliated with Communist, Socialist, or Anarchist parties or groups.

I knew nothing of Spain, and of the war only the highly conflicting accounts I had read in the papers. I decided to start with an open mind and try to learn the situation from the bottom up—not the easiest of chores in the confusion of Valencia. It did not take long to decide that my sympathies were basically with the Loyalists, and they remained so, although I never was able to draw out of the struggle the sense of exaltation that some correspondents experienced. Perhaps this was partly due to an assignment which kept me close to the government. Valencia was a rear-area and headquarters town with all the attending tension and demoralization; its atmosphere was like Cairo and Algiers later in their turn. It seemed to be the cesspool into which everything worst in Loyalist Spain seeped. Madrid, under the enemy's guns and half-starved, was a happier place, and the few excursions I was able to make to the fronts were like holidays after Valencia's enervating frustrations.

Unquestionably, this was a fight against tyranny and oppression, waged with much high idealism. From a legal point of view, here was a people's government coping with a revolt treacherously organized by officers who collected their pay from the Republic while they had plotted against it. But to me, there was also a feeling that Spain was suffering from a horrible disease. Its main cause may have been the stupidity and greed of the elements which Franco represented, back through generations, but it was a malady nonetheless, and a reversion to barbarism on both sides which was bound to have lasting effects. I could not get too enthusiastic over a crusade which had involved so much killing of men for their ideas, no matter how great the provocation.

All this, however, is aside from the international aspects of the Spanish war which again gave proof, if it were needed, of the bankruptcy of the system of collective security in Europe. The idea of the League of Nations had been to generalize local troubles at their start, before they led to general complications. In dealing with the Spanish question this was reversed; it must be considered as just something happening inside Spain, even when Mussolini had more than 100,000 troops there and Hitler was testing his 88-milimeter gun and new model tanks on the Spanish people.

Most churches were charred, and trucks rolled in and out of the cathedral in Valencia, now a military warehouse. One did not ask what had become of the priests; it was a touchy subject. But it seemed clear that the churches had not been burned for being churches, nor priests molested for being priests. I was not in Spain before the war to see what role the Church played, but to those who took direct action, it is certain that most of the Church organization was part of the Franco rebellion and actively participating in it. The custom of burning churches as symbols of oppressive authority is something peculiarly Spanish and difficult to explain outside of Spain. Its difficulty of explanation is one reason for the government's bad press abroad, especially in the early days of the war.

The violence which came from the left as a reaction to the Franco revolt was frightful, but it was perpetrated mostly by lawless and irresponsible elements. Little of it can be pinned on the government; on the contrary, once anything like stable government was reestablished following the disruption of the initial shock of the rebellion, firm steps were taken by the authorities to end the anarchy. Perhaps the sum total of cruelties of the Spanish war is about evenly balanced between the two sides. But on the right it was more wanton and inflicted by elements which should have known better and can be held more accountable.

* * *

The year I spent in Spain was a struggle, against odds, to write objectively, to give as true a picture as I could of what was happening and to avoid the omnipresent propaganda. But there was little room for a neutral in that grim clash. At times, I was bluntly told that I could either write the Loyalist point of view or write nothing. Sometimes I chose to write nothing when I knew that the facts were at a wide variance from the information we might send. I found the censorship most oppressive. The Russian aid to "Red Spain" was negligible beside what Hitler and Mussolini were doing for Franco, but we could not mention it at all. There was a Basque delegation in Valencia, representing a people waging the same fight against Franco in the north, but even that delegation's statements ran into the censor's blue pencil if it did not conform to the Valencia "line."

The defense offered for this kind of censorship was that while it extended beyond military security and was frankly political, this was war and it was necessary. The enemy resorted to such censorship, so the Loyalist government must. I later heard that argument many times—that in a struggle for freedom, it is often necessary to suppress freedom as part of the battle. Assuredly, war imposes discipline, and obviously matters of military security are subject to censorship, but I never have been persuaded that a struggle for truth and freedom necessitates the distortion of facts or the suppression of information other than facts which would help the enemy on the battlefield, and they are few.

Some of the correspondents seemed to have less trouble. John Lloyd, who was doing an excellent job in Madrid for the Associated Press in this period, said, "Well, what if we do lean over backwards to give the Loyalists a break? We know the boys on the other side are having a worse time with censorship. The people can read the stories from both sides and will probably get the idea." The *New York Times* applied this formula to an extreme degree. On the Franco side, its correspondent was William P. Carney, who became inflamed with hatred of the Loyalists in a brief stay on that side in the early days of the war. Assigned to the other side, where he found nobility of character and decency everywhere, he wrote a round-by-round account of the wrestling match of Civilization versus The Snake. He won the Knights of Columbus prize for reporting. Herbert L. Matthews won considerable acclaim—in circles other than the Knights of Columbus—for his reporting on the Loyalist side. When I read the accounts of the Messrs. Carney and Matthews, they seemed to be reporting two different civil wars in two different countries.

* * *

The war and revolution in Spain—which the Anarchists insisted were inseparable and the Communists asserted were two different things—attracted many guest artists, both warriors and revolutionaries. The warriors were in the International Brigade; the revolutionaries were in a press office organization which, in later days, would have been known as the Spanish Republic's Psychological Warfare Branch. Among those waging psychological warfare for the Loyalist cause was Milly Bennett, who came straight from Moscow. Milly had done newspaper work in San Francisco, then went to China to start a newspaper. On her release from a Chinese jail, she made her way to Moscow, where she assisted Anna Louise Strong to put out the *Moscow News*, an English-language newspaper.

Milly was a salty, warm-hearted girl, and I found her extremely helpful. She was still enough newspaper woman to fill in for me with straight-forward stories for the Associated Press on my absences from Valencia. She also undertook to teach me the Real Meaning of the revolution. Once, when I said something about objective reporting, Milly said I ought to know better. There was no such thing as objective reporting. You were conditioned by your environment, by your class. I told her there was a lot in what she said—objective reporting was like sheer perfection in art, something to be aimed at rather than attained. But I thought that the artist who strove for perfection, though never attaining it, would come closer to it than the artist who decided not to try for it since it couldn't be achieved. She could not see it that way.

Covering the government consisted largely of writing stories based on its communiqués and official handouts. The war communiqués, in their sum total during the time I was there, claimed capture of territory approximately equal to the surface of the globe. Other figures—casualties inflicted, prisoners taken—were of similarly astronomical proportions. "Enemy activity consisted of bombing three hospitals and shelling an orphanage," ended one typical communiqué. Not much could be written about the disrupted economic life of the country; that would give comfort to the enemy. When the cabinet resigned, there could be no announcement until a new one was formed. We could write about civilian casualties inflicted in the air and sea bombardments which the capital suffered, and of any enemy "atrocity" we might learn. There were interviews with cabinet ministers and other officials to be obtained, but I found that these—at least the parts of them we could transmit—came out to about the same thing as the official communiqués.

I found it refreshing to spend as much time as possible among the people of Valencia, mostly workers' families, often with a son or two drafted into the Republican Army. I found little real enthusiasm for the war among these families. They had many complaints about conditions in Spain and certainly no love for Franco and his generals. But to most of them, the war had only made life harder; killing men who lived on the other side of Spain and had to fight in Franco's army did not seem a good solution to the country's troubles.

Of all the elements joined in the fight, the Communists were the most disciplined, the most effective. But the Anarchists were the easiest to deal with, for they hated red tape. Uniforms? A badge of servitude; a soldier does not need a uniform, only a stout Anarchist heart. Credentials? Useful only to spies; we trust a man until we know he's a spy. Then we shoot him. And if Anarchism triumphs, how will the world function? Perfectly; there will be no more problems like those of today.

I never was able to obtain from my Anarchist friends a detailed explanation of how that ideal world of theirs would run. They usually began by picturing a factory where there was no owner to exploit the workers; they produced for themselves and other workers, with a technical committee over operations and a political committee to assure every worker justice. No Communist nonsense about everyone producing according to his ability and consuming according to his needs. Everyone would produce freely, naturally, and from his heart under Anarchism, and everyone could consume all he wanted of the earth's lavish bounty once the present oppression was destroyed. If it could work that way in a factory, the same was true with a city, a country, the whole world. They seldom became more specific than this; it was too clear to need further explanation. Only in Spain had Anarchism attracted a wide following, and the movement was a strange combination of idealism and violence. "We are accused of killing," said *Nosotros,* the Anarchist newspaper of Valencia. "It is true that circumstances have compelled us to take direct action at times. But do they not realize that there is a concealed tear in our eye when we do?" The Communists took the sensible view that no social reform introduced in Spain would be worth anything if the war was lost; therefore, all efforts should be put into the war and social measures could await victory. Not so the Anarchists, who seemed to believe that if the reforms were sweeping enough, the war would somehow win itself.

Some of the newspaper people who showed up in Valencia were, like the guest propagandists, odd characters. One, whom we shall call Daphne Davenport, said she had left her husband, a tea planter, to write of the war in Spain for a group of provincial English papers. As she sat beside me in the lobby of the Victoria Hotel sipping a brandy one night, she said: "Don't look surprised when I tell you this, because I don't want to attract attention, but the truth is that I'm not really a correspondent at all. I'm a . . . well, I'm a spy. Please don't tell anybody."

Several weeks after her departure from Spain, Constancia de la Mora, the chief censor, said: "Have you seen the stuff that Daphne Davenport wrote about us after leaving Spain? Her stories are not damaging to us,

but they are the most fantastic rubbish I have ever read. Well, take a look
at them. . . ."

The first clipping of the sheaf went something like this:

By Daphne Davenport
Our Own Correspondent in Spain

Valencia—Ting-a-ling.

It was three o'clock in the morning. I wondered who could be calling
me at that hour. I lifted the receiver and heard the voice of Largo Cabal-
lero, prime minister of Red Spain.

"You must come at once, Daphne," he said. "I need your help."

Throwing a wrap around me, I started for his office. Just then there
was an air raid, but I knew that I must not fail him. Dodging the bombs
and stepping over the bodies, I reached my destination.

I found him nervous and haggard. His desk was strewn with war maps.

We discussed problems of great moment until long after dawn had
streaked the sky.

I cannot, of course, disclose the subject of our conference, as it was
most secret, but I can assure my readers that the conduct of the war was
materially changed as a result of our talk. . . .

Arrests of foreigners in Valencia were fairly common. Some of the foreigners, and many Spaniards as well, unquestionably were spies. Usually
arrests were secret; suspects were taken from their homes or hotel rooms
in early morning hours and once in custody often disappeared for good.
An American girl reporter who wrote for the *Daily Telegraph* of London
and other papers refused to go peacefully when her turn came and was
carried out of the Victoria Hotel screaming and biting. She was a troublesome type, but apparently the suspicion against her was based entirely
on her insistence that she be permitted to go to Minorca, then a forbidden island for reporters. After the American Embassy intervened in her
behalf, she was released but expelled from Spain.

A group of correspondents took up the question of such arrests with
Luis Hidalgo Rubio, head of the press office, and obtained his assurance
that any arrest of a recognized member of the correspondents' corps

would be promptly reported to the correspondents, and the accused would be given a hearing within a reasonable time, which the other correspondents might attend. Not long after this, someone noted the absence of Alkeos Angelopoulos, a Greek journalist assigned to Spain by the International News Service. Inquiries resulted in a reluctant admission that Al Angel, as we called him, had been taken from his room in the usual early morning manner. "Now don't worry," Rubio assured the correspondents. "He is being well-treated."

Lawrence A. Fernsworth of the *New York Times* and the *Times of London,* Don Minifie of the *Herald-Tribune,* and I set out to see what we could do for Angelopoulos. For a week we pressed our demands that any charges against him be made public, but ran into a run-around on all official sides. Even the minister of the interior appeared to be powerless before whatever secret police organization held Angel. As our protests became louder, we were dubbed "the Vigilantes" by those correspondents whose devotion to the Loyalist cause extended to a belief that Loyalist authorities could do no wrong. Angel was at length released and, although charged with no offense, was asked to leave the country.

A month later, Fernsworth, Minifie, and I were lunching when Milly Bennett showed up after an absence in Madrid, irate and bedraggled. "A fine lot of Vigilantes you turned out to be!" she screamed. It happened that Milly herself had fallen into the police net between Madrid and Valencia and had spent several days in jail, with no one to help her get out.

As a result of our intervention for Angelopoulos, Minifie and I found ourselves under suspicion of the secret police. How our actions could indicate that we might be spies was beyond our comprehension, but not beyond Spanish comprehension. We learned that Spanish police don't like interference; anyone interceding for a man in trouble with the authorities may soon find himself in trouble. Minifie's notebooks vanished and reappeared. The linings of my suits were slit in my absence from my room. A friendly detective who lived at the Victoria Hotel confided to me that I was one of the persons he was assigned to watch and report on. It would be easier for both of us, he said, if I kept him informed of my movements. One morning, on calling at his room to report, I found him groaning in bed, semi-conscious. I summoned a doctor. "Looks like some kind of poisoning," said the medico. He cast his eye on a dressing table and saw a half-emptied bottle of a well-known Spanish aphrodisiac, guaranteed to restore youthful vigor. Under questioning, the detective mumbled that a teaspoon dose had worked so well he had decided to take half a bottle. "There's strychnine in it," said the doctor as he prepared an emetic. My detective friend was well within two days.

There were bullfights as usual in wartime Valencia, which meant every Sunday afternoon. The traditional bullfighter's satin costume with white hose and *peruke*[4] had been abolished as too unrevolutionary; the performers appeared in *milicianos'* uniforms. The Spanish friend who took me to my first bullfight deplored the lowered standards the war had brought. All the best bulls were in Franco territory, he said, and all the best bullfighters seemed to be there too.

Patiently he explained bullfighting. I must not expect it to be like an Anglo-Saxon sport, like a boxing match or a football game, where the contestants were evenly matched. Bullfighting was not intended to be a fair fight between a bull and a man. The bull was doomed from the start; even if he escaped death in the ring, he would be slaughtered afterward for meat. A bull is far from stupid; he learns so much in a single fifteen-minute encounter in the ring that he would be too dangerous to put in a second time. Bullfighting, my friend continued, is a sport in which a man flirts with death; it involves the greatest skill and dexterity, and it consists of coming very close to death, but of escaping death by observing the rules and employing the full talent of the *torero*'s art.

One of the bulls proved cowardly, and the spectators shouted abuse and ridicule at the animal. The sight of thousands of human beings, themselves engaged in an internecine contest, berating a beast for not being sufficiently bestial was grotesque. It occurred to me that it also was something like life. As surely as the bull is doomed, every man is doomed in advance to the apparent purposelessness of life. He may, however, defy the fate set out for him and fight it out. He is expected to do so. Though he is bound to lose, he may achieve a moral triumph and give life a purpose by his effort. The thoughts that passed through my mind that Sunday afternoon at the bullfights were rather like the conclusions of the Existentialists that I read about later.

---

4. A wig traditionally worn by bullfighters.

In the summer of 1937 the Loyalist Army launched an offensive to raise the siege of Madrid. It was brilliantly conceived and, had it succeeded, would have destroyed a large part of the besieging force; but supplies, training, and field leadership were inadequate. In the autumn, they made a drive on Teruel. Here they achieved initial success but did not exploit it. From that time on, it seemed certain to me that the Loyalists would never defeat Franco and his German and Italian assistance without support from outside Spain. This was not forthcoming. Had the general conflagration come before the final defeat of the Spanish government in the spring of 1939, history might have been vastly different—and possibly worse for Spain and even for the Allies in World War II. Franco-British intervention on behalf of the Loyalists would have been inevitable, and the speedy reestablishment of the Spanish Republic likely. But on the collapse of France, would Hitler have stopped at the Pyrenees? Here again we enter the unreal realm of "if," and no one can say just what would have come to pass.

I spent the last month of my Spanish year in Madrid. There people had come to accept shellings almost as though they were rainstorms, as something bound to come now and then and something to keep out of insofar as possible. The life of the city went on, for people are adaptable.

Chapter 3

ITALY

ITALY IN 1937 WAS ON THE WAY TO WAR, AND THE ITALIAN PEOPLE were already weary of the adventure. "Better a day as a lion than a hundred days as a sheep," Mussolini told them. He borrowed the slogan from an Italian soldier who wrote it on a wall near the front in 1915. But living like lions, day after day, was too great a strain for the Italians, and as the late John Whittaker of the *Chicago Daily News* observed, they were getting tired of it. The observation caused Whittaker's expulsion from Italy. The Fascists were very sensitive lions, especially when their leoninity was questioned.

I arrived in Rome late that year, this time assigned to the AP's Italian staff. Stung by the Italian rout at Guadalajara, Mussolini had sent more and better soldiers to Spain to redeem the reputation of his warriors.[1] There was no secrecy about Italian intervention now, only a half-hearted insistence that all the Italians going there were inspired volunteers setting out of their own accord. An Italian army hospital ship, it was admitted, was bringing back the wounded in regular runs between Malaga and Gaeta. Even unofficial war comes high, and Italians knew they were paying the bill. Taxes had gone steadily upward, and the effect on prices since my last visit was noticeable.

Our office windows overlooked a side street just as it gave into the Piazza di Spagna. Almost every Italian who passed would stop, adjust his necktie, and slick down his hair to make a *bella figura* as he stepped out into the big square. Mussolini on his balcony presented a *bella figura* to the highest degree. The trappings of Fascism had the grand opera glitter

---

1. In the battle of Guadalajara (March 8–23, 1937) Loyalist troops defeated Nationalist and Italian forces attempting to encircle Madrid.

that Italians love so much. Almost all Italians participated in the big show and enjoyed doing so. They liked to be told they were a great people, no longer to be kicked around but about to come into their glory. This world of have and have-not nations, with the rich ones convinced of their right to eternal enjoyment of their wealth and Italy condemned to eternal poverty, was about to be altered: such was Mussolini's line, and the Italians responded with fervor. At least they did in public.

Some of the younger folk who had known nothing of Fascism went the whole way; most of the older ones had their doubts in private moments. Their Latin skepticism posed questions. I found that most of the Italians whom I came to know well were both Fascist and anti-Fascist. They liked Mussolini's show and the feeling of national importance he gave them; they hoped Italy would triumph as he promised and were eager to participate in the gains. But they knew Italy's tradition of defeat and were fearful of disaster. They hated paying the bill for the show; they were always anti-Fascist then. Two Italians, together with a foreigner like myself, were good Fascists. It was not merely fear of being reported to the secret police that made them so but a reluctance to let down the front of Italianism to a foreigner before one another. Each one, alone, might confess his misgivings, his dislike of Fascism, his contempt for Mussolini's antics, and his bitterness over the loss of liberty.

The Italy of the late 1930s was not only paying for the Ethiopian conquest and for the armed establishment being built up for the much bigger adventure that was to come but also for economic autarchy, the program designed to make Italy as self-sufficient as possible in the impending struggle. Taxes and prices had been mounting sharply since 1935; the pinch was felt everywhere. It was a boast of Fascism that under its regimented economy the worker was protected against inflation; wages always went up in accordance with price rises. It is true that in the spiral, industry had been ordered to pay higher wages, but wages never caught up with prices. Not even the Fascist economy could achieve that. One day the Fascist press jubilantly announced wage increases averaging 10 percent, a new evidence of how Fascism looked after the working man. A week later, another triumph for labor—social security benefits were to be trebled. There was a detail not published by the newspapers—the increased deductions from salaries to pay for the trebled benefits were identical in most cases with the wage increases. The operation, unmasked, was simply the imposition of a new and staggering tax of 10 percent of the national payroll. In return, the government promised bigger pensions—when they were due, which in some cases was not for thirty years.

I wrote these facts and the next day received one of the summonses to the Propaganda Office, which often meant expulsion for correspondents. Giovanni Bosio, whose job it was to crack down on and frequently expel correspondents, thrust a copy of my dispatch in front of me. "That's an anti-Fascist lie," he said. Apparently he himself was not aware of the full significance of the payroll-security jockeying. I told him I knew my facts were correct and suggested that he investigate the government's plans. He told me to return later. When I did, I knew by his expression that any expulsion order which might have been planned had been dropped. Well, yes, there was a modicum of truth behind my dispatch. "But it's the same old story with you American correspondents," he complained. "You couldn't write about the constructive parts, but went looking with a microscope for something which could be twisted against us. This had better not happen again."

More than thirty correspondents—American, British, and French— were expelled from Italy during the period I was there, mostly for reporting information which may have been true but which they could not prove. The Italian Foreign Press Office was fair enough in one respect— you were summoned for a lacing for writing anything they didn't like, but if you could demonstrate it was true, the matter was dropped. The easiest way of proving information to Fascist satisfaction was to cite one of their own publications. Consequently, getting at facts consisted in large measure of looking through fine print for significant revelations. I found a decree in the *Official Gazette,* for example, according pardon to a group of convicts because of their military service in Spain. This made it clear that Italy had permitted jailbirds to "volunteer" to fight for Franco, with a promise of pardon on their return. That story brought me a browbeating too, but no expulsion. "I got it from the *Official Gazette,*" I said with a straight face.

Richard Mowrer of the *Chicago Daily News* was less fortunate when he reported that a detachment of German troops had passed through Italy en route to Libya. This presumably was true; the Germans were secretly training the Afrika Korps at the time and were testing German soldiers under desert conditions. But there were no available documents to prove it, and Dick was given a week to get out of the country. He was secretly engaged to Rosamund Coles of the *Paris Herald*, who, like a loyal fiancée, rushed to Rome to share his expulsion. They decided to marry there and make the departure from Italy their honeymoon trip. Marriage for foreigners involved much red tape in Italy, and they got the formalities completed just under the deadline and drove off with the blessings of the detectives assigned to trail Mowrer.

Despite the Damocles sword of expulsion and the snapping of Fascist officials, life in Rome was leisurely and exceedingly pleasant. The ageless city was mellow and friendly; one always sensed that Rome had been there long before Fascism and would long survive it. There was always a thrill in passing ruins one first came upon in schoolbooks, and always a joy in gazing upon the city from Mount Pincio, where Messalina once held her orgies and where Rome's barbers and butchers now took their girlfriends strolling.[2] The American colony was compact, with its own church and cinema and always a current intrigue to discuss. For a drink with convivial friends after work, there was the choice of Rampoldi's, where tired musicians made every piece sound alike, or the cool *bierstube* of the Albrecht brothers from the Italian Tyrol. There was opera at the Teatro Costanzo in winter and under the pines at the ruined baths of Caracalla in summer. Of all such attractions, only contemporary art exhibits suffered much from the leaden hand of Fascism. The most important exhibit held while I was in Rome was marred by too much of the Duce, on canvas and in bronze, on foot and on horseback, and presenting the crown of Ethiopia to the scared little Victor Emmanuel III.[3]

* * *

The Vatican was as important a news source as the Palazio Venezia, and for much of the time I was in Rome we had a dying Pope to watch. Getting

2. Messalina was a wife of the Roman emperor Claudius; she was often characterized in classical sources as extremely promiscuous.

3. Ruler of Italy (House of Savoy) from 1900 to 1946, Victor Emmanuel III effectively became a puppet king after the rise of Mussolini.

precise information on the condition of Pius XI during the last eighteen months of his life was difficult. Official bulletins were vague, and Professor Arminta Milani, the pontiff's personal physician, would not discuss the matter with the press. Andrew Berding, who had headed the AP staff before my arrival, had learned that a physician of modest practice was a consultant of Milani's. Berding assumed that if he approached this doctor directly for news, it would probably be refused on ethical grounds. So he called on him as a patient, saying something was wrong with his ear. As the physician peered vainly into the ear for the trouble, Berding remarked that as a reporter he was intensely interested in knowing the latest news on the Pope's condition—all the more reason why he needed good ears to hear anything that might be said on the subject. This approach appealed to the doctor's Italian sense of humor and love of intrigue, and he casually gave Berding the information he wanted. Berding paid the regular fee, saying he would return if his ear bothered him again. "By all means," said the doctor. "And if I learn of something good for your ear, I shall summon you."

The physician proved a reliable informant. When I took over the job, I likewise called as a patient, saying my ear trouble was the same as Berding's. The doctor always went through the comedy of examining my ear as he dropped his information; he seemed to enjoy the game. One day he telephoned: "He has had a bad turn and is sinking fast. This looks like the end." Pope Pius died early the next morning, and we were fully prepared for the exhaustive coverage required of the death and obsequies of a pope.

In his final year, the aged pontiff had his good and bad spells; bedridden one day, receiving pilgrims the next. His mind sometimes wandered as he was addressing these visitors. At the time, he was lashing at Mussolini for the Fascist adoption of Nazi racial theories—and Mussolini was hitting back. The pontiff's remarks had to be examined carefully for some new thrust, but his phrases were often so involved that it was not always easy to determine what he had meant.

To report the elaborate ceremonies attending the election of the new Pope, we rented a room—it was a monk's cell—in an old convent facing St. Peter's Square. The buildings there were being demolished for the great Via della Conciliazione development, and this room was the only remaining one close to the square and with an unrestricted view of the balcony of St. Peter's, from which the news was to be announced. We learned that the correspondent of a rival news service, chagrined over our preemption of the vantage spot, had boasted that he had bribed telephone officials to cut off our telephone service at the crucial moment. Richard G. Massock, chief of our home staff, and I were in the room as the moment of the big news approached. As the wisp of smoke rose from the chimney of the Sistine Chapel to signal the election of a pontiff, we found our fears justified; the telephone went dead. But this was of little moment, for we had taken the precaution of having another telephone installed under a different name. That one gave excellent service.

No story of the little world in which foreign correspondents lived in Rome would be complete without a mention of the life and works of Monsignor Enrico Pucci, the able Vatican City correspondent of the Associated Press and every news office to which the Monsignor had succeeded in selling his services—and that included almost all of them, Italian and foreign. Many years before, the Associated Press had been responsible for launching Pucci, an obscure parish priest, on his distinguished journalistic career. The late Salvatore Cortesi, head of the bureau, had encountered great difficulty in getting news from the Vatican. Cortesi, a member of the papal nobility, had excellent connections there, but to Vatican prelates of that time, newspaper headlines were undignified.

Pucci occasionally called on Cortesi seeking alms for the poor of his parish. He liked to discuss Vatican affairs. He appeared well-informed and once or twice let drop a tidbit which seemed incredible at the moment but which later proved correct. It dawned on Cortesi that here was the man he sought—someone who apparently had an inside track in the Vatican and a nose for news. Cortesi explained the interest of American newspapers in prompt and reliable news from the Vatican and of the difficulty in obtaining it. He tactfully suggested that if Pucci could see his way clear to supply the AP with information regularly, he would be glad to contribute a monthly sum to whatever charity the Monsignor might designate.

Pucci readily accepted the offer, said he anticipated no opposition at the Vatican to the plan, and concluded that since he would be performing a professional service, he might as well take the money himself. He went to work with zeal, and for several months Cortesi had unparalleled coverage of the Vatican, well worth the monthly stipend. Before long it occurred to Pucci, however, that if his information was worth money to the AP, it was worth money to others. Soon all foreign correspondents were learning that they could be protected on Vatican happenings only by subscribing to Pucci's service. Their efforts to get to the sources of Vatican news met the same old difficulties; Pucci had an exclusive pipeline. As the Monsignor added client after client among the correspondents and the Italians newspapers, he apparently persuaded Vatican authorities that his set-up was a good arrangement. It was evident that his activities were at least tolerated there. He eventually had two or three assistants, an office in the basement of the Vatican firehouse, and gave day and night service on queries, with prompt answers. His fees went up as his operations expanded. It was no longer a matter of paying for exclusive news; correspondents in effect paid Pucci tribute to keep from being beaten on Vatican stories.

He came close to a fall from favor at the Vatican after the election of Cardinal Eugenio Pacelli as Pope.[4] He issued a box score of the purported votes of the Cardinals at the Conclave—information which the Cardinals are required to keep secret under pain of excommunication. Then he set up an office on the Court of St. Damaso, leading to the papal apartments, and began to issue lists of callers and speculative stories on the purpose of their visits. This procedure may be all right for the White House, but the Vatican was having none of it. The next day, a subdued Monsignor Pucci was out of the Court of St. Damaso and back in the Vatican firehouse basement, and his box-score was authoritatively denounced as being made of whole cloth. He had overestimated the new pontiff's acceptance of American newspaper practices.

Pucci's commercialism was often attacked. Westbrook Pegler, visiting Rome, "exposed" him and asked what people would think if the press secretary of the White House charged money for information.[5] American prelates attempted to break up his system, without success. In defending his commercialism, Pucci insisted that he was not a Vatican attaché but a hard-working newspaperman who was entitled to remuneration for his

4. Pope Pius XII (1939–58).

5. Pegler (d. 1969) was a conservative American journalist who won a Pulitzer Prize in 1941 for his work exposing criminal racketeering in labor unions.

labor. He conceded that he had the Vatican sewed up, but that was only because he was such a hard worker and simply proved his value. While I was annoyed at times by his demands for more money, I rather leaned to his point of view. He had built up his news service by his own efforts, it was certainly a better service than could be expected from any official spokesman, and in Italy all news tipsters expect pay for their information. His take, by American standards, was not enormous. He levied the heaviest tribute of all on his first newspaper love, the Associated Press, and as I recall, we paid him a retainer of $50 a month for a daily bulletin, plus $2 per special question answered.

If the opulence and power of the Vatican and the magnificence of its ceremonies seemed remote from the simple accoutrements of Jesus Christ, at least one had to admire the efficiency of the Holy See as a working organization. Vatican policy was interesting to follow. Its main difference from that of national foreign offices appeared to be the long-term view which fashioned it. Nations seldom look more than a few years ahead in setting their foreign policy—the problems of the moment are pressing, the future uncertain, and governments transitory. The Vatican, with a greater sense of continuity, seemed always to be looking ahead fifty years or so. Tending to support any existing regime which gives the Church a fair deal or better, the Holy See entered into hard bargaining with Mussolini to improve its position in Italy and, having achieved its ends, collaborated with Fascism, though without compromise on matters of faith as it saw them and ever-alert against temporal encroachments. Mussolini was delighted to tie Fascism as tightly as he could to the Vatican, the House of Savoy, and to anything else that seemed secure, to make Fascism's fall a threat to them all. Fascism took the House of Savoy down with it but left the Vatican a stronger force in the country than before. Criticism in democratic countries of the Holy See's apparent benevolence toward Fascism did not perturb the Vatican too much; fifty years from now the issue will be forgotten.

* * *

Life was dull for our colleagues of the Italian press. In Mussolini's words, the newspapers of Italy were "orchestrated," a nice way of saying they could sound no notes that were not in full harmony with his own. The newspapers twice daily received their "directives"—mimeographed sheets from the Fascist Propaganda Office telling them what they must publish, must not publish, how stories should be handled, with what prominence they should be displayed, and giving them other helpful hints on how to run a newspaper. These sheets were theoretically secret and especially not intended for the eyes of foreign correspondents. But among the Fascist journalists there were those who still knew news when they saw it and got some professional satisfaction out of seeing it reported, even if they could not do so for their own papers. Such men invariably tipped us off when any of the directives spilled the beans, as they occasionally did. We found them a good news source. An order like "No mention of the riots in Sicily" might be the first news we had of riots in Sicily.

The Italian papers were not permitted to emphasize Italian crime news, since this conflicted with the Fascist claim that there was little crime under Fascism. They were encouraged, on the other hand, to elaborate on crime in America—provided it did not involve Italo-Americans— and to cite it as another evidence of the chaos which existed under democracy and of the decadence of the United States. When F. Donald Coster, arch-swindler who for years carried on behind a mask of respectability, ended his life as the police caught up with him, the Fascist newspapers went to town on the story. They dropped it, quickly and *in toto,* the following day, when further police investigation disclosed that Coster was in reality one Philip Musica, born in Naples.[6]

In earlier days, Mussolini's own newspaper, *Il Popolo d'Italia,* published in Milan, had been the main Fascist press mouthpiece. The paper also was a source of considerable personal income to the Duce, considering the fact that placing advertisements in it was one manner in which a firm— one after government contracts, let us say—could show its appreciation of the Duce's journalism. But Milan was far from the seat of the govern-

6. Musica was a swindler in the early decades of the twentieth century, running one of the largest bootleg-distribution operations on the East Coast under the aegis of a hair-tonic company. His business dealings made him extremely wealthy and influential; at the peak of his career he owned the third-largest drug company in the world. Eventually, however, his financial machinations were discovered. In December 1937, with federal authorities closing in, he killed himself.

ment, and as the years went on and Mussolini had less need of private sources of revenue, a Rome newspaper, *Il Giornale d'Italia,* emerged as the most authoritative of the Fascist organs.

This was due in no small measure to the energy of its editor, Virginio Gayda. Gayda was no more a member of the Inner Circle of Fascism than Monsignor Pucci was a member of the College of Cardinals. But like Pucci, he was a hard-working newspaperman, and he saw where the opportunities lay. He increased the circulation of his paper by resorting to the only kind of sensationalism the Press Control would tolerate— frantically extreme devotion to the Fascist cause and withering invective against its enemies. His fulminations appeared daily on the front page of the *Giornale.* His style, in contrast to Mussolini's crisp phrases, was involved and sometimes tortured. In berating the "pluto-democracies," or "demo-plutocracies," as he varied the term, Gayda often got rhetori- cally tangled, though there was no mistaking his general idea. In translat- ing such passages, we usually had to split up each of his sentences into two or three. It was by dint of hard work that Gayda made himself the Great Spokesman for Fascism and his newspaper its No. 1 organ. At first he was tolerated, later his usefulness was appreciated, but he was never taken into the higher councils of the party. On occasion, he confessed his puzzlement as to what was really going on at the Palazzo Venezia by sounding out foreign correspondents, who naturally were amused to see the Oracle himself perplexed.

The big issues of the period were the Italian *rivendicazioni*—demands for the immediate cession of Nice, Savoy, Corsica, and Tunisia to Italy— and they were shouted in the streets and before Mussolini's balcony by well-trained demonstrators and repeated every day by Gayda. Only a year before, Mussolini had indicated that Ethiopia had satisfied his colonial appetite, but the Italian proverb *L'appetito viene mangiando*[7] had proven true; now Ethiopia was but the antipasto. The threat was the same as in the Ethiopian grab—France's refusal to come to terms would mean war. The demands were based on flimsy historical and ethnic claims, but greater emphasis was placed on "justice"—Italy's right to the four ter- ritories to relieve her dire lack of resources.

7. "Appetite comes with eating."

The dishonesty of the proposition was so apparent that I decided to have some fun with Gayda. I assembled figures of the resources of the four territories, actual and potential, and called on the Great Mouthpiece. A small man with clipped moustaches, he looked more like a small-town dentist than Italy's leading polemicist but soon was rattling away like one of his editorials on the greed of the rich powers and Italy's right to some of their possessions. No longer could the Italians be kicked about; only by satisfying Italy's just and moderate claims could France be assured of peace and security in the Mediterranean. An underprivileged people was a dangerous people. Italy would be forced to resort to war to get the territories, since she must have them to live.

I showed him the figures and asked him how the annexation of four territories whose resources were on a par with those of Italy would solve Italy's lack of raw materials. He was slippery and hard to pin down, but eventually he conceded that Nice, Savoy, Corsica, and Tunisia would be of little economic value to Italy, that their real use would be as good military positions in a conflict with France, and that on obtaining them, Italy would have to demand other and richer territories if she was to get the resources which she coveted. The interview, in which the Fascist spokesman confirmed the obvious hollowness of the *rivendicazioni,* was widely published. But the validity of Italy's claims was not bothering Mussolini, who pressed them more noisily than ever in his war of nerves and tightened the Italian end of the Rome-Berlin axis.

* * *

Hitler's visit to Rome in the spring of 1938 was probably as gaudy and elaborate an organized spectacle as the Eternal City has ever seen, which is saying a lot. As the Fuehrer's train sped down the Italian peninsula, farmers along the route were mustered to line up their cattle, sporting the Italian tricolor from one horn and the Nazi emblem from the other. At Bologna, fifty locomotives joined in the adulation with a simultaneous whistle salute. At Rome, a special railroad station was erected and a road laid down to receive the honored guest. The subdued ostentation of royalty was blended with the lustier trappings of Fascism as the German and Italian big shots paraded in the King's horse-drawn carriages through the Via dei Trionfi and other thoroughfares to the Quirinal Palace, Victor Emmanuel and Adolf in the first coach. The procession took place in a classic Roman sunset, and the way was banked with a formidable display of uniforms and pretentious decorations. As the carriages passed the Coliseum, a burst of fireworks worthy of that structure's lurid past went up. According to Roman wags, the moss-grown monarch was moved to remark to his companion, "Must remind you of the Reichstag fire."

Each succeeding day brought a new circus—a naval review in the Bay of Naples, a sham battle which tore up square miles of countryside, a visit to Florence to satisfy Hitler's love of art, and a gigantic parade in Rome designed to show off Italy's military might. As a special treat, Italian soldiers did the goose-step, now discovered to have been of Italian origin and renamed the *passo romano*. Hitler looked ill at ease and out of place amidst the bright and bubbling Italian celebration. Mussolini stole the show. Romans were astonished to find Hitler red-haired and red-moustached. They had formed a mental image from his photographs and since red shows black in photographs had imagined him dark-haired. I later found that almost all Americans had similarly pictured him. The visit was said to have cost the Italian taxpayers $20 million.

The goose-step was followed by another German importation, anti-Semitism. Except for some isolated cases of hardship it inflicted, Fascism's adoption of anti-Semitism as a policy was ludicrous. Italy had no "Jewish problem." Its 50,000 Jews were fully integrated socially and economically, and Italians were probably the least disposed toward anti-Semitism of any European people. The Italian racial policy was launched under the rather comic name of *Razzismo* with the aid of a group of professors at the University of Rome, rounded up and egged on by Signor Gayda. Only a few obscure educators could be induced to sign the manifesto, and it turned out to be singularly mild. The Italian people, inhabiting a well-defined peninsula, having common language, culture, and traditions, and practically free from admixture of foreign blood for more than 1,000 years, might be regarded as the Italian race, the pronouncement said. Jews, being outsiders of different blood, did not belong to the Italian race. The professors added that they were not saying that such outsiders were inferior, but merely different. This was sufficient for Gayda to boom that Italy had freed itself from the clutches of the Jewish octopus. The decrees facilitated Fascist despoilment of a few wealthy Jews, but for the most part their application was half-hearted.

In order to enter into any contract, even an apartment lease, foreigners were required to show a "certificate of Aryanism," issued by their consulates. The American consular service refused to issue such a document on the grounds that the United States had no definition of Aryanism. Instead, Americans in Italy requiring the certificate wrote out such statements as "I hereby attest that I am an Aryan," and American consuls witnessed them as they would any other statement. The paper, bearing a consular seal, was readily accepted by Italian officials.

The British, more accustomed to making minor concessions in foreign countries when it helped them achieve more important points, were issuing the certificates. A Reuters correspondent needing one to lease an apartment applied to the British consul. "All right, but show me a baptismal certificate," the consul said.

"I haven't any."

"Then any other certificate that lists you as a Christian."

"I haven't anything like that. But can't you see I am an Aryan? My name is Murphy."

"I must have proof before I can issue a certificate of Aryanism," His Brittanic Majesty's bureaucrat insisted.

Murphy went home, ransacked his effects, and came back with a marriage certificate. "Precisely," said the consul.

With a certificate of Aryanism safely in his pocket, Murphy observed that the marriage certificate proved nothing of his race, but merely the fact that he had been married by a Christian clergyman. "I don't care what it proves," said the consul. "I had to have a piece of paper."

Razzismo included the discovery, presumably by Mussolini himself, that Italians were not Latins. Latium, Gayda explained, was simply the name of the countryside surrounding Rome; its application to a group of European countries had no justification, and Italy had no special link to these countries, especially since France, a selfish and decadent plutodemocracy, was among them. Italians certainly had more in common with the tall, silent Nordics; was not this type often glorified in Italian art? And so Italians became the dark-complexioned Nordics of the South. The slavish admiration of German characteristics and the introduction of Nazi practices which marked Fascist policy in this period probably reflected Mussolini's disappointment with his own people and his contempt for the mixture of individualism, skepticism, and defeatism which made them less useful to his plans. How much more Hitler had to work with! Any hint in our dispatches that Italy was imitating Germany or that German Nazism was dominating Italian Fascism brought a threat of expulsion from the press office. No, the two great powers were marching side-by-side as equal partners. Italians were already laughing bitterly in private moments over that propaganda.

* * *

In September 1938, I had a chance to see how the other half of the Axis lived. Hitler was ready to annex the Sudetenland, without war if possible, as Ribbentrop[8] estimated it was, but willing to have war come if it must. Had World War II begun then, its whole timetable would have been pushed ahead one year, but it is not likely that its outcome would have been much different. All of the powers involved in it had an extra year to make ready, and if the Germans and Russians were throwing more into the preparations, at least Britain and France speeded up the process during the year. It took the fall of France to make the United States begin; if France had fallen a year earlier, our preparations would have started then. The effect of the Munich settlement on history probably was nil.[9]

I arrived in the Sudetenland two weeks before the Munich Conference, part of a staff which the Associated Press was assembling on both sides of the frontier in case war came. The Czech side was under martial law, and public services, including telephone and telegraph, were suspended. I established myself in Eger, which the Czechs call Cheb. The road leading to the frontier was blocked by felled trees. I had to walk several miles each day to Arzberg, on the German side, to telephone my dispatches to Berlin.

8. Joachim von Ribbentrop was foreign minister of Germany from 1938 to 1945. He was found guilty of war crimes at the postwar Nuremberg trials and hanged.

9. In September 1938, desperate to avoid war, British Prime Minister Neville Chamberlain and French Premier Édouard Daladier agreed to cede Sudetenland to Germany.

The people on one side of the frontier were as German as on the other. The subjection of a people as Germanic as the Sudetenlanders to a rule so culturally and linguistically foreign to them as that of Prague was an invitation to trouble. That they had been a well-treated minority is a credit to the Czechs but did not resolve the problem. No one could have expected the peacemakers at Versailles to cede them to Germany, for they had never belonged to Germany. The frontier was not set at Versailles but was the old line which divided Germany and the Austro-Hungarian Empire. It simply happened that Bohemia, with a well-defined natural frontier, from time immemorial had a Czech core and a Germanic rim.[10] The Sudetenlanders, easily enticed by Nazi propaganda, thought of themselves as Germans with a natural desire to "go home." To the Czechs, they were traitors within the country, contemptuous of Czech efforts to treat them decently and bent on a partition which would be the undoing of the Czech homeland. It was another of Europe's insoluble problems—unless the uprooting of the Sudentenlanders which followed World War II can be considered a solution.

The Czech mobilization involved the peculiar chaos of the phlegmatic. Trainloads of Czech and Slovak soldiers were pouring into the frontier region to take up positions against a German attack. The same trains were carrying back hordes of Sudeten youths, called up in the mobilization but not trusted to fight the Germans. They were being sent eastward to harvest the potato crops which the Czech conscripts had been called away from. War was in the air. The Czechs were grim. The Sudetenlanders were making a show of elation. The Germans across the frontier were

10. Sudetenland was an area of more than 10,000 square miles comprising parts of the three Czech provinces of Bohemia, Moravia, and Silesia; it contained more than 3 million ethnic Germans. Until 1918 the Sudeten Germans were thus part of the Austro-Hungarian Empire, which was broken up after World War I. The Czechs wanted their own state, including the highly industrialized Sudetenland; the Sudetan Germans, however, wished to be united with Austria. At the Paris Peace Conference (1919) Sudetenland became part of Czechoslovakia.

In the 1930s Sudetan Germans experienced an unemployment rate of more than 30 percent, which they claimed was the result of discrimination. By that time the Czech government had declared Czech the national language, closed all German-language schools, barred German speakers from government employment, and taken over many German-owned firms. In these circumstances, the Sudetan German Party, financed by Nazi Germany, was able to gain ground rapidly.

confident. Among those stranded in Eger were two French *wagon-lit* conductors, each with a sleeping car on his hands. They had been on the last Paris-Prague express to cross the border before it had been closed; their instructions were to get their cars and themselves back into France as best they could. Fully expecting war and internment before they reached Strasbourg, they left Czechoslovakia with their cars on the tail of a refugee train which the Czechs had permitted to leave.

The *Reichswehr*[11] was massed on the German side, waiting for orders to put on the pincer squeeze which would end Czechoslovakia. The colonel commanding the regiment in the Arzberg area said airily that he regarded the operation as a minor one. I asked him how much resistance he expected. "It will make no difference to us whether the Czechs resist or not," he said with a wave of the hand. Melvin Whiteleather of the AP's Berlin staff, whom I met on my trips to the German side, was convinced that there would be war. I felt certain it would not come; I did not believe that France and Britain would go to war for Czechoslovakia. I offered to make a bet, but Whiteleather refused. He said he wouldn't bet on anything so frightful as war. Then suddenly the settlement of Munich burst upon us. The Czech army along the frontier went to pieces, as any army would under the circumstances. At one moment they had what amounted to a death warrant, for they were to stand against the Wehrmacht's onslaught. The next moment they had a reprieve. At one moment they were soldiers, grim but determined. The next, they were dejected country bumpkins, plodding homeward.

As the Czechs withdrew, truckloads of Nazi flags poured in from Germany in preparation for the coming of the Fuehrer. If Hitler seemed awkward before an Italian background, he was not so here. He was a different man. In this Germanic setting, he was Siegfried after having slain another dragon, he was the Avenging Angel, the People's Liberator, and the Spirit of Germany all rolled into one. Sudetenlanders, quivering with emotion, gazed upon him as upon a god as he proclaimed the arrival of *Der Tag*.[12] For the first time, I was able to comprehend something of the grip he had on the Germans. Mussolini had achieved nothing like it in Italy.

11. The German military force from 1919 to 1935, when it was expanded by Hitler into the Wehrmacht. Here Kennedy seems to use the names interchangeably.

12. "The day," presumably referring to the Sudetenlanders' longing after 1919 for the time when they would be reunified with Germany.

* * *

The fateful year of 1939 opened in Rome with the visit of Neville Chamberlain. To the Fascists, this umbrella-toting fuddy-duddy was a joke and a symbol of a decaying empire, parts of which would soon fall into their hands. Alongside quick-stepping Fascist officials he certainly seemed like that, even to an outside observer. Bourgeois Italians had a certain affection for him and gave him a mildly cordial welcome, which was said to have heartened him and made him feel all was not lost in Italy. Mussolini was courteous but patronizing, and Chamberlain plodded homeward with nothing but the cheers of a small band of Britishers in Rome, who made the old gentleman's eyes moisten as they gathered at the station to sing "For He's a Jolly Good Fellow."

The spring found Mussolini restless and hungry. He had devoured nothing since Ethiopia; meanwhile, Hitler had swallowed Austria, the Sudetenland, Memel,[13] and now the Czechs. There was too much talk about the Germans getting all the benefit of the Axis; he had his prestige to consider. Albania could be snapped up cheaply and almost overnight, and nobody would do much about it. So it was. The only important reaction was Roosevelt's indignant appeal to the two dictators for a ten-year promise of no more aggressions. In return, he promised an international conference to see what could be done about making raw materials accessible to countries like Germany and Italy. Like Hitler, the Duce turned down the proposition in tones of contempt. Laying a cornerstone for the exposition which Rome was planning for the 1940s, he asked whether anyone was fool enough to believe that he wanted war when he was proceeding with such a project. To this he added a snarl that it would take more than an international conference to correct Europe's "pyramidal errors of geography."

Early in May, Joachim von Ribbentrop came to Milan for a meeting with Galeazzo Ciano.[14] The Germans had been pressing for a full military alliance to implement the Axis; Mussolini was proceeding cautiously and

13. A town and surrounding region stripped from Germany by the Treaty of Versailles, now part of Lithuania.

14. Foreign minister of Italy from 1936 to 1943, Ciano (1903–44) was also Mussolini's son-in-law.

did not want it, at least not yet. If Germany scared the British and the French very badly, there was still a chance they might try to come to terms with him at a very fancy price. But some French and British newspapers got wind of a few isolated demonstrations of Milanese dislike of the Germans during the Ribbentrop visit and, wish being father to the thought, published sensational stories on the unpopularity of the Germans in Italy and Italian dislike of the Axis, with exaggerated accounts of the "snubs" offered Ribbentrop. Basically it was true that most Italians were fearful of the Axis and suspicious of the Germans. They were not, however, in a position to express their feelings. The articles caused Mussolini to lose his temper. He decided he'd show the *Daily Express*. He telephoned Ciano to agree to the military alliance. Thus was forged the "Pact of Steel," providing that if Germany or Italy should go to war for any reason, the other would enter the conflict at its side.

* * *

Europe was moving closer to the brink, but newspaper readers were also interested in other matters. One of them was the journey of conductor Leopold Stokowski and actress Greta Garbo. The two had avoided the press, saying they wanted only privacy. By cloaking their travels and intentions in mystery, they got worldwide publicity, and plenty of it. When they settled for a stay at the Villa Cimbrone at Ravello, a group of reporters, mainly from the London and New York tabloids, moved into the village and besieged the villa.

The offices of the news services in Rome received numerous queries from curious editors in America, but the pair refused to discuss personal affairs. Finally, Frank Gervasi of the International News Service, who knew Stokowski well, persuaded him by telephone that it was the aura of mystery that was attracting public attention and that the way to end it was to receive a group of reporters and speak frankly with them. I first met Gervasi at the death watch for Thomas Edison in West Orange, N.J., in 1931, and our paths crisscrossed for many years after that. I have come upon Frank so many times and in so many places that I would not be surprised to encounter him anywhere. Gervasi, Stewart Brown of the United Press, Whittal of Reuters, and I set out for the meeting with the maestro and the actress. Ravello, perched on a cliff high above Amalfi and overlooking a sparkling blue sea, is the most beautiful place I have ever seen, and the Villa Cimbrone and its gardens are the most beautiful spot in Ravello. The present house, property of a British family for the last two generations, is built on the ruins of a Roman villa. The gardens have a tranquility which is not of this century.

Stokowski received us in the villa's great hall and poured a round of vermouths. He said the publicity he and Garbo had been getting was most annoying and that he hoped that by this interview they could satisfy the editors at home and be left in peace. A few moments later, Garbo glided in, clad in black lounging pajamas and clutching a pair of black gloves. "You wanted to see me?" she drawled. "You wanted to ask me some questions?"

We told her we regretted disturbing her privacy but that there was considerable public interest in her trip. Perhaps she considered it none of their business, but one question editors in America wanted answered was whether she and Stokowski were going to marry. "No, you can tell them there will be no marriage," she said. "We are just making a trip together. All my life I have worked very hard—I have never had time to see much of the world. Now, with the prospect that so much beauty may be destroyed, I wanted to see some of it while it was still possible. Mr. Stokowski kindly offered to take me to some of the beautiful places of the world. He brought me here because this is one of them."

Garbo's shyness over publicity had long been regarded by many reporters as merely a ruse to get publicity, and I had come to Ravello thinking that all the mystery over her movements might have been a press agent's plan. I left, however, convinced of the sincerity of the film star's plea that she liked to be left alone. She said frankly—and I believe truly— that she simply did not like people, except for a few intimate friends.

* * *

During the summer, I took a last look around in Paris and London. Everyone knew something was coming but didn't know when and hated to think what. Confidence had risen among the people of both capitals since Munich. Their governments told them they were much better prepared now, and they were inclined to believe it.

On my return to Rome, my temper gave way when the taxi driver who drove me from the station lost his way three times. "You're the people who are going to conquer the world and you can't find your way around Rome," I growled as I paid him. He did not argue back. No great intelligence shone in his big black eyes, but there was sadness and worry. I then felt sorry for him. Like most Italians, he had no ambition to conquer the world, and his fear that Mussolini might call upon him to do so was probably the cause of his nervousness.

The final crisis moved swiftly, and when the war began it seemed like something expected and inevitable, like a sundown. There was even a kind of relief in it—at least the crises were over for good. Alan Rogers, second secretary of the American Embassy, was in the office with me each night to get the latest news. When word came in that Germany and Russia had signed a pact, he said: "The honeymoon of that pair is going to be a rip-roaring affair. But just wait for the divorce—then you'll *really* see something."

Italians were naturally on edge. Under the terms of the military alliance, Italy was to go to war almost automatically. But when the Duce spoke, the word was not war. Hitler had "no present need" for help, and for the moment Italy was taking no initiative. The day after that statement, Mussolini—for the only time in his career—could have been elected president of Italy in an honest election.

In the shift of correspondents occasioned by the war, I was transferred to Budapest. I had grown fond of Rome and the Italian people and was a little sad about leaving. Shortly before my departure, I was riding in a *carrozza* one evening with Sibyl Bingay of the *Detroit Free Press,* who had been touring Europe and was about to leave for home. She believed that anyone who remained on the Continent was a fool—it would all be blown to pieces. As we passed the Trevi Fountain, we each tossed a penny in, at my suggestion. According to legend, if you do that, you will return to Rome. I returned in 1944, under circumstances I could not have imagined in 1939. I don't know whether she ever got back to Rome.

Chapter 4

BALKAN INTERLUDE

UNEASY PEACE REIGNED IN SOUTHEASTERN EUROPE IN THE FALL of 1939. Many there could hardly believe the strange turn of events—a war in Europe going into its second month and still not a shot fired in the Balkans.[1] Amidst the relief there was almost a trace of disappointment among some more adventurous souls that this time the Continent's much-advertised powder keg had not set the conflagration off. Zagreb, the capital of Croatia, was my first stop. The Croats had already got a dividend out of the war, or at least the promise of one. Dr. Vladko Matchek, the Croat leader, had taken advantage of the opening of hostilities to threaten to turn to Hitler for help if he couldn't get satisfaction from the Serbs, who dominated the Yugoslav government. Belgrade agreed to Croatian autonomy.

My first lesson in the intricacies of Balkan politics was that, despite all that was written outside Yugoslavia about Yugoslavs, inside the country there was no such thing as a Yugoslav. There were Serbs, Croats, and Slovenes, and all three looked upon the designation "Yugoslav" with suspicion. The three peoples lumped together after World War I had been forged into a nation only on paper. Basically, there was scarcely any difference between the Serbs and the Croats. They spoke the same language, though they wrote it in different alphabets. Religion served to identify one from the other. In the borderline area, if a man was a Roman Catholic, they wrote him down as a Croat; if Orthodox, as a Serb. But even religion was not the real barrier between the two. It lay in the fact that the

1. This is a reference to the assassination in Sarajevo in June 1914 of Archduke Franz Ferdinand of Austria, heir to the throne of Austria-Hungary, by a Bosnian Serb nationalist. The assassination led Austria-Hungary to declare war on Serbia, which was the beginning of World War I.

Croats, once integrated in the Austro-Hungarian Empire, had achieved a European veneer. Hence they considered themselves more civilized, more cultured, and generally superior to their uncouth Serb cousins. To the Serbs, who had never succumbed to the Habsburgs, the Croats were softies and smoothies, not to be compared to Serbs as fighters or rulers.

* * *

After a week in Yugoslavia, I reported to the AP office in Budapest, which was charged with covering all southeastern Europe. It was headed by Bob Parker, beside whom I had worked in Paris. In succeeding months, I filled a roving assignment in the region and was away from Budapest most of the time. Like Germany and Italy, Hungary was a have-not nation, another casualty of World War I and the peace treaties. She had a larger percentage of her people under foreign rule than any other European country. The fact that she was too small to do anything about it by herself only increased her bitterness and conviction of the righteousness of her cause. Despite century-old antipathy toward the Germans, Hungary's course in World War II was set. Apart from German proximity and pressure, Revision was an obsession with Hungarians, and Hitler stood for Revision.[2] By my arrival, Budapest had already played jackal to Hitler, and the pickings in Slovakia and Ruthenia whetted its appetite for a feast in Transylvania.

To central European peoples, playing both ends against the middle is but common sense and essential to survival. While moving ever closer to Germany, Hungarian officials tried to keep on the best possible terms with the United States and even with the British. Each move toward Germany was accompanied by ever greater politeness toward American diplomats and correspondents. Throughout southeastern Europe, British and German agents were busily at work. The Germans were counting on the region for supplies and laying the groundwork for the manner in which they intended to use it in their later assault on Russia. The British,

2. Revision was a reaction to the Treaty of Trianon, which sharply reduced Hungary's territory in the wake of World War I and led to large numbers of Magyar-speaking peoples living in other countries. Hungarian sentiment toward the Treaty of Trianon was intensely hostile, especially in the interwar period.

hampered by the muddling ways of the Chamberlain government, were making a half-hearted attempt to thwart German plans. Here and there they purchased vital materials to keep them out of German hands. Espionage was actively pursued by both sides. Here the British seemed to have the edge. Now and then we had evidence that British intelligence was at work, and it seemed to be at work effectively.

The absence of any organized American intelligence in a region so full of information and of clues to the future was strange. An organization was ready-made for it. American prestige in southeastern Europe was high, and Americans generally were trusted. In all of the countries there were thousands of citizens of "double nationality"—nationals who had gone to America, been naturalized, then returned to their homelands. They called regularly at the American Legations. The sum of information which might have been obtained from them was considerable, but as far as I could determine, no effort was made to get or coordinate such information.

Our position in world affairs and the inevitability of our involvement in the war was such that the value of an adequate intelligence organization in southeastern Europe was obvious. At times I suspected that such an organization might exist—and might function so smoothly as to be invisible. This was not the case. We had no intelligence system. We had a motley group of diplomats and military attachés, some good, some bad. Our military attaché at Budapest was recalled for indiscreet remarks to the German military attaché, which spilled the beans on a confidential matter. Our minister in Budapest was John R. Montgomery, the Carnation Milk millionaire, who was rounding out his career with a fling at diplomacy. He was a likable and dignified figure, but hardly the man for the rough-and-tumble of the place and time. Concerning the information which he transmitted to Washington, one of his aides remarked that his motto, quite naturally, was "All that I have I owe to udders."

During this period, Czechia, comprising the provinces of Bohemia and Moravia, had been annexed to the Reich, but Slovakia remained outside as a German "protectorate." Few correspondents had visited Slovakia since it was given its new status, and there had been little news from there. Cy Sulzberger of the *New York Times* and I decided to see what might be happening in the protectorate. The timid little Slovak minister in Budapest was reluctant to give us visas. When we told him that a refusal to let correspondents in would inevitably be interpreted as meaning that his country was trying to hide something, he seemed frightened and yielded. We hired a car and driver and set off over icy winter roads. The car skidded off the road at one point and slid down an embankment. Even after that we could not induce the driver to put on the chains. He had previously been a locomotive engineer, he said, and didn't believe in them.

The Slovaks, poor country cousins of the Czechs, had not been accorded much participation in the administration of Czechoslovakia. The Czechs said they lacked the qualifications for it, which was largely true, as a result of their long bondage under Hungarian feudalism. Now they had a country of their own—of a sort—and not much experience to enable them to run it. We found the new Slovak officials clumsy and scared. At Presov we were arrested by the newly organized Slovak Gestapo, which was trying hard, but not very successfully, to emulate its German counterpart. For one thing, the phlegmatic Slovaks did not seem capable of getting angry at their prisoners. Cy and I were questioned separately for several hours and accused of various crimes, apparently on the off chance that we might break down and confess something. The interrogators told me that they knew that I was a well-known Hungarian terrorist in disguise.[3] Eventually we were released, but for the rest of our journey through Slovakia we were marked men, studiously avoided by all good Slovaks trying to keep out of trouble. The main fear seemed to be that any association with us might incur the displeasure of the German Gestapo, which had agents everywhere in the country. Our trip was publicized by the Nazi newspaper in Slovakia, *Der Grenzebote*, which described us as two British agents in disguise.

On arriving in Bratislava, the Slovak capital, we were received by the youthful propaganda chief of Slovakia. He also apparently suspected us, for he set a blonde girl to watch us. Cy and I dubbed her the Slovak Mata Hari and amused ourselves by going through a series of mysterious movements, which had the poor girl beside herself in perplexity. We left Slovakia the next day, with little information except that it was getting by as best it could under the German shadow.

---

3. Kennedy was accused of being a terrorist by the name of Kenedi, a common Hungarian surname.

* * *

"When in Rumania, always remember that the exact opposite of what people say is not necessarily the truth," said Fred Hibbard, counselor of the American Legation at Bucharest. He was the best-informed man I met in Rumania and easily the ablest American diplomat in the Balkans. *Domnul* Fred[4] was a tolerant man and immensely fond of Rumanians—he had stood up as godfather for dozens of little Rumanians, the sons and daughters of waiters, taxi drivers, and bartenders. I asked him if the corruption in Rumania was really as bad as I had heard. "Well," he said reflectively, "I can't say, because I don't know how bad you heard it was. But it's pretty bad . . . pretty bad."

The Legation itself was following the Bucharest custom of making a weekly payment to the cop on the beat. It had drawn the line, however, when police attempted to extort *baksheesh* from American visitors entering the Legation. Bob Parker called Rumania the "Bribery Coast." On my first visit, he and I entered the country on a Rumanian dining car, without lei, but with dollars. The official rate of exchange was then 142 lei to the dollar, but in Rumania no one sold dollars at the official rate. The black bourse[5] rate of that period was about 500 to the dollar, and later it soared to well over 1,000. The head waiter insisted he could give us only the official rate. We agreed, but demanded the Bank of Rumania receipt, which we knew he was obliged to issue on all transactions at that rate. At first he denied there was any such form, then he offered a slightly higher rate if we would forego the receipt. After dinner, we remained in the diner drinking Scotch mixed with Perla de Borsac, a heavy, bubbling Rumanian mineral water. Before ordering each round, we negotiated the sale of another dollar, each time at a higher rate. We saw the dollar quotation climb from 142 to 200, 240, 290, and finally 300 lei during that pleasant evening in the dining car. The head waiter seemed to enjoy the bargaining as much as we did. It must have been a profitable evening for him too, for in addition to his currency dealings, we noticed that he was falsifying the duplicates of our checks.

4. Mr. Fred.
5. Black market.

Modern Rumania emerged in the nineteenth century from the long night of Ottoman domination and the Crimean War's setback of Russia. The country was given a German king, Charles of Hohenzollern-Sigmaringen, and a constitution modeled after Belgium's.[6] Rumania was no Belgium. Her soil was rich, but not adapted to the cultivation of that fragile flower, democracy. Some political and economic progress was nevertheless made, and the country had singularly good luck. Oil proved a source of considerable wealth. Territorial gains were made in the Balkan Wars. In World War I, Rumania cast her lot with the Allies. Although her record was one of defeats and a humiliating capitulation to the Central Powers, the country came out of the Peace Conference with Bessarabia from Russia, the Bukovina from Austria, and Transylvania from Hungary. Luck was again with the Rumanians, and they came up with a country doubled in area and a population of 19 million. She was the size of Italy and had greater natural resources. With her gains she got troublesome minorities of 4 million potential seeds of destruction of the new Rumania.

Modern Bucharest was an imitation Paris, gaudy and meretriciously built. One of its proudest monuments was an Arch of Triumph. In view of the Rumanian army's record on the battlefield, many foreigners ridiculed so pretentious a commemoration of nonexistent victories. Apparently they had never taken the trouble to read the monument's inscription. It bore no list of triumphs like Napoleon's Arch in the Place de l'Étoile, but proclaimed, freely translated, that after being kicked around for a good many centuries, the Rumanian people had finally put one over on their neighbors. That was Rumania's triumph.

To compare Rumanian politics with the Augean stables would probably be unfair to the stables.[7] There was, however, one sincere movement in the direction of decency and democracy during the period between the two world wars. It was launched by the National Peasant Party, headed by Dr. Iuliu Maniu. Maniu, a Transylvanian who had fought against Magyarization before the deliverance of the Rumanians of that area,[8] prob-

6. Charles ruled as king of Rumania from 1866 to 1914; he was enthroned with the support of the German chancellor, Otto von Bismarck.

7. The fifth labor of Hercules was to clean the stables of King Augeas.

8. In 1918, during World War I, Hungary made a forceful attempt to impose Magyar culture and language in the region of Transylvania. The attempt was met with equally

ably was the only honest politician that Rumania has ever had. His party stood for fair elections, liberation of the peasantry from its serfdom and debt oppression, a free press, local autonomy, abolition of anti-Semitic measures, good treatment of minorities, and administrative efficiency— all radical reforms in Rumania.

In 1928 the National Peasant Party came to power, but its undoing followed shortly after. The old gang in Bucharest wanted nothing so little as its program. Sentiment in Rumania for King Carol's return from exile was a factor in its fall.[9] Maniu consented to Carol's return on his promises of a limited monarchy and the non-return of the notorious Magda Lupescu. But once Carol was back and felt strong enough, he slipped out of his promises on a King-can-do-no-wrong basis, recalled Lupescu, and ousted Maniu. Carol, gifted with Hohenzollern cunning for promoting his own interest, reinforced his power in the series of crises through which Rumania passed in the 1930s. Not strangely, a form of Rumanian Nazism arose during this period in the Iron Guard, headed by the zealot Corneliu Zelea Codreanu.[10] The movement grew strong and terrorized the country for a period, but there was no room in Rumania for both Carol and a Nazi regime, and Carol won out.

Codreanu and a dozen of his leading thugs landed in jail. When the movement remained active, Carol decided on a stronger repressive measure. The Iron Guard leader and his lieutenants were moved from the prison in a truck and mowed down on a lonely road—"shot while attempting to escape." The quality of Rumanian marksmanship alone made that explanation unacceptable. But Codreanu eventually came into his own, in true Rumanian fashion. After Carol was ousted in 1940, the Iron Guard had the Rumanian Orthodox Church canonize the dead leader and his gorillas. It was comforting to have the church's guarantee that all thir-

---

forceful resistance. After the collapse of the Central Powers and the disintegration of Austria-Hungary in the wake of the war, Transylvania became part of Rumania.

9. Carol II (d. 1953) had renounced his right to the Rumanian throne in 1925, in the wake of the scandal that erupted over his very public affair with Magda Lupescu, a pharmacist's daughter. He returned from exile in 1930 and was immediately proclaimed king. His relationship with Lupescu endured, and they were married in 1947.

10. Charismatic far right Rumanian politician and founder of the nationalistic and anti-Semitic Iron Guard organization.

teen were now in Heaven, doubtless staging anti-Semitic riots, their chief diversion on this earth.

Rumania, with its oil, wheat, minerals, and oleaginous plants, was the richest Balkan prize. The Germans had already clamped a trade treaty on the country which assured the Reich the lion's share of her exports. The British were buying goods here and there to keep them from the Germans. German technicians were everywhere. Not only were they occupied with speeding up the flow of supplies to the German war machine, but with long-range plans which were part of the New Order that Hitler was going to impose on Europe. One of these experts, my chance companion on a long train ride, outlined the program in detail and with enthusiasm. "It's what this part of the world needs," he said. "It will put the Balkan countries on their feet in a manner that England, France, or America, under the old system of trade, never could. It's true that this is our *Lebensraum*,[11] and we have got a right to it. But it's equally true that Germany is Rumania's *Lebensraum*. We must be assured of the raw materials, and they need our finished products."

I remarked that while I did not doubt that the economies of Rumania and Germany could be made to complement each other, the advantage would be Germany's rather than Rumania's. I said that any such plan was bound to halt much of Rumania's industrial development. Assigned an agricultural role by Germany, her living standards could not be raised much. "Not at all," he replied. "It is true that some Rumanian industries will be permitted to languish, but only the uneconomic ones. For every industry we destroy in this country, we shall give them a better one. For example, they have a razor blade factory. That is too fine an industry for Rumanian craftsmen, who are clumsy, and Rumania is too far from the Swedish ore. We can supply them with better razor blades for less money than they can make them. But take the case of sugar refineries. There is an industry which Rumanians can handle efficiently—under German supervision, of course. They are at present shipping thousands of bulky carloads of sugar beets to Germany. Why not refine the sugar here? That is economically sound. We are going to establish dozens of sugar refiner-

11. "Living space," referring to the Nazis' belief that additional territory was required for Germany's continued economic prosperity.

ies in this country." The German technician spoke as though Rumania were a German possession. Under the terms of the trade treaty, they were not so far from the truth.

Another German expert showed me plans for reorganizing the retail trade in Bucharest. These included the closing of some established stores, the founding of new ones, and the merger of two of the capital's department stores. Neither the Rumanian government nor the owners of the shops had as yet been consulted, but the program had been drawn up with German thoroughness. Such were the blueprints for the New Order that never came.

* * *

I spent the early part of 1940 in Bulgaria, Turkey, and Syria. In Syria, the French Middle East army, headed by General Maxime Weygand, had been widely advertised as a powerful fighting force 200,000 strong. Beirut and Damascus bristled with French uniforms, but my feeling was that the show was mostly bluff. Without any military information to support my hunch, I estimated the effective fighting force at about two divisions, not very well equipped and badly led. After the collapse of France, this was shown to be the case.

Weygand accorded me an interview but had little to offer except whining complaints that the United States was sending supplies to Russia— he cited some figures which were absurd. There was little doubt that he considered Russia a greater enemy than Germany, and one which might momentarily enter the war on the German side. He indicated confidence that France and Britain could defeat both powers. One of the grandiose French projects of the moment was the bombardment of the Caucasus oilfields by French aircraft from Syria.

Most of my Weygand interview was never published because of a feud between French civil and military authorities. The general approved of my dispatch, but civil censors butchered it secretly at the telegraph office because the commissioner-general's office claimed censorship authority. Having no Germans at hand to fight, the two branches of French officialdom in Syria and Lebanon were putting all their energy into a lively feud that was symptomatic of the French of that period.

I thought I had seen the ultimate in comic opera countries in the Balkans, but Beirut was like burlesque of a Balkan capital, with Oriental scenic effects. An *îlot* of Christian Arabs in a sea of Moslem Arabs, it was the worst advertisement for Christianity I have encountered. Even Christian Arabs conceded that they trusted a Moslem over a fellow Christian Arab. Beirut newspapers rivaled religious sects in numbers and in sincerity. The city had about twenty-five dailies. The exact number was difficult to determine because newspapers came and went rapidly, depending on what cash might be picked up in subsidies granted by public or private quarters for publishing—or not publishing—information.

One night a fire extinguisher fell from the wall of a movie house. There was a pop as its cap came off, and a few startled persons in the audience arose from their seats, then went back to looking at the film. One of the Beirut papers carried an item the next day that the theater had burned to the ground, with several persons missing. Jim Boardman, a serious young American who taught journalism at the American University, met the editor a few days later and said: "That was a terrible exaggeration you published. Why do you deceive your readers that way?"

"Nonsense," the editor replied. "We didn't deceive our readers at all. They all knew perfectly well that the theater had not burned."

* * *

Early in May 1940 the Germans published the text of a purported telephone conversation between Chamberlain and Daladier which they said had been tapped by their spies. The alleged conversation concerned Allied plans for a landing of French and British Middle East forces at Salonika for a thrust into the Balkans. The German "disclosure" was pure fantasy, part of the cover plan for Hitler's impending assault against the Low Countries. Apparently it was intended to turn Allied eyes eastward in the belief that Germany was building up an excuse for a thrust of her own into the Balkans. It fooled practically nobody, but on the off-chance that something might happen in Salonika, the Associated Press instructed me to go there. I went reluctantly, certain that the assignment would be a dull one.

I was right. Each morning I walked to the waterfront and scanned the horizon for the Anglo-French invasion which I knew was never coming.

My visits aroused the suspicions of Greek naval guards, who arrested me for questioning and released me a half-hour later. Other than that, nothing happened. My vigil ended on May 10, when, as I sat chatting with the American vice-consul, Edmund Gullion, news arrived that the Germans had struck at Holland. The Phony War was over and the battle of Europe had begun, far from tranquil Salonika. I went to Athens. The Metaxas dictatorship might be best described as an unlovely regime.[12] It was a deadening thing, but it did not go into every corner of life as Nazism and Fascism did. Speech was still relatively free; one could hear Metaxas criticized openly in cafes. Outside of official circles, one heard practically no expressions of support for the government. It seemed to exist chiefly by default. The opposition was incapable of organizing.

I got into trouble with the regime by filing a dispatch which said that troops along the Albanian frontier were being reinforced as a purely defensive measure and that airplanes were being moved from airfields at night and concealed under trees as a precaution against surprise bombings. Both statements were true, and the measures were no more than proper precautionary ones for such a period. But the government feared that the Italians might regard even such innocent moves as a provocation and issued a communiqué denying their truth. No country tried harder than Greece to give the Axis no reason for attack.

In view of Greek fears that Mussolini might attack their country, I asked the Italian minister in Athens, Mazzi, what he thought about the prospects. He was a bombastic, ultra-Fascist type who had spent some years in New York as Italian consul-general. "Why should we attack Greece?" he asked. "After this war we shall be Master of the Eastern Mediterranean, and all the countries on it will have to obey us." On the outlook for Italy's entry into the war, he said: "When the Germans hit the British Empire on the head, we will grab it by the tail." With Hitler's invasion of England, he expected Gibraltar, Malta, and Egypt to fall into Mussolini's hands like ripe plums.

An Italian could talk that way then without provoking laughter, for with the German army pouring through the Low Countries, the situa-

12. Ionnis Metaxas was a general and prime minister of Greece from April to August 1936, when he declared a state of emergency, dissolved Parliament, and declared the Fourth of August Regime. He remained dictator until his death in 1941.

tion looked bad for Britain—and Italian prowess had not yet been tested. Few who saw the Greek army, with its mule-pulled, rickety hay-wagons, would have thought it could successfully resist the Italians as it did. Six months later it was Mazzi who gave an elaborate reception at the Legation in honor of the late composer Giacomo Puccini, apparently designed to disarm the Greeks, as the Italians were moving into assault positions along the Albanian frontier. At 3 a.m., a few hours after his Greek guests had gone home, he called on Metaxas, got him out of bed, and delivered Italy's three-hour ultimatum. The Italian army was already marching on Greece as he presented the note, which Metaxas rejected on the spot.

After his return to Italy, Mazzi fell into disgrace. When things went badly for the Italians in Greece, Mussolini apparently held him partly responsible—either because he did not scare the Greeks into acceptance of the ultimatum or because he had underestimated Greece's ability to resist. When I last heard of him, he was living in Venice, a broken man, insisting that he had really been anti-Fascist all the time.

Chapter 5

THE MIDDLE EAST

EGYPT IS THE NILE AND THE NILE IS EGYPT, THE SAYING GOES. I saw proof of this before setting my foot on Egyptian soil. For hours the plane winged over a tawny expanse of desert, an overwhelming emptiness. Then I saw a green ribbon with a glistening silver thread running through it. That was the Nile and its green borders, the 5 percent of Egypt which supports 95 percent of its people. No river ever did so much for a people and got worse treated in return. Besides being Egypt's lifeblood, the Nile is Egypt's sewer, the giver of its food, the recipient of its offal and its dead cats. The river has had its revenge for the ill-treatment, for it is the breeding place of the bilharzia worm, the bladder parasite which has undermined the health and stamina of a large part of the population.

In a world fast losing national costumes and all the quaint old individuality sought by tourists, Cairo stood out all too raucously. Here the old and the new were mixed as though they had been in a head-on collision. Hotels, apartment houses, and shops which would do credit to Paris looked out on streets teeming with *fellaheen*[1] in nightshirts, street magicians with their snakes, donkey carts, and camel caravans. Shops bulged with goods; nightclubs and bars were crowded. Prices were high and business was booming. Nobody seemed much worried about the war. The Egyptians weren't in it, and the British, no matter how little the outlook justified it, seemed confident. I reached Cairo on September 3, 1940, five years to the day of my arrival in Europe. My first task was to go through the formalities of being attached to the British army as a war correspondent.

The head of public relations for the army was Major (later Colonel) Philip R. Astley, an aging playboy of finely chiseled face and graying hair.

---

1. Peasants or agricultural workers.

He was of the Guards and favored officers from the better regiments as his aides. A former husband of Madeleine Carroll, the film star, the Astley of younger days was effusively described by the actress Gertrude Lawrence in her autobiography, *A Star Danced*. "Philip was in the Guards," wrote Miss Lawrence, "everything a knight in armor should be, as dreamed of by a romantic young girl. He was born at Chequers, which is now the official country seat of all British Prime Ministers. He was christened in the robes of Oliver Cromwell and educated at Eton and at the Royal Military College, added to which he was desperately good-looking and had unparalleled charm."

I did not see Astley in quite this light at our first encounter, though he was unquestionably a gentleman of considerable charm. I gauged that his experience with the press had been limited to reading the births, marriages, and deaths in the *London Times*. He impressed me as one who would make an excellent customers' man for a topnotch investment house and a great aid and comfort to the dowagers as they clipped their coupons. Undoubtedly it was this quality that had led to his selection as head of public relations in the Middle East. Whitehall regarded correspondents, especially American correspondents, as necessary nuisances who had to be held in check but handled politely. "There's really nothing to it, you know," Astley said, explaining how censorship functioned. "You'll get used to it in two days, and then you'll see how perfectly simple the whole thing is."

There was this to it: The censorship was carried on in the name of the Egyptian government—with the "advice" of the British. If a dispatch contained military information, one submitted it to the British army censor. If it contained anything about the Royal Navy, it went to the naval censor. Any mention of the Royal Air Force required the stamp of the RAF censor. Then there was an "Anglo-Egyptian" censorship for political matters (exercised by a British officer). Each of these censors had an office in a different part of the city, and they observed different office hours. None had much authority, and they had to refer to higher quarters almost anything which deviated from the official communiqués. One had to take dispatches personally to all of the censors to answer the questions or argue any point that might come up. It was almost a day's work, and sometimes more, to get through censorship a dispatch giving a general picture of the situation and therefore falling into the fields of all the censors. But more important than that, it was practically impossible to write anything but British propaganda. In less than the two days set by Astley I saw how perfectly simple the whole thing was.

Protests by correspondents resulted in the consolidation of three of the censors in a common office. As a result of an endless struggle by correspondents, censorship did improve, slowly and slightly, through the years of the Middle East campaigns. But it remained basically bad and dishonest, admittedly political, and exceeding the needs of military security. Worse than that, it was exercised with the characteristic that seems eternally bound to all censorship—stupidity.

* * *

The Italians had a quarter of a million soldiers in Libya and almost that many more in Ethiopia. Egypt lay between them, and a junction of the two armies in the Nile Valley would have given Italy a clean sweep in Africa from the Tunisian frontier to the Indian Ocean, control of the Suez Canal and the Mideast oil. With France out of the way, Mussolini was free to hurl all his navy and air force, his total war resources, at the British in the Mediterranean. To defend the Middle East, the British had a field force of 50,000 or so in the western desert, a fleet based at Alexandria that represented no more than one-fifth of the British navy and but a token air force. A division of Australians and one of New Zealanders had come in, neither ready for battle. With the closing of the Mediterranean, a sea trip of two to three months was required for reinforcements from Britain, and only a trickle was arriving.

If numbers—numbers of soldiers, warships, airplanes, and guns—meant anything, Egypt and the Suez Canal were as good as in the Italian bag. To the American minister, it seemed only a matter of time when he would be functioning as envoy to an Egypt under Italian occupation. King Farouk,[2] according to reliable informants, was pinning his hope of holding his throne on his final talk with the Italian minister, who had assured him that Italy understood his position under the British and would be

---

2. Farouk I ruled Egypt from 1936 until 1952, when he was deposed in the Egyptian Revolution. He died in Italy in 1965.

well-disposed toward him, provided Egyptian aid to the British was held to a reasonable minimum.

If such awe of Italian prowess now seems absurd, it must be remembered that the abysmal weakness of Italy had not yet been revealed. Mussolini was still the conqueror of Ethiopia and Albania. To a few, there was a portent in the fact that Italy, on declaring war in June, did not spring to action. The British were stunned then by the fall of France, which had taken down with it the main land force of the Allies in the Mideast, the Weygand army in Syria. In the desert, Mussolini might be waiting for more favorable weather in the autumn, but he did not even attempt to take Malta, on his doorstep. Instead of grabbing the British Empire by the tail, as forecast, the Italians took the safer course of grappling with a prostrate France. They proved poor even at that. The whole story of Fascist Italy's incapacity to complete its preparations for World War II has since been laid bare. Mussolini, realizing his weakness, banked on a speedy collapse of Britain. Then Mediterranean loot would not merely be cheap— it would be free. At the time, the odds seemed good. But like many who have sought something for nothing, he ended up with nothing.

The Italians in Libya burst out of their lethargy on September 13, with what the Fascist press acclaimed as a full-scale invasion of Egypt. They advanced for three days along the coastal shelf against only skirmish action by the British and halted at Sidi Barrani, a Bedouin village seventy-five miles inside the Egyptian frontier. Here they settled down to mass supplies, building desert fortresses around their holding and a road the length of the strip. They were still three hundred miles from the Nile Valley.

* * *

Mussolini, wearying of Marshal Rodolfo Graziani's whines about the difficulty and risks of continuing without long preparations, impetuously launched his attack on Greece. Again he was attracted by something cheaper, again he was disappointed. The Greeks, the most wantonly aggressed of all victims of the Axis, soon had thrust the Italians back into Albania and were talking about driving them into the sea.[3] The British,

3. After overrunning Albania in 1939 and making it an Italian protectorate, Mussolini invaded the northwest mountains of Greece in late 1940, only to be driven back by the Greek army.

giving their new Greek allies as cheerful a welcome as circumstances permitted, had little to spare in the Eastern Mediterranean. The Greeks, in
turn, were chary of British aid on a scale which might bring the Germans
down on them. An agreement for limited assistance was made. The British loaned the Greeks a few RAF squadrons and were permitted to occupy
Crete and establish a naval station in Suda Bay there.

While we were waiting for something to happen in the desert, Alan
Moorehead of the *Daily Express* and I were selected by Public Relations
and told in a whisper that we might accompany General Sir Archibald Per-
cival Wavell, the commander-in-chief, on an inspection trip to Crete. We
took off from Alexandria in a big Sunderland flying boat and winged over
the sea that Mussolini said was his without interference. Wavell read a
volume of Browning and chatted discreetly with us as tea was served. We
put down on Suda Bay.

Moorehead and I visited units camped in the island's pleasant olive
groves and at length encountered a captain overflowing with efficiency
and helpfulness. "It was really none of my affair, you know, but here was
Wavell coming and no decent arrangements made for him," he said. "So I
found this well-concealed farmhouse. Nice little shack, don't you think?
I persuaded the family to move out—the natives are really quite fine
that way. I got some workers and had them clean up and do a little paint
job, too. I requisitioned a few odds and ends. Nothing really official, you
know. I suppose the British army will pay up. If not, we can give the stuff
back or make it up some other way." He showed us the bedroom he had
prepared for the general, all in true military simplicity, with a neat iron
bed and a table with a couple of well-selected books in English on it.

The next day, as we were departing, the captain arrived at the wharf
with the commander-in-chief. By this time he seemed to be handling all
details of the visit and doing it well. As Wavell stepped on the launch, a
large camera appeared in the captain's hands. He started to pose Wavell
for a picture. I knew instinctively that he was a newspaper photographer—all newspaper photographers have unmistakable mannerisms. I
was right. He was Geoffrey Keating of Fleet Street, in the army as a War
Office photographer. He later headed the British army's corps of photographers through the three desert campaigns.

It soon became plain why Wavell had permitted two correspondents to accompany him to Crete. His trip was a deception mission. He was up to his neck in plans for an offensive in the desert, a secret so well kept that not more than a half-dozen men on his staff knew anything about it until it was ready to be launched. Wavell was still hopelessly outnumbered, but the Greeks had shown the way in throwing the Italians back and made him decide to take a gamble. There was no possibility of establishing adequate supply lines across the vast stretch of desert; neither the supplies nor the transport was at hand. His plan, a daring one, was to attack with only a few days' supplies and count on capturing from the enemy the wherewithal to keep the drive going. Borrowing from strategy employed by Edmund Allenby, under whom he had served in the Mideast in World War I, he moved troops by night to places close to the Italian forts, where they lay hidden as long as forty-eight hours, half-buried in the sand.

The attack came at dawn on December 9 and was directed at Niebeiwa, a fortified camp containing a force under General Pietro Maletti, picked to spearhead the Italian drive to the Nile when it got underway. The camp was overrun before the Italians recovered from the surprise, Maletti dying as he fought it out behind a machine gun. The art of military deception, at which the British excel and of which the Italians were easy victims, helped make up for the great odds. The Italian spies in Cairo were mostly known to the British. They were not rounded up, but left in circulation and fed what information the British desired the Italians to have.

As Niebeiwa was attacked, a feint was made at Maktila, the easternmost of the strong points that the Italians had established around Sidi Barrani. For this there was a company, partly inside dummy tanks of wood and canvas which they moved about by walking. The outlines of eight pieces of artillery also appeared on the desert horizon. One was a real cannon; seven were of wood. The object was to occupy the 2,000 Italians there to prevent them from reinforcing Barrani. The operation's success was beyond expectations. The Italians at Maktila were not only kept from Sidi Barrani—they surrendered outright. The whole coastal strip which the Italians had occupied in Egypt was cut to ribbons in two or three days, as small British armored columns skirted its southern edge and made thrusts to the sea in several places. Forty thousand confused Italians, and all the equipment and stores they had built up for the march to the Nile, were taken.

This first desert campaign was on a small scale compared with the size of later operations, and the number of correspondents accompanying the force was correspondingly small compared with the hordes in the field in the later phases of the war. There were Christopher Lumby of the *London Times*, Arthur Merton of the *Telegraph*, Alex Clifford of the *Daily Mail*, Moorehead, George Laycock, and I. With every desert-worthy vehicle that could be scraped up needed for the operation, it was to be expected that the transportation made available to us would have something wrong with it. Public Relations sent us off to war, under the watchful eyes of our conducting officers, in Ford station wagons too badly jounced by desert travel to be of much value to the army. Luckily, a small baggage truck followed these vehicles, and as each foundered, its occupants got into the truck. Soon we were all in it, wedged among the camp beds and rations. We were designated as a self-sufficient unit, expected not to draw on the limited supplies in the desert. That meant we had to carry everything we needed, including gasoline and water. We slept on our camp beds in the open; the desert army was an untented one in those days. Our army rations consisted almost exclusively of corned beef, but we shared in the loot, and soon we had loaded our truck with the best pickings of the Italian officers' messes, including a barrel of wine, which we carried on the roof.

The few Italians who escaped capture in Egypt were chased over the frontier. Here, in front of the ruined Fort Capuzzo, Mussolini had erected a triumphal arch with imperial eagles on it and bearing the inscription "As far as here, O Mother Rome, thy voice is heard." The success in Egypt, especially the amount of supplies and vehicles taken, whetted Wavell to drive into enemy country. The first obstacle was Bardia, "key to Libya," containing a heavily armed force of 40,000 with six months' supplies, behind a formidable double perimeter of steel, concrete, and barbed wire twenty-five miles in length and running to the sea at either end.

The Australians, now ready for combat, joined the desert army and, with British armor, cracked Bardia open and overran it in two days' fighting. Two weeks later, on January 27, Tobruk, seventy miles to the west, was reduced in a similar attack. Its defenses were even stronger than those of Bardia. As we awaited the assault on Tobruk, I joined a party of Australian correspondents. It was quite cold—freezing just before dawn—and we lived in a cave which apparently had been used, off and on, since the Stone Age. Inscriptions and hieroglyphs marked its walls, but with a bright fire burning it was a comfortable nook, free from the two great desert plagues of flies and sandstorms. As the zero hour approached, a forward-looking officer of the Pioneers[4] had his men digging a neat row of graves in the sand. "After Bardia I had a devil of a job for the small force that I've got," he said. "This time we're getting a head start."

With the fall of Tobruk, the collapse of the Italians in Cyrenaica was amazing, the eagerness with which they surrendered almost unnatural. In the first days of the campaign, some correspondents had amused themselves by rounding up willing prisoners in batches of fifty or a hundred. Now it was necessary to shoo them away to get any work done. Every Italian unit, every tank, seemed to carry a white flag as standard equipment. At Tobruk, high officers packed their bags as the fighting dwindled and were ready to go when the last shot was fired. A black-bearded colonel, seated on his valise at the roadside, arose, saluted, and offered his surrender as we walked through the town. His tunic bore five rows of medals. "You must have been in a lot of battles to get all those medals," someone said. "Not all are for battles," he replied. "Some are for earthquakes."

Derna, ninety miles farther into Cyrenaica, is at the end of the desert and the beginning of the green country, and the first populated place of any importance west of Alexandria. Here the Italians could not be cut off, because armor could not cross the great gulch which runs south from the town. They held out for several days, dropping heavy artillery fire over a ridge which protected them, and then withdrew by night, blowing up the road leading down into the town.

It was the fashion of those early days of the war for correspondents to write hair-raising stories on "How I Almost Got Killed Today." With many soldiers *getting* killed, I could not see much point to the lurid accounts of the personal escapes of onlookers. But such stories were in demand, especially in England. British propaganda officials seemed to encourage

---

4. The Pioneer Corps performed a wide range of tasks during the war, primarily involving light engineering projects such as building roads or bridges. They also served as stretcher-bearers.

them, perhaps because they thought they let the people at home and in America know that the Phony War was over and the British now were fighting in earnest.

Outside Derna I walked into one such experience without seeking it. The day was peaceful, the air was crisp, and the desert had been washed by a winter rain. Squadron leader George Raughton of RAF Public Relations and I were strolling across the airport, already in British hands. The artillery over the ridge suddenly opened heavy fire on the field. We jumped into a rickety Italian shelter. I suppose it was our imagination, but every shell seemed aimed at us. For forty-five minutes they fell, knocking off part of the shelter roof and bringing down debris on us. I know I trembled with fear, but my main feeling was one of irritation for having exposed myself to such fire without good reason.

The withdrawal of the Italians gave Derna's 12,000 natives their first taste of freedom in a long time, and they enjoyed it in accordance with their traditions. Looting of Italian houses began on a restrained scale in the morning and increased when the first Australian patrols to enter indicated no great disapproval. Some Australian soldiers were obligingly battering down doors for the fun of seeing the ragged, screaming, fighting Arabs rush in and carry off every movable object. By nightfall the Italian quarter of Derna looked like a locust-ravaged field, and even some of the Arab shops had suffered. Order was restored quickly, however, as the town major and his occupying forces showed up.

* * *

The Italians had withdrawn to Bengazi. The fall of their Libyan strongholds of Badia, Tobruk, and Derna had left this city and all that remained of Cyrenaica untenable. The British were still 150 miles away, and the coast road was protected by demolitions and rear guards. Counting on enough time to do the job, the Italian command organized a methodical withdrawal into Tripolitania. Part of the Italian civil population was flown to Italy; the rest accompanied the army on a 500-mile trek for Tripoli. A British armored force, however, made a brilliant and grueling march across the desert far inland and reached the Tripoli road, 50 miles outside Bengazi. It was a close race. An hour and forty minutes later, the great cortege, comprising all that Mussolini had left in Cyrenaica, ran smack into the waiting armor. The Italians attempted to break through, but their confusion was too great. At the end of the battle, 10 miles of the road was littered with wrecked vehicles and bodies, and the survivors were begging for capture.

This first desert victory annihilated an Italian army 150,000 strong and provided a big and badly needed boost in morale for the British at home, then undergoing the worst of the bombing. Coupled with the brave struggle of the Greeks, it exposed, completely and for good, the Fascist myth of the Italians as a warrior people and Italy as a formidable military power. It spelled the effective end of the Axis, for it divested Italy of any pretense of parity in the combination and reduced Mussolini to undisguised German domination. On the day Bengazi fell, the first units of the Afrika Korps arrived in Tripoli to take over the war in the desert—a supreme humiliation for Fascist arms.

If war can be romantic and adventurous—it seldom is to the soldiers who fight it—the Wavell campaign probably came nearer to being so than any other of World War II. The old regimental spirit of the British army was strong. Units bearing such anachronistic names as Guards, Hussars, and Yeomanry fought with fierce pride and rivalry to add new glory to their lists of battle honors. Above all, the British learned the desert, tamed it, and made it their ally. The Italians planned and fought in terms of colonial warfare. They followed practices which had been effective in their subjugation of the rebellious Senussi tribesmen[5] but which were bound to fail against a modern army. Far from making the desert their friend, they feared it, and locked themselves up in strongholds such as Bardia and Tobruk. The application of mechanized warfare to the desert made operations not so different from those at sea. In giving up their mobility the Italians placed themselves at the worst of disadvantages. The mass of Italian soldiers fought without much heart and fell below their British and American opposites in resourcefulness and stamina, but the weakness of the Italian top was greater. Captured documents revealed Graziani's intelligence as extremely bad. Staff work, planning, and rear-area organization had been shot through with bickering incompetence

---

5. Members of a Libyan sect that led the country's resistance to the Italian invasion.

and petty feuding. If Fascism had given the Italian armed forces a new facade of confidence, it had also endowed them with its own corruption.

* * *

Life in the desert—at least for correspondents—was a holiday compared with working in the enervating headquarters atmosphere of Cairo. On my return to Cairo, an inspection of what the censors had done to my dispatches was disheartening. The word "wells"—a cablese form whose context made clear that it stood for "as well as"—was deleted for violating the rule against mentioning water resources in the desert. The fact that the Australians had used the word "kangaroo" as a password during a certain operation was blue-penciled; they might want to use the word again. Headquarters felt that any indication that the Italians were not always the fiercest of fighters minimized the achievement of their British victors. Any factual matter to this effect was struck out. And it was feared that any unkind remark might goad the enemy to greater resistance. So our dispatches, as abbreviated and amended by censors, spoke only well of the Italians.

Army censorship in Cairo was by this time in the hands of a major selected for the job because he had once broadcast cricket matches. He was assisted by a young subaltern whom Bob Casey of the *Chicago Daily News* has described as "arrogant, humorless, sarcastic, and overinflated," with unlimited opportunity to develop his character in his role as a censor. His deletions, often based on his incapacity to understand our copy, were bad. But I felt that his alterations and "improvements" went beyond even the official conception of what censorship should be. I protested. "Those few changes were put in to help you," the major explained. "You weren't here, and the only alternative was not passing the dispatch at all. I have never met more unappreciative people than you correspondents."

A story which I had written about the arrival in the desert of plasma made of blood donated by Americans had been submitted to a high medical officer to assure its scientific accuracy. He found nothing wrong with the facts but added a few frills to my literary style and wrote into the dispatch this observation: "The fact that some British soldiers show signs of an American accent is, however, more likely due to the influence of Hollywood films than to the fact that they now have American blood in their veins." Instances like this one confirmed my theory that if you give a man a blue pencil and the authority of a censor, strange things happen to him.

* * *

Cairo was as bustling and carefree as ever. Egyptians shared in the jubilation over the victory in their own detached way. One Arabic newspaper, commenting on Egypt's contribution, pointed out that while Britain had supplied the men and arms, Egypt had furnished the desert for them to fight in. An Egyptian cartoon showed an embarrassed Mussolini complaining, "But Greece is too mountainous," and an angry Hitler replying, "Yes, and Egypt was too flat." Everything, it seemed, was available in Cairo for a price. *Everything.* One shop, in letters four feet tall, advertised "Coronation Robes for Royalty." Let a stray king pass by on his way to be crowned, and Cairo had a robe ready for him, war or no war.

GHQ, Middle East, was entrenched in an enormous eight-story apartment house development taken over as construction was completed in 1939. The several buildings were enclosed behind a barbed-wire perimeter, like a little Tobruk in the midst of Cairo. New arrivals, especially Americans, were shocked to find that GHQ observed Egyptian office hours—five hours for lunch. Gray Pillars, as headquarters was known, got in a good morning's work, knocked off at noon, and functioned again for two hours in the early evening. There were efforts to change this system, but they always failed. It was defended as the most practical and efficient schedule for Cairo's heat. I could never decide whether it was or not.

Cairo probably offered the best facilities of any city on earth for keeping officers from their work. The bars and terraces of the Turf Club, Shepheard's, and the Continental-Savoy were jammed with men in uniform at lunchtime; for those who wanted to make an afternoon of it, there was the Gezira Sporting Club on an island in the Nile. In the evening, a vast array of Bacchanalian and Sybaritic attractions were available and well patronized. Weekends brought horse races at two tracks. A good percentage of the girls regularly seen with members of the armed forces were reputed to be spies, and occasionally they disappeared, presumably falling into the toils of the Counter-Intelligence Corps. Espionage was not

easily controlled. At the start of the war, it was against the law in Egypt
to spy on the Egyptian army, but there was no law against spying against
the British army. This was later remedied. After the British reverses in
the desert in 1942, General Sir Claude Auchinleck, blaming matters partly
on the pleasure-loving officers of Mideast headquarters, ordered them to
abandon their city offices and apartments and live in tents in the desert
outside Cairo. But the Gezira grenadiers were never ones to surrender
easily in such matters, and the plan was dropped.

* * *

The keystone of British policy in the early part of 1941 was to get the assistance of the United States. Standing alone, save for the Dominions,
and faced by an overwhelming German superiority, this was Britain's
only hope of victory. The Lend-Lease Bill was before Congress. Britain's
plea, heroically voiced by Winston Churchill, was: "Give us the tools and
we will finish the job." This was a dishonest statement. Churchill and everyone else knew that given no matter how much material aid, Britain
did not have the manpower to beat the German army. Roosevelt was no
less dishonest in implying that the furnishing of arms to Britain might
spare the United States from war. Both knew that Lend-Lease was a stepping stone to our entry into the conflict. But the insincerity of the public
utterances of the two leaders was merely a facade erected to meet the exi-
gencies of the moment. Behind it, there is no doubt that both were acting
in what they believed the best interests of their respective peoples. And if
Lend-Lease brought war closer to the United States rather than staving it
off, at least it bolstered the British until our gigantic preparations were in
full swing. In less guarded moments, even the censors disclosed that all
British actions were bent in one direction. After I had argued lengthily
with a high censorship official that a dispatch which I wanted to send
contained nothing affecting military security, he said petulantly, "Yes,
but that story certainly won't help get the United States into the war."
That was final. The dispatch didn't go.

I felt that the American correspondents in the Middle East bore a
heavy responsibility. I was convinced that the United States was inevitably moving toward war and inescapably bound to become involved in it.

Nevertheless, the American people were in the course of making the momentous decision. They certainly had a right to the fullest information that could be given, short of military data of value to the enemy. They were relying on us for information from the only area in which the British supplicants and prospective partners were in direct contact with the enemy by land, sea, and air. In theory, British officials agreed with this argument; in practice, they almost always found some run-around technique for suppressing any news they desired suppressed and had intricate machinery for slanting much of the rest.

The American Legation might have exerted considerable pressure to improve censorship, but it was of little help. Alexander Kirk, who succeeded Bert Fish as minister, gave the American correspondents some lip-service at first but soon made clear that his assignment, as he saw it, was to promote American entry into the war. When I asked him to intercede in getting a certain dispatch through censorship, he conceded that the dispatch was legitimate news but expressed fear that "some mealy-mouthed isolationists in the Senate" might quote it, to the embarrassment of the Administration. I said that since we were not yet at war, I thought that even an isolationist, no matter how mealy-mouthed, had a right to his views. Kirk agreed in principle, of course, but made no move to get the dispatch passed.

* * *

In early 1941 Mussolini was stymied in the mountains of Albania, but Hitler was massing troops in southeastern Europe to redeem the Axis in Greece and get set for his attack on Russia. In one way or another, Britain had failed to save the Czechs, the Poles, and the Norwegians. In the Balkans, a British guarantee had come to be regarded as a liability. Should Britain now fail the Greeks, British prestige in America would be low indeed. So Rule No. 1 of British policy dictated the sending of a force to Greece. The decision was made by Churchill, not for love of the Greeks, nor in hope of stopping the thirty-six divisions that Hitler potentially had available. The course was set for its effect on the United States.

I sailed for Greece in March, in a trawler escorting one of the convoys in which Wavell shifted half his Mideast force across the Mediterranean.

We were bombed on the trip. I have never encountered finer men than those of our trawler. When Britons are backed at bay, they are superb. The army sent to Greece had a division of Australians, mostly veterans of the Desert Campaign; a division of New Zealanders new to battle; a British armored brigade; and other odd lots of British—60,000 in all. It was under the command of "Jumbo," the bulky General Sir Henry Maitland Wilson. He commanded a number of operations in World War II, and almost all of them went badly. Yet competent military men, including critical American observers, seemed to retain a fairly high opinion of his ability. He was good at explaining his failures and making the explanations stick.

We correspondents attached to the Expeditionary Force were immobilized in Athens almost a month. We were not even permitted to inform our offices of our whereabouts. The presence of the force was officially a secret, although uniforms were visible everywhere and the German Legation functioned normally, for Germany and Greece were still at peace. The German military attaché, who spoke perfect English, visited a New Zealand encampment and on his departure presented the stupefied officers with his card. The "secrecy" was due to a Greek desire not to "provoke" the Germans to attack.

Cy Sulzberger of the *New York Times* was in Greece when we arrived. He became accredited to the British army so he might report on the new force when it went into action. During the "secrecy" period he drove to Belgrade, where, free from British and Greek censorship, he filed a full account of the presence of the British in Greece. It was published prominently by the *Times*. British officials were furious. They accused Sulzberger not only of evading censorship but of revealing British troop movements and positions which he had observed during his trip. They muttered of dire penalties to be imposed on him if he fell into British hands and even held his disclosures partly responsible for the British defeat in Greece. This accusation seemed absurd to me since the British went into Greece knowing they would be defeated.

Some of the correspondents in Greece, bitter over Sulzberger's journalistic triumph at their expense, added their denunciations to those of the officials. They demanded that he be deprived of British army facilities in the future. I did not join in the protest. Not having heard Sulzberger's side of the story, I did not know what justification he might have had for sending the dispatch. And I certainly did not believe it in the interest of a free press for chagrined correspondents to gang up with censorship officials against another correspondent when the whole pretense of the secrecy of a British force in Greece was absurd. It was a fact, I believe, that the British, in accrediting Sulzberger, had through an oversight neglected to obtain his signature on the formal agreement to abide by the rules of censorship. This was a technicality, of little moral weight. In defending his action, Sulzberger said the arrival of the Expeditionary Force in Greece was common knowledge in Belgrade, which was emphasizing the strength of the force and encouraging correspondents to write about it. He argued that he did not see why the fact that he had seen some of the force should bar him from writing what every other correspondent in Belgrade could write.

The Germans did not have to fight their way the length of Yugoslavia. The Bulgarians had accepted a German occupation, and the Germans had massed a force in the southwestern tip of that country. One prong raced down the Vardar Valley to Salonika. Another drove through the Monastir Pass in southern Serbia. The Yugoslav army went to pieces; generals wandered along roads looking for their divisions. The thrust through Monastir split the British and Greek forces and was the end of the so-called Olympus line in northern Greece. When the Germans struck, we were liberated from our Athens imprisonment; the presence of a British army in Greece was at last officially divulged. We reached Larissa in time to see all that remained of the RAF in Greece—a squadron of Hurricanes— destroyed by German fighters on the airfield. At Tyrnavos, some miles north, we were barely able to advance against the military traffic speeding pell-mell in the opposite direction. The British were falling back to attempt to establish a new line from Thermopylae to the Gulf of Corinth— a good natural line, well buttressed by mountains.

When the mayor of Tyrnavos told us that the only news he had was that he was appointing a committee to deal with the Germans, we decided we might as well turn back and get a vantage point on the new line. That night we reached Thermopylae. Since school days, I had imagined the famous pass to be a gap between two mountains; I was surprised to find it was a shelf between the mountains and the sea. The hot springs from which the place takes its name ran through a concrete spillway. Nearby was a small amusement park, closed for the war. We took a bath in the spillway and camped in a grove. On succeeding days the Luftwaffe bombed and strafed the roads at will; all opposition had been knocked out of the sky. We were black and blue from jumping into ditches.

The Greeks are a mercurial people. Their victories over the Italians exalted them to the greatest heroism. The German breakthrough plunged them into despair. On April 22 they gave up. They requested the British to remove all troops from the Greek mainland. The King and government left for Crete. The withdrawal from Greece was one of the great sagas of the war. It was Dunkirk on a smaller scale, but no less heroic. It was the British army at its very best: in adversity. The Australians and New Zealanders, who had come 7,000 miles to be thrown into this hopeless battle, came through the debacle with unflagging determination. Three-fifths of the Expeditionary Force escaped, an achievement of high order in the circumstances. Most of the troops avoided Athens and headed straight for the Peloponnesos Peninsula, to be taken off the beaches by every craft that the British navy could gather. Kent Cooper, general manager of the Associated Press, scanning the reports in New York, apparently got panicky. He ordered me to leave Greece at once. A little Greek vessel, the *Elsa,* chartered by the British, was leaving Piraeus, the port of Athens, that night. I arranged to get on it.

In the afternoon I met my old friend of Spanish days, Angel Angelopoulos. After his release from jail—he credited Farnsworth, Minifie, and myself with saving him from likely execution on the trumped-up charge of espionage—he had returned to Greece. There he had set up in business, supplying Greek newspapers with American comic strips—strips in which Greek words came out of the mouths of the characters familiar to all American newspaper readers. We went into the deserted bar of the King George Hotel. I told him about the ship and asked him if he wanted to come. He considered the matter, then rejected the suggestion. "It isn't very pleasant to look forward to living under German occupation," he said. "But this is my country, and I think I'll stay and take my chances." He came through the occupation and is now International News Service correspondent in Athens.

I took aboard the *Elsa* with me Mary Brock, wife of a *New York Times* correspondent, a refugee from Belgrade; Peter Tompkins, an American writer; and Mary's dog, Slatko. We drove to the docks in Tompkins' car, threading through a labyrinth of streetcar tracks twisted out of their beds by recent bombings. Tompkins abandoned the car on the wharf. The *Elsa* was jammed with Australian soldiers and a strange mixture of civilians. In its hold were 150 captured German soldiers. We slid slowly out of the harbor on a night which was, luckily, moonless; scarcely were we outside the boom when the port got another bombing. The *Elsa* was the last vessel of any size to get away from Piraeus.

* * *

By my return to Egypt most of the land gains made by Wavell in the desert had been wiped out. General Erwin Rommel and his Afrika Korps had gone into action. They were of a different metal than the Italians. Taking the British route in reverse, they had recaptured Cyrenaica. The Germans had not, however, destroyed an army. Most of the newly arrived Australian division which was holding the desert had taken refuge behind the perimeter of Tobruk. The most remarkable siege of the war followed. The Tobruk force not only held out for seven months but harassed the enemy and built up supplies for an eventual breakout. What must have galled Mussolini, the Australians proved the worth of the Italian fortifications. They did so not by locking themselves up behind them but by organizing a mobile defense which could be moved quickly to meet a penetration at any part of the perimeter.

Hitler tossed victory away half a dozen times. His greatest mistake was his greatest victory, the Battle of France. Had he permitted the Phony War to continue in the West and marched against Russia with assurances that this was his real fight, British and French apathy of the first eight months of the war would almost certainly have deepened. There would have been no terrifying jolt to bring Britain to action. Chamberlain would probably have remained pleasantly at the helm, perhaps according Russia a good-luck cheer, but surely not much more. Large segments in both countries would have been, and perhaps quite openly, on Hitler's side. After his victory in France, Hitler might again have assured victory by invading Spain, taking Gibraltar and sealing the Mediterranean. But here he apparently relied on the Italian navy, and while the Mediterranean route was almost cut off for a long period, enough [ships] got through to turn the scales for the British in the Middle East at critical periods.

Greece was a miniature Battle of France, both as a victory and as an error. Had the Germans kept out of Greece and instead put a little more strength into the desert, there is little doubt that they could have taken the Middle East while the best half of its defenders were in Greece. A thrust into the Nile Valley at that time would have cut off Wavell's troops from their base and stranded them in Greece, a worse fate than the rout which befell them. Once the Germans had taken Egypt, the whole Middle East was theirs, for the rest of it was practically undefended. The Mosul and Persian oil would have been assured and the way opened for a two-pronged assault of the Caucasus, which almost certainly would have turned the balance at Stalingrad. Erwin Rommel and his Afrika Korps, however, were left poised on the Egyptian frontier, waiting for reinforcements and supplies. The Germans crowned their Greek victory with a spectacular airborne conquest of Crete. Then they cast their eyes toward the Caucasus along the shortcut route of Syria, Iraq, and Persia. They tried to ripen this area for their penetration as they had in the Balkans. They were at a disadvantage; there was no Wehrmacht close at hand to back up their diplomatic moves with the terror of immediate invasion.

Persia harbored many German agents, the Shah's hospitality to them springing from his fear of Russia. The Germans had the means of controlling the Vichy French in Syria. Between these two countries lay Iraq, where Abdul Illah, regent for the boy King, played the British game.[6] The Germans had in Baghdad a figure bent on emulating Lawrence of Arabia. He was Fritz Grobba, an old hand in the Middle East, who was distributing gifts ranging from Mercedes Benzes to bicycles to sheiks, depending on their importance. Iraqi officers dining at his house found bills from five to fifty pounds under their plates, depending on their rank and usefulness. Grobba was successful with Prime Minister Sevyid Rashid Ali El Gailani. Iraq was bound to Britain by a treaty which had replaced the British mandate in the 1920s, but Rashid Ali took his cues from Grobba. The

---

6. Faisal II became king of Iraq in 1939, at the age of three, upon the death of his father in a car crash. Abdul Illah was his uncle.

British and Abdul Illah lined up enough support in the Iraqi Parliament to overthrow his cabinet.

Rashid Ali proved more trouble out of office than in. In April he achieved a coup d'état with the aid of Grobba and the Iraqi army, and the regime of Rashid Ali and his Golden Four began. The four were Iraqi generals. The regime was enriched by a guest participant, El Hag Effendi El Husseini, the deposed Mufti of Jerusalem, long a thorn to the British. The Mufti had escaped from Palestine disguised as a woman; the French in Syria had permitted him to proceed to Iraq. With the aid of two conspirators of the caliber of Grobba and the Mufti, finding a good reason for the revolt was no big problem for Rashid Ali. He charged the Regent with plotting to usurp the throne of his five-year-old nephew, Faisal II, deposed him, and named an aged sheik in his place. Abdul Illah, fearing for his life, fled to the American Legation in pajamas. The American minister, the late Paul Knabenshue, and his wife hid him under a lap robe in their car and spirited him from Baghdad to the safety of the big RAF base at Habbaniyah.

The British met the situation by landing troops at Basra, Iraq's port on the Persian Gulf. Rashid Ali, not yet ready for armed conflict with Britain, accepted the landing as being in accordance with Britain's rights under the Anglo-Iraqi Treaty. A few weeks later, when more British troops debarked at Basra, Rashid Ali put his foot down. As he interpreted the treaty, Britain might land troops once, but not a second time. He cut off the pipeline from the Mosul oilfields to Haifa, where the British Mediterranean Fleet refueled. The Iraqi army occupied heights dominating Habbaniyah and shelled the airfield, without much effect. The British replied with the only artillery they had—a pair of old cannons ornamenting the Administration Building.

The British right to an airbase at Habbaniyah also was written into the Anglo-Iraqi Treaty. The base, a convenient stop on the way to India, is set in the dustiest of desert terrain on the banks of the unlovely Euphrates, sixty-five miles west of Baghdad. Like many British outposts, it was more English than England. In peacetime, RAF officers even rode to hounds in traditional hunting regalia, a desert jackal replacing the fox. The British force at Basra started a march up the Tigris Valley toward Baghdad. Another force set out from Trans-Jordan for the relief of Habbaniyah. Iraqi troops fell back slowly before both groups. The small garrison at Habbaniyah was composed of Assyrian mercenaries. Until I went to Iraq, I did not know there were Assyrians left in the world; I had classed them with the Philistines and the Toltecs. But here they were, and as a Christian minority in Iraq they enjoyed shooting at the Iraqi. They held Habbaniyah without much trouble until an attack by a few antiquated RAF bombers drove the Iraqi from the heights.

A Luftwaffe detachment arrived to aid the Iraqi. The jump from Greece was too long to make without a stop, so the planes landed at Aleppo, in Syria, where the French permitted them to refuel. The help was not very effective; the German flyers apparently were not used to desert conditions. The end came in Iraq when the British force from Trans-Jordan reached a desert post and found a military telephone still connected with the War Ministry in Baghdad. The British commander had one of the Arabs in his force speak on the telephone, representing himself as a member of the retreating Iraqi army. He sounded an alarm of the arrival of mighty British reinforcements—20,000 men and eighty tanks. Panic spread rapidly among Rashid Ali, his Golden Four, and the Mufti. That night they took all the cash they could carry and fled into Persia, leaving Iraq without a government.

To many a citizen of Baghdad, the absence of authority was the dream of a lifetime. There followed forty-eight hours of looting, rapine, and killing—a carnival unequaled elsewhere in World War II. The Jews, who numbered one-fourth of the capital's population, were the main victims. As units of the retreating Iraqi army fell into the city and saw what was going on, soldiers joined in the pillage. Word spread to the desert, and whole tribes of Bedouins started for the city to get their share. The retreat brought in an orderly company of the army under a strict Kurdish commander. He ordered a few bursts of machine-gun fire on the looters, and peace was restored rapidly. The Kurds, another minority in Iraq, are likewise not reluctant to fire upon Arabs. When the British arrived, the Regent resumed his post and a new government was installed.

When I reached Baghdad after the disorders, the killings were estimated at anywhere from two hundred to two thousand, many of them women and girls thrown out of windows after being raped. No precise figures were available; they seldom are in Iraq. The story of the massacre,

reaching America after a delay and in sketchy form, attracted little attention. A British censor, deleting many details from my story, said: "Now
that the thing is all over, we don't want to advertise it, because we've got
to get along with the Iraqi, and you know how sensitive they are." His eye
fell on a phrase in my dispatch attributing the carnage to "lawless and
irresponsible elements." "Yes, that's a good way of putting it," he said.
"Anyone who knows anything about Baghdad will know that 'lawless and
irresponsible elements' means 90 percent of the people, and yet when
you phrase it that way, you won't offend the Iraqi."

* * *

As the campaign went into a lull, we moved into a hotel in Haifa and
drove to the front every other day or so. Compared with the desert, this
was war with modern conveniences, including hot showers daily. Driving
south from Haifa to visit some camp or other, we crossed a triangular
plain, formed where Mt. Carmel recedes from the sea. Hugh Laming,
our conducting officer, who was an amateur strategist, said: "What an
ideal place for a battle! If I were a general, I'd choose this as the place to
make a stand along this coast." Looking at a map a few days later, I saw
that the plain had a name. It was Armageddon. In Palestine, we soon got
used to having familiar Biblical names bounce up when least expected.
Sometimes they were on signs, such as "Intoxicating drinks for H. B. M.'s
Forces. Reuben's Tavern, Nazareth. 5 kilometers."

At length the French persuaded themselves that they had held out
long enough to preserve their honor and asked for an armistice. The peace
meeting was held at the British army barracks near Acre. The British
troops were instructed to receive the French delegates with full military
honors but could not bring themselves to do so. The buglers lifted their
instruments to their mouths, but they were mute, having been stuffed
beforehand. Wilson had offered generous terms, including repatriation
of all French soldiers who preferred to return to France. He thought the
French were ready to accept them, but once the meeting got underway, it
turned out that they came to haggle. At one point, the political delegate,
Conti, remarked that no agreement made at Acre would be worth much,
since it was obvious that the Germans were going to win the war. Wilson

exploded. "If you feel that way, go back to Beirut and I'll shell hell out of you," he said.

Late that night, the armistice agreement was completed. Photographers were permitted in the room to record the signing. One of them plugged a high-powered lamp in the lighting system and blew it out. Several officers started out of the barracks for the power house, but a Palestinian police sergeant on guard at the door blocked the way. He had been refreshing himself during his long vigil and apparently had confused himself with a Scotland Yard inspector. "When the lightsh go out, nobody ish to leave," he said. "'Ow do I know you 'avent shtolen the jewelsh or murdered somebody?" The power plant seemed beyond repair. A motorcycle was wheeled into the conference room, and its headlight was beamed at each delegate, in turn, as he signed.

* * *

Beirut gave the Australians a noisy welcome on its "liberation" and settled down to swindling them. One enterprising Levantine went too far and almost had his establishment wrecked. His fancy posters announced the exhibition of a mermaid. Australian soldiers gladly paid their money and swarmed in, expecting to see a fish-tailed lovely swimming in a tank and, if they were lucky, to have a conversation with the unusual lady. Instead they found a stuffed sea-lion with two freak protuberances which might remotely—very remotely—be said to represent a mermaid's breasts.

A British public relations officer, Major Roselli, was assigned the task of supervising Beirut's four French-language dailies. The papers had perforce been filled with Vichy propaganda, and on the day we entered, their pages were crowded with articles denouncing the British in biting terms. Roselli speedily furnished them with an amplitude of prepared editorials greeting the liberators, telling of Britain's respect for the Arab peoples and recalling the glorious old Anglo-French amity. The mechanical facilities of the newspapers were limited, and they had a supply of the old Vichy articles in type. To avoid waste, Roselli graciously permitted them to use up the supply, and on the second day of the British occupation both pro-British and anti-British offerings were scattered through the papers. "You seem to have done a good propaganda job on the local press," said

Alan Moorehead, pointing to one of the favorable articles and trying not to laugh. "Oh, it's fair," said Roselli. "I hope to do still better tomorrow."

With the generosity they have so often displayed in giving away other people's property, the British invaded Syria voicing promises of independence for Syria and Lebanon. They obtained from General Charles de Gaulle an assurance to this effect. Once Syria was occupied, British and Free French interpretations of these promises differed widely as to their effective date, as to the terms on which the French would relinquish their mandate, and as to Britain's role in the states after independence. Some months later, when it served British interests, General Sir Edward Spears, the British representative in the country, actively encouraged native demonstrations against the French, beaming on the demonstrators and saluting them as he whizzed by in his car. To assure worldwide publicity for these demonstrations, the British government officially helped correspondents to evade French censorship. An RAF plane was made available daily to carry dispatches to Cairo, where British censors had no objection to accounts of unrest and anti-French sentiment in Syria. Not only censorship but the evasion of others' censorship can be an instrument of governmental propaganda.

Cornelius Van H. Engert, the American consul-general in Beirut, had done an able job under the Vichy regime and aided in bringing about the armistice meeting which ended the conflict. Shortly after the British occupation began, he inaugurated an American censorship, although we were not then at war. Engert was drawn into this by the British, who adopted a practice of submitting to him any dispatch concerning American policy or American activities in the Middle East, which were becoming considerable under the Lend-Lease program. They had attempted to get the American Legation in Cairo to do the same thing, but Kirk had consistently refused to exercise censorship, even in an advisory capacity.

I asked Engert if the State Department had authorized him to function as a censor. He denied, of course, that he was performing censorship. He was merely telling the British censors, at their request, what he thought ought not to be published in America, and they were following his recommendations. He wanted to help both correspondents and censors and further the joint interests of the two countries against aggressors. The fact that an American official had established an unauthorized censorship certainly was legitimate news. Had I written it, it would have been highly embarrassing to Engert, all the more so since the British would have submitted the dispatch to him for approval or suppression. After considering the matter, I decided not to embarrass him and never wrote the story.

Once Iraq and Syria were cleaned up, such German agents as were operating in Persia could do little harm to the British. The real menace to British interests in Persia, which included the vast oilfields of the Anglo-Iranian Oil Company, owned partly by the British government, and the refinery at Abadan, the largest in the world, was not the Persians or German agents but the possibility of a Russian invasion. Since neither Russia nor Britain trusted the other in Persia, they reached an agreement to attack on the same day, the British dashing for their precious oilfields. It was a bald aggression, in some respects like the German-Russian invasion of Poland. German activity in the country offered a convenient excuse. Both countries agreed to get out after the war, and eventually they did, some pressure being required to obtain the Russian withdrawal.

A young Rhodesian pilot named Pelling flew me to Basra. A British force made up mostly of Indian army units, had been massed there for the attack. Every small Arab craft that could be bought or borrowed along that part of the Persian Gulf had been lined side-to-side to form a pontoon bridge across the Shatt Al Arab, the wide river formed by the junction of the Tigris and the Euphrates. Despite all these preparations, the Persians were taken unawares. The Abadan Refinery, just over the frontier, was taken in a few hours of fighting.

The stoutest resistance came from Admiral Aly Bayendor of the Persian navy, reputedly the only man in Persia who could talk back to the headstrong Shah and get away with it. Aly, educated in England, had induced the Shah to let him build up a navy for Persia. He had assembled a fleet of second-hand gunboats and destroyers, half a dozen in all, and had trained crews. His fleet was moored on the left back of the Karun River; he was asleep in his home in Khoramshah, on the opposite side. The vessels were boarded by Indian army troops in a surprise attack and set afire. No alarm had been given as the raiders approached; the key officers of Bayendor's staff had been bribed in advance by British agents. Aly awoke to see his life-work and pride, the Persian navy, in flames. He seized a rifle, joined a Persian infantry unit, and fought it out. The British found his body in a heap of others. They gave him a funeral with military honors. There were moist eyes among the British officers attending. The case of Aly Bayendor was simple: His country was invaded, and he had fought unto death to defend it. "He died like a bloody Englishman," a Tommy said.

Few Persians were of the metal of Bayendor. As we advanced on Ahwaz over seventy miles of untidy desert rife with gazelles, word came that the Shah had asked for an armistice. The Persian campaign lasted three days. Seven of us—five correspondents, a driver, and our conducting officer, Captain Kim Mundy—bounced back over the desert in a station wagon with our stories. We had no compass, but we knew that if we went in a westerly direction we would reach the banks of the Shatt. Then it would be easy to find the bridge. We pointed our car toward the sun until it set, then selected a star just above the sunset point and kept our eyes on it. Soon the star set—all of us had forgotten that stars set, too—and we were lost. After many hours, we found the river.

Chapter 6

OFF FOR TRIPOLI

AGAIN I FOUND THAT CAIRO HAD NOT CHANGED MUCH. THE RICH Egyptians had got richer from war profits, the poor had become poorer from the high cost of living. Important reinforcements had arrived, and the capital was more crowded than ever. American uniforms were now in evidence—a United States Military Mission had been set up to handle Lend-Lease supplies. Wavell had been removed from the Middle East Command over the reverses in Greece and in the desert, which were due far more to political decisions made in London than to any failing of his. He was succeeded by Lieutenant General Claude J. E. Auchinleck, whose record indicated a capable officer but not the man of imagination and initiative needed in the Middle East. He lacked Wavell's magnetism. Everyone felt that he knew Wavell; nobody came to feel that way about "The Auk."

The importance of fighting in the Middle East now was being more fully appreciated at home. The Associated Press decided to establish a full bureau there. I was named its chief. The territory under the new Cairo bureau stretched from the mobile desert front to India and from the Turco-Bulgarian border to Central Africa. Madagascar apparently was thrown in, for we were once asked to cover a story there. In the early days in the Mideast, Larry Allen and I had covered the territory. He took the Navy and Alexandria; I took the Army, the Air Force, and Cairo. Larry had four ships "shot from under him," and his descriptions of Mediterranean naval battles were among the war's most vivid and exciting stories. Preston Grover and Bill McGaffin, both excellent reporters, also spent periods in the Mideast. Grover was attached to the Navy for a time and, like Allen, was cast into the sea when his ship was torpedoed. Rescued, he came ashore, wrote his story, and left almost immediately on another operation.

Rommel,[1] poised on the Egyptian frontier, was completing his build-up of men, equipment, and supplies for a thrust to the Nile Valley. The British, adequately reinforced, equipped, and supplied for the first time, were planning a new effort to destroy the enemy in Africa. The desert force, which had borne the newspaper-given name of "the Army of the Nile," was designated the Eighth Army. Lieutenant General Sir Alan Gordon Cunningham, the conqueror of Ethiopia, was made its commander. Cunningham, of rosy face and clear blue eyes, looked like a healthy English squire. At a press conference in Cairo on his departure for the desert, he exuded confidence to a point of foolishness. He saw little difference between desert warfare and the bush warfare he had waged successfully in Ethiopia; in fact, he saw no very serious problems at all. He seemed to overlook the circumstance that he now was not pitted against a demoralized Italian colonial force, but against the best-organized and best-led Panzer force the German army had.

The British opened their offensive before dawn on November 18, 1941, as a weird electric storm added flashes to those of the artillery. Rommel was caught by surprise; he was massing a large part of his army for an attack on Tobruk and was not too well placed to meet the onslaught. In its general outline, the British plan was to surround, or almost surround, the enemy force between the Egyptian frontier and Tobruk and destroy it. The attack on the frontier was to be followed up by a break-out from Tobruk. More than 100,000 fighting men were engaged on each side, the British having a slight superiority in men and equipment.

In the first few days of fighting, before the battle was decided, fantastic claims of victory emanated from the "Cairo spokesman," which meant Army Public Relations. Rommel was contained to the extent that one contains a bear by grabbing its tail. The surrounding wall was too thin. A series of British mistakes caused British units, including the all-important armor, to be split up. After gauging the situation and disposing of his effectives to meet it, Rommel lunged eastward into Egypt and threw British operations into confusion. The battle raged like a free-for-all dogfight. Soldiers were captured, liberated, and recaptured within a

1. German Field Marshal Erwin Rommel, known as the "Desert Fox" because of his many successful campaigns in North Africa.

few hours. A desert hospital changed hands three times in a night, and a tank battle took place between its tents without scratching a patient.

Auchinleck hurried to the desert to find out what was going on. Cunningham confessed he didn't know; he did not know his own dispositions, let alone the enemy's. The bewildered commander of the Eighth Army recommended giving the whole thing up as a bad job, withdrawing, and starting again later. Auchinleck sacked him on the spot. To avoid an adverse effect on the morale of the troops, it was decided to attribute Cunningham's removal to illness, and he agreed to enter a hospital. He made the story true by suffering a nervous breakdown in the hospital. Invalided to England, he recovered and filled home commands later in the war. Churchill would never give him a field command again, but when the Labour Party came to power, Cunningham was assigned the thorny Palestine commissionership-general.

Godfrey Anderson,[2] Edward Ward of the British Broadcasting Corporation, the late Hal Denny of the *New York Times,* and six South African correspondents were captured in the melee. Denny, the only American in the group, was released by the Germans, since the United States was a few days short of being at war with the Axis at the time of his capture. Anderson and Ward remained in a German prison camp until the end of the war.

Auchinleck picked Major General Neil Ritchie, a black-moustached and colorless figure who looked like a London bobby, to succeed Cunningham. Ritchie took over an almost hopeless tangle. He decided to strike before the Germans could reorganize. This was fairly effective but caused the British to use up supplies in advance of schedule. After inflicting considerable losses on the British and taking some heavy bangs, Rommel got most of his force out of the trap and fell back skillfully to El Agheila. This was the point near the dividing line between Cyrenaica and Tripolitania which Wavell had reached. Auchinleck thus regained all the lost territory. He took Cyrenaica in half the time that Wavell had required. But territory meant little in the desert. He failed to destroy the Afrika Korps, which was his object. Wavell had annihilated an army of 150,000. Auchinleck had inflicted losses of 35,000 on Rommel, but only 10,000 of these were Germans, the remainder Italians. His own losses approached 25,000. It

2. Anderson was a member of the AP's London bureau.

is true that Wavell was fighting Italians, and Auchinleck Germans, but Auchinleck had resources vastly superior to Wavell's.

By late January 1942 Rommel was probing eastward at Agedabia, a British position some sixty miles from El Agheila. His actions seemed preliminary to a counter-offensive, but British officials were reassuring. Oliver Lyttelton, minister of state in the Middle East, said no German tank reinforcements had arrived. In actuality, they had arrived and British officials knew it at the time. Brigadier Eric James Shearer,[3] who was responsible for a large part of the misinformation made public from the Middle East, said at a press conference that the situation was not comparable to that of the preceding year; the British now had supply dumps at hand and were in a strong position to repulse any enemy attempt to come back.

The facts were that adequate supplies had not been established near the front. Efforts to get Bengazi into operation as a base had bogged down. A vast amount of gasoline stored under the desert sand near Agedabia was lost through leakage. The British army's gasoline can was a cheap, flimsy, cumbersome metal container that punctured easily. The Germans had a sturdier, more serviceable can. Some of the American observers held that the loss of gasoline at Agedabia turned the balance there; it immobilized the British when the German armor attacked. In any case, the German gasoline can—the so-called Jerry can—was adopted by the American Army, manufactured by hundreds of thousands in the United States, and used until the end of the war.

Having routed the British at Agedabia, the Afrika Korps pushed ahead two hundred miles, recapturing half of Cyrenaica. It stopped at the Gazala Line, where the British had taken positions with good natural defenses. There the opposing forces stood watching each other for months, tormented by a blistering sun, choking sandstorms, and the desert's worst pest, flies. The very factors which enabled the British to defeat the Italians in the desert were in large measure responsible for their undoing at the hands of the Germans. The British had courage and spirit; they were desert-minded. But they fought as brigades and were brigade-minded rather than battle-minded. They thought of armored warfare too much in terms of cavalry battles. Famous Hussar units were all too ready

3. Shearer was director of military intelligence in the Mideast.

to execute a Charge of the Light Brigade, with the do-or-die heroism that went with it. Rommel harbored no such illusions. His regiments were not Hussars, dragoons, or uhlans; they had no sentiment about the trappings of the past. The pride of his men was in the Afrika Korps as a whole. They did not seek jousting matches, tank against tank, and let the best tank win. Their faith was in close coordination of armor, artillery, and infantry; their delight was to lure British tanks into ambushes where artillery could finish them.

The Germans also appreciated the vital importance of rapid and efficient tank recovery units. They had the equipment for picking up disabled tanks; they had mobile workshops near the front for repairing them. This organization often functioned in the midst of battles. The exaggerated British figures of enemy tank losses—the total claimed during the Auchinleck operations far exceeded the number of tanks the Germans had—may have been numerically correct. But many of the tanks were back in action the next day. The British had no comparable tank salvage system. Apparently, they hadn't thought of it.

Apart from the British devotion to tradition, there was, of course, an important psychological reason for German superiority on the battlefield. The Germans had lost the last war; their goal was to do better this time. The British had been on the winning side of World War I and almost every other war. Only with difficulty could many of them escape from the conviction that if it was good enough in 1917, it's good enough today. Some went back further than 1917.

* * *

Pearl Harbor did not so much hit Americans in the Mideast as sneak up on us. One day we were unofficially at war; the next day it was official. The United States Mission became the United States Middle East Command. Its chief was the same: Major General Russell L. Maxwell, of the Army's Service of Supply. Maxwell was soon up to his neck in censorship and loving it; he personally read and blue-pencilled our dispatches. He once passed a dispatch for Joe Levy of the *New York Times* and rejected one of mine which was substantially the same. "You don't know how to do it," Joe said. "Just lead off with a couple of paragraphs emphasizing Maxwell's importance, and he'll pass the whole story."

American projects in the area included an enormous repair base in Eritrea which was to be "the arsenal of Democracy in the Middle East." Millions upon millions were poured into it; we heard prodigious stories of the way money was being spent. The total contribution of this development to the war effort, I was told later, consisted of the repair of one tank and one airplane. I wrote a story about the base, which was well outside of German bombing range, and Maxwell personally passed it—the story emphasized that he was in command of the whole works. After it had been printed in many newspapers in the United States, the War Department issued a "kill" on it. Some papers removed it from later editions. Others refused to do so on the grounds that once it had been published, "killing" it for reasons of military security was absurd.

The Cairo AP bureau grew. Harry Crockett, Don Whitehead, Toby Wiant, Paul K. Lee, and George Tucker arrived to join our staff. I hired Stephen Barber, a precocious English youth of nineteen, who was soon one of the best newspapermen in the Mideast Theater. We also received one of the country's best news photographers, Weston Haynes. Haynes grew a big black beard and amassed a collection of uniforms that would have done credit to the wardrobe of a grand duke. His assortment ranged from kilts to a naval costume fit to grace an admiral. His expense accounts were a problem; it was hard to convince New York of the validity of such items as "hire of six Egyptian laborers to move ship in Suez Canal which was blocking my view." Haynes fascinated Barber. He once told Stephen that he was about to marry but did not want to beget children since he feared a strain of insanity in his family. But he and his fiancée loved children, and in casting about for a suitable man to father a "eugenic" baby, they had picked Barber. Barber was agog with excitement until he learned that the offer was just another of Haynes' little jokes.

I have long regarded news photographers as members of a race apart and have never understood them. I suppose a man has to be different to be a news photographer—some of the things they are expected to do would keep normal persons away from the *métier*. One American photographer in the Mideast—this one was not Haynes—was ordered by his home office to proceed to India at once. In explaining why he could not carry out the order, he cabled: "Laid up with the flu. Doctor says must stay in hospital two weeks. If need me meantime address me Venereal Disease Ward Fifteenth General Army Hospital Cairo."

Early in 1942, we had a little military campaign in Cairo which the censorship wouldn't let us report. So far as I know, it never has been made public. The British decided that a return of the Waft Party to power in Egypt would provide a stronger and more cooperative government.[4] In addition to British encouragement, the move had popular support. King Farouk, however, had not forgiven Nahas Pasha, the Waftist leader, for once calling him "a headstrong boy" and refused to ask him to form a cabinet.

That night British troops marched on the Royal Palace. They surrounded it with tanks and armored cars. Guns were pointed at its windows; a gate was smashed down. In this setting, Sir Miles Lampson, the British ambassador, and General Stone, commander of the British troops in Egypt, called on Farouk. They told him that a warship waited at Suez to take him and his family into exile if he stood in the way of the British war effort. The monarch graciously consented to a Waftist cabinet. Nahas knew his standing would be impaired in Egyptian eyes if it were known that he owed his office to the British. So the Egyptian people were given the story in reverse: the British had attempted to prevent Farouk from accepting Nahas. The youthful monarch, according to this version, had stood firm even against the display of arms and had had his way.

* * *

As some high British officers were explaining that neither side could fight a desert campaign in the summer and that the lull on the Gazala Line would continue until autumn, Rommel attacked. The date was May 26, 1942. Ritchie had decided against a continuous chain of defenses at Gazala. Instead he sowed a solid minefield from the coast to a point thirty-five miles inland. Immediately behind this minefield was a series of "boxes," protected by mines and barbed wire, supplied to withstand a siege and prepared to meet attack from any direction. The Germans, it was

4. The Wafd (or Waft) Party was a nationalist movement that arose after World War I, when Egypt was a British protectorate, to push for Egyptian independence. After the protectorate ended in 1920, the Wafd Party became the dominant political party in Egypt, but it gradually lost much popular support because of the 1936 Anglo-Egyptian Treaty and because of its leaders' willingness to cooperate with the British during World War II, both of which undermined its avowed nationalist aims.

argued, could not overrun all these boxes. If they bypassed any of them, the garrisons could sally out and maul the German rear. The German armor went first for the southernmost box, Bir Hacheim, held by the Free French Foreign Legion under General Marie Pierre Koenig. After several days of terrific battering, the French withdrew. To the identifying shout of "Vive la Legion," to keep from fighting one another, the Legionnaires broke through the German ring at bayonet point in the dark of night.

From Bir Hacheim the Germans smashed northeastward. The battle was decided at the Knightsbridge Box, where Rommel lured the British into a trap in which their armor was at the mercy of his guns. All but seventy of their three hundred tanks there were destroyed. Rommel outfought them and outclassed them; he was the undisputed master of desert warfare. The British went into a headlong retreat of almost four hundred miles. This time Tobruk did not stand; its garrison of 25,000 men, mostly South Africans, crumpled. A defensive position had been laid out at El Alamein, about seventy miles from Alexandria. This was a reserve line; it was the last stand that could be made before the Nile Valley. It had a big advantage over other desert lines—an inland anchor, the Qattara Depression, an enormous and impassable sub–sea level chasm in the desert floor. The fleeing British were too disorganized to take up positions on the line. For at least twelve hours, the way to the Nile Valley was open. One fact saved Egypt: the Afrika Korps had spent itself. It did not have the strength or supplies to move into the Nile even without opposition.

At the end of the retreat, I went into Cairo. There the panic exceeded anything among the fighters in the desert. Thousands of Jews and other civilians who feared the Germans had fled—to Suez, Palestine, Luxor, Khartoum, anywhere that was distant. Those who had obtained airplane transit sold their automobiles at the airport for $10 or anything they could realize. Business establishments were sold at one-tenth their value. GHQ was in a dither. So many documents—including the censors' files of our dispatches—were burned that a haze hung over Cairo and the day was dubbed "Ash Wednesday." In the courtyards of Gray Pillars, soldiers were feeding bales of papers into flaming ashcans. Various headquarters offices started to move to the Suez Canal Zone or farther. The Navy left Alexandria for Port Said, destroying many valuable installations.

The actions of Maxwell's staff were anything but a credit to our country. Officers abandoned automobiles and other property in Cairo and boarded airplanes for Khartoum, spreading alarm as they departed. American headquarters seemed to have no direction; almost every officer apparently was left free to flee if he chose. Kirk, the American minister, remained at his post, telephoning American civilians and making transport arrangements for them if they desired it. The American Legation, including the Office of the Military Attaché, acquitted itself with more grace, coolness, and common sense than the United States Middle East Command.

Frank Gervasi arrived in Khartoum en route to Egypt after a visit home. He encountered the arriving hordes of Mideast refugees, military and civilian, and filed a dispatch giving details. The dispatch was censored in Cairo, where a British censor deleted all mention of the British, but passed the account of the fleeing Americans. I returned to the front— the new front so convenient to Cairo—in a car which I had purchased at panic prices. The British, and especially the New Zealanders, were rapidly reorganizing. The Alamein Line was held fairly securely. Barricades of cotton bales had been thrown up outside Alexandria. There was no panic now, but a grim determination to hold on. Auchinleck, the poor picker of field generals, sacked Ritchie and took command in the desert himself, blaming the newspapers for exaggerating the importance of the defeat.

* * *

During the retreat an event of considerable interest, especially to Americans, took place. It was the first battlefield encounter of World War II between the German and American armies. Only a token force of Americans was involved, but the engagement was nevertheless an American victory, since the Americans inflicted considerable losses on the Germans and came off practically unscathed. The Americans, new to battle but men picked from armored war training centers at home, manned nine General Sherman tanks. They were brought to the Mideast under the command of Senator Henry Cabot Lodge of Massachusetts, who was doing a tour of duty as an Army officer on a leave of absence from the Senate. After their combat experience, they were to return to the training centers as instructors. Lodge managed the men well and earned their respect; on the battlefield they were under the command of a combat officer, Captain Stelling. Their assignment was to cover the withdrawal of South African troops from the northern end of the Gazala Line, and they acquitted themselves well.

The Americans gave me a graphic account of their battle. All the American correspondents naturally wanted to get the story out; it was held up pending its release by the War Department. Lodge was compiling a report on the test encounter and wanted all the information he could get. I wrote my own account in the form of a news story and gave it to him with the understanding that it might serve as a supplement to his own report and that upon release of the news by the War Department it would be turned over to the Associated Press in Washington. In due time the news was announced by the War Department in a brief communiqué. The Department simultaneously gave my dispatch, much fuller and with first-hand descriptions by the combatants, to the AP. It was the main story in almost every newspaper in the country that day.

Rival correspondents were angry. Leon Kaye, chief of the United Press bureau in Cairo, stung by the biting messages he had received from his New York office, lodged a formal complaint against me of violating censorship. I was given a hearing and, of course, cleared. The American War Department itself had released my story. Lodge, in Washington, said he would have done the same service for the United Press if he had been asked. It was the first of a number of such incidents which I experienced. None of them involved military security, but merely the wrath of Army brass or riled correspondents—or both—that someone had been alert enough to find a legitimate way through the maze of obstructions set up for suppressing information.

* * *

Once it became apparent that there was a chance of holding the Mideast, American supplies poured in more heavily than ever. An American Air Force command was established in the Theater, and groups of fighters and medium and heavy bombers were diverted there to bolster the British. Major General Lewis H. Brereton, who commanded this force, was placed under Maxwell. Brereton and his combat officers naturally disliked being under a supply general, especially one whose organization was so shot through with politics and incompetence as Maxwell's. The friction soon became an open row, and both generals burned up the cables to Washington with recriminations. They were ordered to compose their differences and fight the enemy instead of each other. Lieutenant General Frank M. Andrews, one of the Air Force's ablest senior officers, then arrived to take a command over both Brereton and Maxwell. The atmosphere of American headquarters changed on his arrival; the self-important hierarchy of non-combat officers which Maxwell had assembled while he was enthroned was no more efficient but became less overbearing.

I suppose that almost every war correspondent suffers qualms of conscience at one time or other. We were forever extolling the heroism of the soldiers, emphasizing that their fight was to save all Civilization. If it was, why didn't we get in and give them a hand, instead of cheering them on from the sidelines? During the Andrews regime in Cairo I was offered a commission. The rank mentioned—that of major—frightened me. I knew I had no military qualifications or training to warrant such a grade. After some reflection, I decided that the duties which I would be assigned would probably contribute no more to the winning of the war than my work with the AP. I turned down the offer.

Churchill came to the Middle East in the summer of 1942 and found GHQ uneasy, morale low, the soldiers despondent. The arrival of important reinforcements and supplies made little difference: the men had no confidence in the command. A result of Churchill's visit was the removal of Auchinleck. General Harold R. Alexander took over the Mideast Command; Lieutenant General Bernard L. Montgomery assumed command of the Eighth Army. The situation, as it appeared to me at the time, was this: Daring initiative and terrific drive was imperative if Rommel was to be knocked out. Montgomery would be given a chance. If he succeeded, the Middle East was saved. If he failed, Alexander was there to make the best of a bad fate. Alexander was a specialist in evacuations; he had won his spurs at Dunkirk and in Burma.

Montgomery's first act was to cancel the elaborate plan drawn up for evacuating Egypt in case the Germans broke through the Alamein Line. He ordered the Eighth Army to hold the Line; there would be no withdrawal. He took vehicles away from units at the front; they would have no use for them. "If we cannot stay here alive, we will stay here dead," he said. The desert veterans had had their fill of pep talks, but there was something different in this cocky little man. He did not spare his predecessors. "Our failures have been due to bad generalship and bad staff work," he said at a press conference. "Our soldiers have been let down." If this was "not cricket" to the officers of GHQ, it was language that the fighting men could understand. There seemed to be something more than bluff in the studied audacity of the new commander. The atmosphere in the desert changed immediately—one could feel the change. From the start, there was no doubt in my mind that the Eighth Army had at last found a commander worthy of it.

At the time, there was no way of knowing exactly how much of the change was due to Montgomery, how much to Alexander. Some correspondents thought Alexander was the brain, Montgomery the front man. In any event, Montgomery was running the show in the desert, and Alexander was content to let him take the spotlight. It was apparent that they worked well as a team. Montgomery's assurance, sometimes bordering on the theatrical, was calculated to give the soldiers a desert hero other than Rommel. It had that effect. On August 31 Rommel, not appreciating the change which had come over the British, attacked with the apparent intention of smashing into Egypt. Montgomery had anticipated the time and place of the attack. He borrowed Rommel's own tactics. The Germans were sucked into an ambush, and British guns took a fearful toll on their tanks while they were tangled in a minefield. The heavy loss of German armor made possible Montgomery's offensive in October.

* * *

Meanwhile, Larry Allen had been taken prisoner during a naval raid on Tobruk. He was aboard the destroyer *Sikh,* which was disabled by shore batteries and boarded by the enemy. By October 23 Montgomery was ready for his great offensive. He had built up a new, powerful armored force equipped with the latest American tanks. His troops were hardened by intensive training, and their morale was tops. "My plan is simple: I propose to destroy the Germans in Africa," he told us at a press conference.

Rommel was absent when Montgomery struck; he was at home, apparently explaining the failure of his attack and trying desperately to get reinforcements. There was a fortnight of fierce fighting. Montgomery did not hesitate to change his plan when circumstances required it. The engagement ended in a German rout. Remnants of the Afrika Korps retreated in disorder as far as Mersa Matruh, 150 miles westward. Here Rommel pulled his remaining forces together, and from then on his withdrawal across all of Libya and into Tunisia was orderly and skillful, but each stand the Afrika Korps attempted to make collapsed before the superior power of the Eighth Army. After his breakthrough, Montgomery exhibited a cautiousness which increased as the war went on. It was understandable; the victor of Alamein had too great a reputation to take a risk which might destroy it forever.

The desert was strewn with wreckage in Rommel's wake. Near Mersa Matruh our party of correspondents—George Lait, Chester Morrison, and I—loaded a truck with fine foods from a German ration depot. Products of the occupied countries of Europe were there—Danish hams, Dutch cheeses, French wines, Norwegian sardines, Czech sausages, and canned Hungarian goulash. Outside Mersa we ran into a German pocket which gave us a rain of mortar shells, while Lait and our conducting officer, Captain Bill Warrener, were pulling a badly wounded British officer to safety. Lait, Shan (Alexander) Sedgwick of the *New York Times,* and Aubry Hammond, an English correspondent, were wounded by fragments. Morrison and I were untouched. We all sent stories of the incident, and the next day some playful correspondents at the press camp fixed up a telegraphic form addressed to me and bearing the signature of Kent Cooper, head of the AP. It read: "Kennedy: Lait and Sedgwick getting big play for being wounded. Why you not wounded? Explain at once how you sat back and permitted opposition to score this beat. Affectionate regards. Kent Cooper."

As our AP staff grew larger, I was compelled to remain closer to headquarters to look after the many details connected with running it. Don Whitehead took over the coverage of the Eighth Army and did so superbly; he was one of the best correspondents of World War II.

Tripoli, the great prize of Montgomery's Libyan offensive and the triumphal end of the British Mideast struggle of almost three years, fell in

January 1943. The news was given out at headquarters at an unexpected hour, and I was lucky enough to be the only correspondent in the press room at the time. This fact, and a good break in communications, gave me an hour's lead on the story. The next day I flew to Tripoli to see Churchill gloat over the conquest. The greatest city and last strip of Mussolini's new Roman Empire had been torn from him. While there, I received news that Harry Crockett of our staff had been lost at sea when the destroyer *Welchman*, in which he was traveling from Malta to Alexandria, had been sunk by a torpedo.

* * *

That was the winter of my strange fever. Almost everybody picks up un-usual maladies in Egypt. Mine was a fever which went up and down. I still don't know whether it was grippe, dengue, or something else. The doctor who was treating me in my hotel room suggested that I get a thermome-ter and give him an hourly record when he called the next day. The events which followed led to a widely told story, which like most widely told stories, lost nothing in the telling. According to the standard version, in-cluded by Bob Casey in a recent book of such stories, I sent a bellboy to a drugstore for a thermometer, put it in my mouth, and found that I had a fever of 108 degrees. I sent for a second thermometer, which registered the uncomfortably low temperature of 85. A third instrument showed 101, and when I sent that one back, a note came from the druggist: "You have tried our high-reading barometer, our low-reading one, and our me-dium one. Just what do you want?" It didn't happen that way. It was true that every thermometer the bellboy bought seemed permanently fixed, but only because I didn't know about the little trick of flipping the mer-cury down before placing a thermometer in the mouth.

The war had moved more than 1,000 miles away from Cairo. The area was in no apparent danger, and there was little information there that could have been of value to the enemy. But Cairo remained a great war center, bulging with army bureaucrats, British and American, who whiled away the time sniping at one another. And Middle East censorship got tighter than ever. Maxwell was recalled to Washington and left blaming the correspondents for his troubles. His successors, first General Ralph

Royce, then General Benjamin Franklin Giles, were of the same stripe in their notions of their importance and their zeal in suppressing information which might place them in an unfavorable light or otherwise displease them.

As British censors were banning "anything susceptible of making the Greeks think about Cyprus," Giles issued an order forbidding correspondents from writing about the Greek internal situation.[5] The fact that he had issued such an order was itself censored. He took the view that his own official reports to the War Department were adequate; the Department could give the American public such information as it might deem advisable. Giles banned observance of the Fourth of July in 1944 on the grounds that it might hurt the feelings of the British. I missed this glorious decline of the Middle East as a war theater. When the Eighth Army went under General Dwight D. Eisenhower's North African Command, the Mideast and North African staffs of the Associated Press were combined and I was asked to go to Algiers and take charge.

5. The island of Cyprus was at that time a British colony. Greek Cypriots, a majority of the population, wanted union with Greece (*enosis*).

Kennedy in British army's desert uniform, Cairo, 1940.

Kennedy visiting the Acropolis, Athens, 1941.

Kennedy saluting, Crete, 1941.

Kennedy in Napoleonic pose, Crete, 1941.

Kennedy (right) and Jack Hetherington of the *Melbourne Herald* during bombing in Crete, 1941.

Kennedy (left) and Geroge Laycock on the porch of the Tiberias Hotel, Tiberias, Palestine, June, 1941.

Kennedy and unidentified AP staffer react to bombing at Anzio beachhead, February, 1944.

Kennedy at Anzio, Italy, 1944.

This is to certify that

Mr. *Edward Kennedy*

of *ASSOCIATED PRESS of America*

is officially accredited to the
MEDITERRANEAN FLEET as War
Correspondent; is subject to Military law
and is entitled to be treated as an officer.

Certified true likeness of

Mr. *EDWARD KENNEDY*

Charles S. Rowe

Lt-Cdr. Charles S. ROWE, R.N.V.R.

FLEET PRESS LIAISON OFFICER

P K Enright

CAPTAIN OF THE FLEET.

Kennedy's ID card for British forces in the Mediterranean, 1942.

Participants in the signing of the German surrender, May 7, 1945, at Reims,
France. The Germans are seen at one side of the table, backs turned. Seated at
the other side, left to right, are British Lt. Gen. Sir Frederick E. Morgan, French
Gen. Francois Sevez, British Adm. Harold M. Burrough, U.S. Lt. Gen. Walter
Bedell Smith, presiding; Russian Gen. Ivan Susloparov (in the act of signing),
Lt. Gen. Carl A. Spaatz, Air Commander-in-Chief, and Air Marshal J. K. Robb. At
the end of the table are British Maj. Gen. H. R. Bull and a Russian interpreter,
Susloparov's aide. Lt. Gen. Ivan Chermiaff, sits behind the interpreter.

Three German principals sign the surrender. Left to right: Maj. Gen. Wilhelm Oxenius, Col. Gen. Gustaf Jodl, and Gen. Adm. Hans von Friedeburg. Behind them can be seen the war correspondents who witnessed the event. Kennedy (with glasses) peers over the shoulders of two correspondents holding papers.

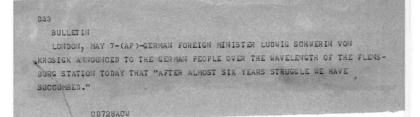

```
D22
    BULLETIN
    LONDON, MAY 7-(AP)-THE FLENSBURG RADIO BROADCAST AN ORDER OF THE
DAY BY GRAND ADMIRAL KARL DOENITZ TODAY DIRECTING THE COMMANDERS
OF ALL GERMAN U-BOATS TO CEASE HOSTILITIES.
                                        CD701ACW
```

```
D23
    BULLETIN
            NEW YORK, MAY 7-(AP)-THE FCC REPORTED A BROADCAST BY THE
FREE DANISH RADIO TODAY WHICH SAID "IT HAS JUST BEEN ANNOUNCED
THAT THE GERMAN FORCES IN NORWAY HAVE CAPITULATED."
                                        CD702ACW
```

```
D24
    BULLETIN
            WITH THE U.S.THIRD ARMY, MAY 7-(AP)-THE FOURTH ARMORED
DIVISION IN TWIN STABS NORTH AND NORTHEAST TODAY REACHED BREZ, 50
MILES SOUTHWEST OF PRAGUE, AND BOSCHOWITZ, 52 MILES SOUTH OF THE CZECH
CAPITAL.
        CD702ACW
```

```
D33
    BULLETIN
    LONDON, MAY 7-(AP)-GERMAN FOREIGN MINISTER LUDWIG SCHWERIN VON
KROSIGK ANNOUNCED TO THE GERMAN PEOPLE OVER THE WAVELENGTH OF THE FLENS-
BURG STATION TODAY THAT "AFTER ALMOST SIX YEARS STRUGGLE WE HAVE
SUCCUMBED."

        CD728ACW
```

These are flashes and bulletins from a larger series signaling the surrender of Germany and the end of the war in Europe on May 7, 1945, which unfolded swiftly. An hour and 36 minutes elapsed between the first message from London and Edward Kennedy's bulletin, datelined Reims, France.

```
D57
   BOYLE'S NOTBOOK
BUST
   BUST


D57
   BULLETIN
   FIRST LEAD CAPITULATION (FIRST LEAD EUROPEAN)
BY THE ASSOCIATED PRESS
   LONDON, MAY 7--GERMAN BROADCASTS SAID TODAY "ALL FIGHTING GERMAN
TROOPS" HAD SURRENDERED UNCONDITIONALLY, AND THE WORLD WAITED FOR AN
OFFICIAL ALLIED ANNOUNCEMENT EXPECTED FROM THE BIG THREE CAPITALS.
   R816ACW
```

```
FLASH
REIMS, FRANCE--ALLIES OFFICIATLY ANNOUNCED GERMANY
SURRENDERED UNCONDITIONALLY.
                         R836ACW
```

```
REPEAT FLASH
REIMS FRANCE--ALLIES OFFICIALLY ANNOUNCED GERMANY
SURRENDERED UNCONDITIONALLY.
                         R836ACW
```

```
D63
   BULLETIN
            BY EDWARD KENNEDY
   REIMS, FRANCE, MAY 7-(AP)-GERMANY SURRENDERED UNCONDITIONALLY
TO THE WESTERN ALLIES AND RUSSIA AT 2:41 A.M. FRENCH TIME TODAY.
   R837ACW
```

The key message is contained in bulletin D36 (not pictured), announcing that
Flensburg Radio was broadcasting that Germany had "capitulated unconditionally." Within two hours of Kennedy's bulletin, SHAEF had declared that the AP
report was not "authorized" but did not deny its veracity. (AP 30, Original Wires
Collection, Associated Press Corporate Archives)

Kennedy and daughter, Julia, on a visit to St. Augustine, Florida, 1957.

Chapter 7

NORTH AFRICA

ALGIERS, FOR ALL ITS NATURAL CHARM, WAS DRAB COMPARED WITH Cairo. In Cairo, civil life went on through the war, no more than a little hemmed in; in Algiers, it was ground down until it was hardly noticeable. The military was in full control and in possession of almost every large building and countless homes, of the railroads and almost all vehicles, of shops now serving soldiers and restaurants converted into messes, of movie houses reserved for the troops and even of dental offices. The occupying armies were theoretically friendly, but never have I seen a city that looked so thoroughly occupied, or met people less enthusiastic over their visitors.

The Supreme Command was established in the rambling St. George Hotel on the wide avenue that wound steeply up the hill from the waterfront. The St. George had been built sporadically, planlessly, and without much effort to get any two rooms on the same floor level. Some of its cubicles and narrow corridors seemed to have been salvaged in downtown house-razings, carted up the hill, and nailed on. Its congestion was so great that indoor traffic signals were required. The big, grimy-gray building of the Algerian Agricultural Administration had been taken over for the press. *Stars and Stripes* occupied one floor,[1] Public Relations and the correspondents another. Above us, a floor was reserved for the Psychological Warfare Branch. Here General Eisenhower had a hard-boiled cavalry colonel to take charge of all the propagandists and civilian idea men sent out by Washington and London.

The Americans, who usually favor directness, wanted to mount a cross-Channel invasion in the fall of 1942. The British cabinet would not

---

1. *Stars and Stripes,* founded in 1861, is an independent newspaper operated by the U.S. Department of Defense reporting on matters affecting the U.S. military.

have it. Churchill never ceased talking about Fortress Europe's "soft underbelly," the Mediterranean. He was even more fascinated by its Balkan tail. The Americans were thinking in terms of a single objective in Europe—defeating the Germans. The British were thinking and planning in terms of national survival and welfare, future as well as present, of the whole European political picture, and of their empire, their lifelines, their foreign interests. The Americans ruled out an offensive up the Balkan peninsula as an absurdly roundabout, costly, and difficult way of getting to Berlin. Churchill, foreseeing the postwar world, even then was dreaming of containing the Russians; we certainly were not. Despite our disillusionments after World War I, we were waging our second war in Europe with our same old naiveté: once the monster of Nazism was destroyed, democracy would flourish again and peace would have a chance. We did, however, agree to go first for the monster's underbelly instead of directly for his heart. The result was Operation Torch, the invasion of French North Africa, timed to coincide with Montgomery's desert offensive.

By the time I arrived in Algiers, a front had become stabilized in Tunisia. In the Mideast we had only scanty reports of what was happening on the other side of Africa; when I got there, I found a war being waged in circumstances as fantastic as anything in the Middle East. Militarily, everything was bigger and more powerful. Here the predominating influence was American. There was none of that British penny-pinching, understatement, or diffidence. The daily garbage of the Americans was enough to feed the British Eighth Army for a week. The communiqués were longer and more dramatic. Censors came not by two's or three's but by the dozens.

At the moment of the landings, it happened that shifty-eyed Admiral Jean-François Darlan was in North Africa to visit his son, stricken by poliomyelitis. His was a voice that the French officers commanding the defense of North Africa would heed. The Allied Command acted swiftly to make use of the fine bird it had trapped. Darlan was induced to order the end of resistance; the action was effective in Algeria and Morocco but not in Tunisia, where Germans were pouring in to come to grips with the invaders.

The price paid for the order and for the prospect of efficient military collaboration and civil order in North Africa under the incumbent leaders was the acceptance of a Little Vichy, turncoat but not much different in ideology from Big Vichy. Darlan headed it, surrounded by a galaxy of officials and officers who had been high in the favor of Pétain and Laval.[2] General Giraud, free from the Vichy taint but no less reactionary than the others, who had slipped out of France believing he was to be given command of the whole Allied North African operation, accepted command of French forces in North Africa.[3] The uproar in the United States and Britain was terrific. The deal looked like a sell-out to the very elements which our soldiers at the front were fighting; certainly it was a sell-out of those French—in North Africa, France, and elsewhere—who were struggling hardest against Nazism. The arrangement, a military exigency which probably saved 10,000 American and British lives, was another of the contradictions of a baffling world. Had the invading force been compelled to fight it out with the French who held Morocco and Algeria, the Germans might have moved enough strength into Tunisia to imperil the whole North African operation. To most Americans, De Gaulle then personified French patriotism. It nevertheless would have been folly to fight a civil war to install him in power.

As Roosevelt was assuring the American people that the acceptance of Darlan was but a temporary expedient, Providence intervened through the medium of an unbalanced youth who sent three bullets into the admiral's chest. The Allied Command was greatly relieved by the event yet mindful of possible repercussions among various French elements. It applied an old favorite remedy: censorship. But "because we knew there were Axis agents around, it became unwise to try to withhold the news of Darlan's death," General Mark W. Clark, who was supervising the arrangements, explains in his memoirs. "We didn't want Berlin or Rome to sound off first."[4] Had it not been for the Axis agents, one is led to assume, Clark might have tried to hold up the news of the assassination until the end of the war.

2. Marshal Philippe Pétain (d. 1951) was chief of state of Vichy France. Pierre Laval (d. 1945) was a high-ranking member of the Vichy government; he was executed for treason after the war.

3. Henri Giraud (d. 1949) was captured fighting the Germans in 1940 and held as a prisoner of war until 1942, when he pulled off a daring escape and made his way back to France. He later commanded French troops in Operation Torch.

4. General Mark W. Clark, *Calculated Risk: The Story of the War in the Mediterranean* (1950; reprint, with a new preface by Martin Blumenson, New York: Enigma, 2007), 108.

Prompted by Churchill, the generals decided to cast suspicion on the enemy in making the announcement. "It is not yet known from preliminary investigation whether the assassination was of German or Italian inspiration," said the communiqué. This phrase, which fooled nobody, was one of those tortures of the truth at which military spokesmen are so adept. It is in a class with Brigadier Shearer's description of an engagement in the Mideast in which the British ran into a German ambush and suffered disastrous losses. "We compelled the enemy to disclose his strength," said Shearer's communiqué, without amplification. Girard succeeded Darlan, becoming *commandant-en-chef, civile et militaire,* surrounded by the same old Vichy group and responding to Anglo-American pressure for liberalization and reform with the eagerness of a banker to lend money to a gypsy. De Gaullists who had risked their lives for the Allied Cause before the landings were still in jail, and more were being arrested. Even the Nuremberg racial laws were slow to go. Giraud's first reaction to American protests on this score was indignation over intolerable meddling in French affairs.

For a period, the Allied Command sought to hide the more grotesque features of the political tragicomedy of Algiers by political censorship. This was justified on the grounds that the situation was too fragile to withstand the publication of "inflammatory" information. As pressure against it mounted at home, Eisenhower formally ended the exercise of political censorship by the Allied Command. Shortly thereafter, the promise was made by Roosevelt that American censorship would be confined to matters of military security, that there would be no political censorship by American commands abroad. After almost three years of British political censorship in the Mideast, it was like coming out of a fetid room to fresh air to be able to write of political events without fretting over the stupidity and tyranny of censorship. The removal of the Army's political censorship in North Africa caused no upheavals and no collapses, nor the slightest impairment of the war effort.

* * *

The AP staff which had accompanied the Allied Force to North Africa from the British Isles and the United States was a highly capable one. It in-

cluded Wes Gallagher, Noland (Boots) Norgaard, Hal Boyle, Bill King, and
Dan DeLuce. To these were added Don Whitehead, George Tucker, and
Paul Lee, who had come across from the Mideast as the Eighth Army
and Eastern Mediterranean Fleet moved into the new theater. Later Joe
Morton, who had been at Dakar; Relman Morin, released from Japanese internment in Indochina; Kenneth L. Dixon, and Lynn Heinzerling
joined us. Joe Dynan, also released from Japanese internment, came to
cover French politics. I believe this staff was the best group of reporters
ever assembled; I was extremely proud to be the head of it. The staff won
three Pulitzer Prizes. Larry Allen, by this time chafing in a German prison
camp, got it for his brilliant stories of Mediterranean sea battles. DeLuce
won it in 1944; Boyle in 1945.[5]

For the enormity of the story which we were covering, the staff was
small. It was limited by a rigid quota system imposed by Army Public
Relations; it took long arguments and cajolings to get each new man into
the Theater. The home appetite for news from North Africa seemed in-
satiable. We were sending up to 20,000 words a day. There was the headquarters story, purporting to give an overall picture of the campaign each
day, first-hand accounts by members of the staff at the front, countless
"features," and reams of news of regional interest containing a never-end-
ing flow of names of soldiers, their exploits, experiences, and thoughts.
It was in this period that Ernie Pyle, whom I had known in Washington
ten years before, achieved tremendous success with his daily article on
how the soldiers lived. He had written a column for years without great
renown, but when he applied his unaffected touch to the war, his following skyrocketed. His simple stories about soldiers meant more to most
people at home than studies of high strategy, pronouncements of generals, or the endless recital of gains and losses.

Boyle, after finishing his other work, found recreation in writing a
column of similar substance. Hal was an indefatigable worker; it was not
unusual for him to put in an exhausting day at the front, return to a
chilly press camp tent and bat out a big quota of news stories, then turn

5. Morin won two Pulitzers after the war, in 1951 for his coverage of the Korean
War and in 1958 for his reporting of the Little Rock school crisis. Whitehead also won
two Pulitzers, in 1951 for his reporting of the Korean War and in 1952 for his coverage of
President-elect Eisenhower's secret trip to Korea.

out a column of bubbling humor, sharp satire, or moving sentiment, as his mood dictated. I regarded Boyle's writing as superior to Pyle's and his observations more penetrating; Ernie, however, had a popular appeal that no other correspondent achieved. Boyle added to the legendry of the Tunisian campaign by delivering a political speech to a horde of ragged Arabs. In advance of the troops, he and other correspondents entered a village evacuated by the enemy. The local population surrounded their jeep, cheering. Hal, who has the face of a rakish cherub, replied with a ringing oration which ended with an improvised rhyme:

> Vote for Boyle, the son of toil
> Honest Hal, the Arab's pal.

Arabs are quick to memorize a phrase they don't understand. When the troops arrived, they were astonished to hear the natives applaud their entry with Boyle's ditty.

As living quarters for the AP staff, Norgaard had obtained a gaudy villa which a wealthy Algerian had built as a love nest for his French mistress. Its pink marble bathtub was almost a swimming pool; its main bedroom, which I occupied as head of our household, might have graced the finest bordello of Paris. We were allowed to draw Army rations upon payment and once every two weeks got a good supply of canned goods. The best items, like tinned chicken, were hard to obtain, but we could get unlimited amounts of the less desirable products, such as five-pound cans of hominy. We converted the hominy into fresh meat by using it to fatten a flock of chickens which we had obtained in the country and kept in the garden. A tight friendship bound the members of our little group, and our *esprit de corps* was the envy of other news staffs. Such merit as I might have had as head of this superb staff was based largely, I believe, on one point: I never got in a man's way when he had a good story.

I was faced by a serious administrative problem a few days after I reached Algiers: a charge of attempted murder against Wes Gallagher. It was brought by a high-strung woman correspondent who alleged—not to prosecuting authorities but to all who would listen—that Gallagher had placed her where he knew she was sure to be bombed. In reality, Gallagher had merely found quarters for her in the overcrowded city. De-

Luce and I eventually persuaded her that Wes had not sought her doom.

Another problem arose from the fact that shortly before my arrival an Associated Press photographer had produced a vivid battle picture, replete with explosions, wounded, and dead. The photograph had been forwarded through Army photographic channels to the Associated Press, which issued it to newspapers. It was a marvelous shot; its only flaw was that anyone who knew anything about news photography could tell it was a fake. It had been "reenacted" a hundred miles from the front, with the generous cooperation of an Army unit with plenty of explosives on hand.

The Associated Press was so delighted with the prominence with which the picture was published throughout the country that Alan J. Gould, assistant general manager, cabled congratulations. That was before rival photo agencies exposed it as a phony simply by pointing out a number of features that proved it was not a combat picture. After the exposure, Gould recalled the photographer in a burst of lofty moralizing and severe condemnation. He did not mention the fact that the fake picture, with its give-away features, had been passed by AP officials before being distributed.

The photographer's plaintive story was that he had risked his life for weeks at the front without obtaining a single good combat picture. Such shots are elusive and often a matter of luck. He insisted his picture was true in this respect: it was a faithful reenactment of what was happening at the front. Some moralists have argued that anything is true if it illustrates the truth, and our photographer doubtless was a follower of this school of thought. His point of view, if carried to its logical conclusion, would have eliminated the need of war photographers, for Hollywood could have provided an adequate supply of reenacted battle scenes. That would never have been accepted. Yet a good percentage of the war photographs published in American newspapers were reenactments, in one way or another. This is not to deny that there were also countless photographs of stark authenticity and naturalness, taken at a cost of high casualties among photographers. When Giraud and De Gaulle shook hands at Casablanca, several photographers missed the scene and asked them to repeat it. That was a reenactment. A large part of the British army's excellent film *Desert Victory* consisted of reenactments. I saw the photographers borrow a group of Italian prisoners from a cage and have them go through their surrender again, emerging timorously from dug-outs holding white flags.

In peacetime no less than in war, a large part of news pictures are reenactments. Every good news photographer is an incipient Hollywood director—he has to be to bring in what editors want. It would be hard to draw a line between truthfulness and fraud in photographs. In my early days in newspaper work, on one of America's most respectable papers, our city editor sent a photographer to the zoo on Groundhog's Day with orders to get a picture of a groundhog looking at his shadow. The photographer failed at the zoo, so he went to the museum, borrowed a stuffed groundhog, concealed its mounting with shrubbery, provided the shadow by artificial light, and even managed to capture an expression of surprise on the animal's face. The picture was a success, with no questions asked.

* * *

By April our forces in Tunisia were hardened and seasoned and ready for the grim work of destroying the enemy in Africa. Enough men, planes, guns, tanks, ammunition, and supplies had arrived to give us clear-cut superiority over the Germans. Not until then could we beat them. This was the general pattern of our operations against Germany to the end of the war. We won no victories against superior enemy strength. Perhaps brilliant successes against greater strength no longer are possible in war. Our course was the wisest and safest one—we knew we could produce the stuff, so we waited until we had it before risking lives. Our home front, industry, natural resources were the biggest factor in winning the war, for here we were able to achieve overwhelming superiority. This does not, of course, belittle the contribution of the fighting men.

I left Algiers for three weeks in Tunisia toward the close of the campaign. As in the Mideast, a feeling of peace and tranquility descended over one on departure from headquarters. The nearer the front, the less the red tape, the more forthright and sincere the men, the friendlier the atmosphere. The winter was gone, and the fields were carpeted with the brightest wildflowers I have ever seen—mostly in patches of bright reds and yellows. I took an airplane trip back over the western desert, once so familiar. The desert was fast erasing the signs of the three campaigns; slit trenches already had filled with sand, and only a little tell-tale wreckage marked the scenes of battles.

In the last days of the campaign, Wes Gallagher suffered a broken back when his jeep struck a rock, throwing him out. He was in a cast for weeks, then in a corset, but recovered fully. George Tucker received head injuries in an airplane collision on the Algiers airfield. They seemed slight at first, but a blood clot in the brain developed. He was flown home to have part of the skull removed, the clot flushed out, and the skull piece replaced.

* * *

Giraud's masquerade as a popular leader daily became more absurd. A straight-laced soldier of unquestioned integrity, he was without much comprehension of politics, economics, or anything else outside the Army. The pressure of De Gaullists and of American and British liberal elements against the still-strong tinges of Vichy in North Africa did not diminish. Washington's backing of Giraud began to wear thin. The *commandant-en-chef, civile et militaire* sought clumsily to meet the situation by inviting De Gaulle to share in his power. De Gaulle arrived late in May and proved for a few hours that the bulk of the French in North Africa were for him. The double bed of authority was a lion-and-lamb resting place, and the lamb was the bewildered Giraud. We now heard tales of effective resistance in France which indicated a well-organized Underground. We heard of no outstanding personality in the movement, but I thought I could detect signs of a strong leader. I asked De Gaulle about it. "Yes, there is a leader of Resistance in France," he said. "Naturally I cannot disclose his identity—very few people even in the movement know that—but I can assure you that he exists and the effects of his work can be felt."

I departed for a few weeks' leave in America, my first trip home in years. In New York I was asked to broadcast and as a subject chose this mysterious leader of the French Underground. It appealed to the network people; they embellished the program with dramatized episodes and the strains of the "Marseillaise." After the liberation of France, I learned the identity of this figure and the fact that he had fallen into the German net shortly before my broadcast. He was Max, the man who almost single-handedly drew Resistance groups together and probably played a more important role in the war than De Gaulle. His name is scarcely known today, even in France.[6]

On my return to North Africa, the big Army transport plane put down at Marrakech, the main transatlantic airfield in Morocco. The field was alive with a choice bit of gossip—General Patton, it seems, had struck and insulted a shell-shocked soldier, and Eisenhower had made him apologize, not only to the soldier but to his whole army. On arriving in Algiers, I found that everybody knew the story, but no correspondent had attempted to publish it. Censors had not specifically ruled that it could not be sent, but the Army had made it plain that it looked with disfavor on seeing the news of the incident in print.

That afternoon I discussed the matter with Captain Harry C. Butcher, Eisenhower's naval aide. He said Eisenhower would like to have my views, and we went into the general's office. I urged Eisenhower to release the story as a matter of good public relations for the Supreme Command and for General Patton. I pointed out that information of this nature, already known to tens of thousands, was bound to break into print at home. I said that if the news came through regular channels, the effect would be good. The American public would certainly understand that a general might have a fit of unreasonable temper in the heat of a campaign; the important point was that he had made amends. Publication of the information, I said, would enhance rather than diminish respect for Patton at home and increase confidence in the Army and its censorship. On the other hand, I continued, if the news broke in an irregular manner, the emphasis would be on the fact that it had been suppressed. The reaction, I said, would be unfavorable to the Command and to the correspondents.

Eisenhower discussed the matter in his usual frank and friendly manner. He agreed with me in principle but couldn't bring himself to the point to approving publication of the story. He seemed to cling to the Army reluctance to air such matters, to the old West Point tie. "I'm not defending Patton's action," he said. "I think it was despicable, and I have told him that. I have written him a personal letter telling him just what I thought about it and ordering him to apologize. He has done that. Geor-

6. "Max" was Jean Moulin, who was captured and tortured by the Germans in 1943 but refused to disclose any information about the Resistance. He died of his injuries near Metz in a train headed to Germany.

gie Patton is the best field commander we have. He can get men moving faster than anyone else. We want to call on him for a great deal more in this war. It would be a pity to lose him over something like this."

Eisenhower's conclusion was this: He had issued no order prohibiting correspondents from sending the story. He would consider the points which I had raised and send word to all correspondents should the Command decide to release the story. He thought the best form might be for Patton himself to discuss it at a press conference. He would consider any attempt by a correspondent to publish the story in the meantime as an embarrassment to Patton, to himself, and to the war effort. This effectively tied the hands of correspondents. No decision to release the news came. But the story, as was inevitable, broke in America. On November 21, Drew Pearson, in his Sunday evening broadcast, said Patton had struck a soldier, been "severely reprimanded" by Eisenhower, and removed from his command of the Seventh Army. Pearson expressed the opinion that Patton would never command troops again.

The Pearson broadcast caused a sensation. We were flooded with messages asking if the story was true and, if so, why we had not reported it. The reaction of the Supreme Command was to clamp total censorship on the case until an official statement could be concocted to meet the situation. Eisenhower was not in Algiers. His chief of staff, Major General Walter Bedell Smith, known as "The Beetle," drew up the statement after communicating with him by telephone. It was as follows: "General Patton is commanding the Seventh Army, has commanded it since it was activated, and is continuing to command it. No reports have ever been received at this headquarters of any soldier refusing to obey an order by General Patton. General Patton has never been reprimanded at any time by General Eisenhower or by anybody else in this theater."

It would be difficult to imagine a more dishonest statement. It lacked even the perverted courage of a straight lie. Each of its three sentences was technically correct, yet its whole intent was to deny the Pearson report by deceit. It was true that Patton had never been formally relieved of the Seventh Army command, but the Seventh Army was inoperative, its troops and equipment transferred to the Fifth Army. The question of whether or not any soldier had disobeyed Patton was not at point. Patton had been reprimanded (as the dictionary defines that word) by

Eisenhower, but his excoriation had not been put in the form of an official Army Reprimand. By order of General Smith, correspondents were forbidden to comment upon his statement. We could send only the bare statement, which we knew to be untrue.

The next day the uproar at home was so great that the War Department advised the Command to come clean. Smith came to our press room, airily apologized for what he called his "tongue-in-cheek" communiqué of the preceding night, cast a few sneers at Pearson and the press in general, and told us we might now tell the truth about the slapping incident. Censorship was off as regards Patton, but it was still on as regards Smith. We were not permitted to identify the author of the brush-off statement. As was to be expected, the unfavorable comments at home were directed against the AFHQ's suppression of the news rather than against Patton. The Army had an answer to this. Major General Alexander D. Surles, chief of public relations in Washington, blamed it on the correspondents, who he said had been free to send the story. I was rebuked by the Associated Press for not having informed the home office on the situation before Pearson scored his beat.

Chapter 8

RETURN TO ITALY

WITH NORTH AFRICA AND SICILY IN THE BAG, PREPARATIONS WERE pushed for something bigger, Operation Avalanche. It was to be the first thrust into Hitler's Fortress Europe. Handing out assignments for each offensive chilled me. I never could be sure that I would see all members of the staff again. Our arrangement was that Dan DeLuce would land on the Italian toe with the British Eighth Army, Pat Morin would go ashore at Salerno with the American Fifth. Hal Boyle was to get into Italy by his own devices, Ken Dixon to cover the invasion from the air. Don Whitehead was to be aboard an American naval vessel, Paul Lee with the British navy. Noland Norgaard and I were to handle the headquarters story in Algiers.

In the breakneck race among the press services to be first with the news, we all had bulletins announcing the invasion written out and ready to slam in the censors' basket the instant the news was released. The first dispatch in the basket was the first to go. Since the radio transmission frequently broke down, that might mean a lead of many minutes or even hours. We knew the invasion was *en route*. When a special communiqué was announced for 5 p.m., the press room was on edge, correspondents nervously fingering their prepared bulletins.

There had been indications that Italy might pull out of the war. I knew that the only way which she could do so was by unconditional surrender. So to be on the safe side, I also prepared a bulletin announcing Italy's surrender and guarded it under my typewriter. To the dismay of correspondents who had no appropriate bulletin prepared, the special communiqué did not announce the invasion of the Continent, but Italy's surrender. I thrust my flash into the basket, a censor stamped it, and off it went to New York and the world. It took only a few seconds for other correspondents to dash off their flashes, but by that time the censors had received an order to hold up all stories until after a special broadcast to the Italian people urging them to turn on the Germans. My bulletin could not be recalled. The hold-up order on the other correspondents' dispatches was rescinded after a few moments of loud protest on their part. My scoop on the Italian surrender was less publicized than that on the German surrender. Several hours later, the invasion of Italy was announced. Again we were first, this time only by a split second and only because I won the rat race to the censors' basket.

I never had illusions about this kind of journalism—it was imbecilic by any sensible standard. But it was what the AP, the UP, the INS, and Reuters wanted; it was what we were paid to do. Get a beat of a minute or two on any important story and congratulations poured in from New York. All three of the American agencies would regard such a feat as important enough to take a full-page advertisement in *Editor & Publisher* to crow over it. The fierce competition was heady stuff. I admit I liked it. The race required meticulous preparation and the greatest alertness. In more philosophical moments, I reflected that it was a losing game—the day would come when I could no longer qualify to be an AP correspondent because younger men would outrun me. I made a firm resolve to quit and take a more sedentary job when I reached the age of forty. There were, however, aspects of our work other than split-second scoops, and some of these I regarded as of genuine and far-reaching importance. One was that by all-out zeal and effective teamwork our AP staff was producing daily a full and well-written account of a stupendous drama for millions of eager readers. Another was our relentless and vigorous struggle against the constant attempts of censorship to go beyond matters of valid military security.

I went to Italy with a military government detachment, arriving in Salerno as a German counter-attack almost wiped out the beachhead. Major Harry P. Cain, who later became a United States senator, was in charge of the civil administration of Salerno. His biggest problem was that the town was still under shellfire and the Germans had kidnapped its Fire Department and were holding it in a cave in the hills. Troops attached to military government made a sortie and delivered the firemen and their equipment. Gordon Waterfield of Reuters and Dave Driscoll of Mutual Broadcasting were with me. Our conducting officer was Captain Richard Llewellyn, the author of *How Green Was My Valley*, who entered into our adventure with full zest. Waterfield and I had known prewar Italy as correspondents, Llewellyn had worked in the kitchens of Italian hotels in an attempt of his youth to learn the hotel business from the bottom up. We set out by truck to visit all of liberated Italy and see what Fascism had left in its wake.

The Italians were giving the British and Americans a boisterous welcome. To them it was being reunited with old friends, and since the old friends were known to be wealthy, they looked forward to handouts with the anticipation of children descending the stairs on Christmas morning. That any of their new co-belligerents could harbor ill will against them for having fought on the opposite side was inconceivable. *That* was merely the doings of the wicked Fascists. And now, it turned out, all Italians had been anti-Fascist all the time. "I was such a strong anti-Fascist that even my best friends were afraid to be seen talking to me on the street," said one. "I was so much against the Regime that I gave up smoking," said another. "I didn't want the government to get the tobacco tax." We met only one man who admitted he had been a Fascist. He couldn't very well deny it, since he was still wearing the uniform of a captain of the Blackshirt Militia, but he did not lack an explanation. "I was a Fascist extremist," he said, "because I thought that was the best way of ending the Regime. Some of us decided to do our best to push Fascism along the extremist road, knowing that all the sooner it would be dashed over the cliff."

The war posters told the story of Italy's flagging zeal for the war. The older and more weather-beaten ones bore Fascist boasts and slogans of conquest. The recent ones displayed a turn toward religion and exhortations for fortitude in adversity. Taranto, because of its naval base, had been a target of many Allied bombings, and a large part of the city lay in ruins. The townsfolk acted hurt rather than angry. "Why did you bomb us?" one after another asked. The easiest answer was, "Because Italy declared war on us." This seemed only to puzzle them. Italians saw nothing untoward with Italy's switch from one side to the other. "The way the Germans are now treating us, you'd think we were traitors," an Italian colonel said.

We learned that King Victor Emanuel and Marshal Pietro Badoglio[1] had reached Brindisi after their escape from the Germans and the new

1. Prime minister of Italy after King Victor Emmanuel III removed Mussolini from the government in 1943, Badoglio signed the armistice with the Allies.

Fascist Republic. We went there and found Badoglio eager to talk to us—he wanted to assure the American and British peoples of the friendship and good faith of the Italians and to appeal to them for support. Lieutenant General Sir Frank Noel Mason-MacFarlance, head of the Allied Control Commission, who also was in Brindisi, got wind of our plans and forbade the interview. He couldn't permit Badoglio to hold a press conference yet, he said, since he didn't know whether the Allies were going to accept him. The Allies did accept him, of course, and the doddering monarch along with him. It was the Algiers story over again, and the same good reasons were given. The inclination of American and British policymakers to bolster decrepit and discredited leadership in liberated countries was remarkable.

For months our bureau straddled the Mediterranean, as headquarters remained in Algiers, while operations took place in Italy. Eventually, headquarters moved to the big palace at Caserta, which the kings of Naples had modeled after Versailles, and Public Relations set up shop in Naples. Eisenhower left for England to prepare for the Channel invasion and was succeeded by Jumbo Wilson. The only operation which Wilson had launched in the Middle East after I had left there was an assault against the Dodecanese which proved a dismal failure.[2] Wilson's arrival in the Italian Theater was marked by a slowdown in military operations and a new tendency toward political censorship.

Stories of vigorous Yugoslav resistance under a mysterious new leader named Tito had been filtering through to us for some time. General Draja Mihailovitch, who earlier in the war had waged a resistance to the Germans based on Serb nationalism, by now was a minor figure, hiding in the mountains. It was apparent that Tito had united Serbs, Croats, and Slovenes as no one else had, in peace or in war. Dan DeLuce obtained passage across the Adriatic, spent a few days in territory held by Tito, and returned with a series of five dispatches, the first reliable news story of the struggle of Tito and his partisans. I submitted the first four of the dispatches to the American censor, who passed them. The next day the censor lost his job. The British Middle East Command claimed Yugoslavia as part of its theater of operations—and the right to censor Yugoslav news. The

2. The Docadenese Islands, which belong to Greece, are located in the Aegean Sea.

fifth part of the series was sent to Cairo, where censors deleted practically everything but the dateline. The series won DeLuce the Pulitzer Prize.

Since Tito's operations were part of the war, we naturally wanted to report them. Tito desired a representative of the American press at his headquarters. Joe Morton made arrangements with Tito's representative at Bari to go to Yugoslavia, but British Mideast authorities forbade it. They picked two correspondents in Cairo to be assigned to Tito at such time as they should deem proper. The British, suspicious of Tito, were attempting to get concessions from him to check Russian influence. The granting of his request for an American correspondent at his headquarters, I learned later, was one of the concessions which the British Foreign Office was offering in return. The press was a pawn. As the negotiations dragged on, we hit on a way of getting Tito's story. DeLuce, Morton, and I compiled twelve questions covering military, political, and social aspects of his movement and his postwar aspirations. These we submitted to Tito's agent in Bari, who forwarded them to Yugoslavia. Within a few days we had the answers, signed "J. B. Tito, Marshal of Yugoslavia." This was Tito's first public declaration of what he was fighting for; it gave clues to his postwar course.

We had violated no regulations in submitting the questions to an agent whom the Allied Command accepted at Bari, but British officials were infuriated that we had pierced the wall of censorship they had built around Tito. The Allied Command refused to pass a dispatch based on our questionnaire. After a long battle, I succeeded in getting censors to pass a dispatch, saying that we had statements addressed to the American people by Tito but could not send them because of Allied censorship. This story aroused protests at home which compelled the Command to release our answers from Tito.

* * *

That winter was cold and wet in Naples, and Neapolitans, living on poor food and with scarcely any fuel, suffered much. But Neapolitans are used to poverty and its inconveniences. They pulled through without too much grumbling, though worn expressions replaced the carefree smiles of earlier years. The Army brought out a new DDT lice powder to combat the spread of typhus. Civilians were dusted with it by tens of thousands; its ashy grey on their necks and faces made them look like ghosts. The winter was much worse for the troops at the front, blocked at Cassino despite several ill-planned and disastrous attempts to break through. After efforts by the land forces failed, a terrific air attack was launched. Air generals announced that the Cassino stronghold was blasted away, but when the troops advanced on it, they found it as strongly held as ever. Recriminations between the ground and air forces and between Allies followed. The fact that stray bombs had killed Allied troops only added to the bitterness.

In the frustration of the Cassino deadlock, the Allied Command ordered the destruction of Monte Cassino Abbey, a sanctuary of learning and culture for 1,400 years. In justification of this act, it was charged that the Germans were using one of its towers for observation. There were so many natural high points overlooking the Allied positions, it is difficult to see how the Germans could have gained much advantage from use of the towers. Lynn Heinzerling, who watched the bombardment through field glasses, said he thought he observed men in German uniforms running from the monastery. Workmen who dug out the ruins much later reported finding the bodies of 163 refugees and 7 German soldiers. The Command's assertion that there were German concentrations on the Pope's summer estate at Castel Gondolfo proved to be incorrect; in that case, it was refugees and not German troops who were bombed. The demolition of the abbey did not enable us to break through at Cassino.

The Americans were not enthusiastic about the Italian campaign. Had the decision been wholly in the hands of the United States, the drive up the peninsula probably would have been halted at Cassino. Emphasis would have been placed on the air offensive and preparations for the Channel crossing. But attacking the "soft underbelly" remained an obsession with Churchill. He viewed the Italian campaign as the equivalent of Wellington's Peninsula campaign, "the bleeding sore" which weakened Napoleon sufficiently to cause his undoing at Waterloo. The Italian campaign was in truth a bleeding sore, but for the Allies as much as for the Germans. It was largely trading man for man. There was little likely profit in a drive up the mountain-locked Italian boot, against the weight of military history. It is true that it resulted in the destruction of a number of the Wehrmacht's best divisions. Whether this weakening turned the tide in the Battle of France could be debated indefinitely.

The side-run by sea had been effectively employed by Montgomery in overcoming land barriers in the Eighth Army's progress through the Italian toe. Churchill insisted that it be tried in a thrust at Rome which would jar loose the stalemate in Italy. Possession of the Eternal City was of little military value, but the prime minister coveted it as a psychological prize to offset growing impatience on the home fronts, in countries under German occupation, and in the Kremlin. It would be a shot in the arm until the Channel invasion began. And there was a possibility that German forces between Rome and Cassino might be trapped.

The landing at Anzio was made in January 1944. It brought some of the war's fiercest fighting and most sublime valor but was not a notable success. Launched amid confusion at the top, it had originally been keyed to a proposed offensive on the main front but later was made an almost unrelated operation. The debarkment went well and took the enemy by surprise. Major General John P. Lucas, in command, appeared not to have been given clear directives on how much he was to bite off during this period of little opposition—whether or not he was to dash for positions on the Alban Hills and cut off all of the Pontine Plain. It has been argued that he followed a wise course in establishing a compact beachhead, for if he had extended his lines too far and too thinly, he might have lost everything piecemeal. The Germans massed great strength around the perimeter and counter-attacked heavily, almost wiping out the beachhead. Their mistake in making their main assault in the most strongly held sector was an important factor in saving it. Lucas was removed. How much of the responsibility was his when things went wrong is an unanswered question of the war. At the time, we felt that a large part of it was higher up.

Don Whitehead made the landing and got the first press dispatch off the beachhead. When Anzio was undergoing its severest test, the alarm at home was greater than at Anzio itself. A statement by Roosevelt that the fate of the beachhead was "critical" brought a series of panicky cablegrams from AP General Manager Kent Cooper ordering me to call all Associated Press personnel off it. By this time DeLuce had replaced Whitehead and we had a photographer there. The beachhead had not been given up. On the contrary, the troops there were battling resolutely to hold it. It was obviously the duty of war correspondents to remain with them and continue to tell their story. A pull-out by the Associated Press at that time, as ordered by Mr. Cooper, would have cost the AP the loss of all prestige in the Theater. The presence of correspondents had an effect on the morale of combat troops—it made them feel that they were not forgotten, that the people at home were following their every move.

I felt that it was imperative that the AP be represented on Anzio while there was important news there. Yet if I did not obey the instructions, I would be responsible for any casualties which might occur. I was up to my neck in Naples in details of running our service, but the only solution was to go to Anzio myself. I left that night on an LST.[3] It was a lucky break, for the three weeks which I spent on the beachhead were the most moving of my life. Press headquarters was in a building which leaned against a squat cliff which ran down to the beach. We could see the front from its roof. The whole beachhead was under shellfire. While the odds of getting hit were actually small, there was no way of getting out of range and scarcely any sure shelter. This fact seemed to be impressed on every man: they were all on the same beachhead. There probably never have been 50,000 men who lived together with greater devotion and consideration toward one another. Eventually Anzio's perimeter became strongly fixed, and the German battering diminished. There was another deadlock, and the Command built up the beachhead's force and supplies for a breakout in connection with a later offensive on the main front.

* * *

The reporting of World War II was at its worst, in my opinion, in the so-called Headquarters Story. This was the daily overall picture of what was happening in the Theater, as woven together from the communiqués, the flood of Army handouts, and the vocal emanations of the official spokesmen, designed to provide the correspondents with "background." Sometimes the spokesmen, by slip of tongue, referred to this "background" as "directives." As the war progressed, the public relations machinery for

3. Landing ship tank, a World War II naval vessel that delivered troops and equipment directly onto the shore, sometimes irreverently called a "Large Slow Target."

providing information for the headquarters story grew greater and more elaborate. The headquarters press rooms looked like classrooms, the correspondents sitting at desks and the spokesman of the moment standing before war maps like a teacher, pointer in hand. Even as he spoke, enlisted men distributed sheaf after sheaf of mimeographed pages, providing still more information for the correspondents. Generals, admirals, and other luminaries were brought to the press rooms to add their word, frequently "off the record."

In the early days in Cairo there was but one press conference a day, and that often consisted merely of the announcement that there was "nothing to add to the communiqué." Along the Algiers-Naples-Rome-Paris trail, the number of daily conferences increased to two, three, four, and sometimes five a day. The number of "special" handouts increased from one or two a week to twenty or thirty a day, some running to sixty pages. This flood of written and vocal matter, in the main, was the Army's opinion of the Army. It was usually a high opinion. The reputations of generals were safe in the hands of the spokesmen and the handout writers. Every reverse had its explanation, every error its excuse.

Not all the material handed out was dispatched as news. There are some things which even a headquarters correspondent will not swallow. But the Army line was mixed in with solid news; often there was no way of checking facts. Since press communications from the front were slow, the headquarters story usually was ahead of the accounts from correspondents on the scene. The headquarters story was a roundup, conveniently set forth by the Army. Reporters at the front could see only a small segment at a time. Consequently, it was the headquarters story that drew the big headlines. When the real story—or as much of it as got by censors—arrived two or three days later, it was often buried in the back pages.

Headquarters correspondents developed techniques of their own. Some became expert in separating the wheat of official announcements from the chaff, often bringing out important information by careful interrogation of the spokesmen. Others did not. In the spring of 1944, I experimented on moving the headquarters story a little nearer the front. Eighth Army was then inactive. News of both the main and Anzio fronts of the Fifth Army were available at Fifth Army headquarters. We started putting out the general story from there. The plan failed, partly due to slower communications from Army headquarters, partly to an apparent demand at home for some of the embellishments and amplifications which Theater headquarters provided. Fifth Army had its own set of public relations officers, zealous in promoting publicity for General Mark W. Clark. They insisted that "Fifth Army" be part of the dateline; occasionally it was written into dispatches as they passed through censorship. Sid Feder, who had joined our staff, said: "When we get to Pisa, I'm going to satisfy these boys. I'm going to dateline my story 'With General Mark W. Clark's Fifth Army in the Leaning Tower of Pisa.'"

The Air Forces maintained public relations staffs big enough to man ten metropolitan newspapers. Their handouts not only described operations in detail but often included chatty little interviews with the participating airmen. When correspondents entered Foggia, they learned that one of the victims of the Allied bombings of that city had been a circus midget. This fact inspired a British correspondent to write a parody of an American Air Force handout. It was no more far-fetched than many of the dramatic narratives produced by Air Force Public Relations. It follows: "When the sirens sounded in Foggia, Giovanni Piccolo, the littlest man in Italy, was in a cafe. Others fled. Being a brave man, Giovanni remained to finish his beer, then strode resolutely to the nearest shelter. At that moment our heavy bombers attacked. Bombardier Joe Doakes, son of Mrs. Doakes of 100½ Main Street, Wolfbane, Mo., describes it this way: 'I was looking through my bomb-sight when I saw the little fellow crossing the street. He couldn't have been more than three feet high. I let him have one of my blockbusters, right on the noggin. You should have seen him fly to pieces. Boy, will Mom be proud of me for this!'"

Many of those in public relations were good and honest newspapermen. But their role was similar to that of civilian journalists in a totalitarian state. Sometimes—if the facts did not conflict with the official line—they turned out stories of merit. But in the aggregate, public relations journalism was cramped by the hand of officialdom and scarcely distinguishable from the war reporting in the Fascist and Nazi press.

That spring afflicted the Neapolitan *campagna* with an extra woe: the worst eruption of Vesuvius in generations. As a spectacle it surpassed anything I saw in the war. As a destructive force it was more gripping, if only minutely as extensive. I was awed to see a pulsing stream of molten lava thirty feet high crush the houses of a village, then bury them within itself as it continued its snakey course down the fertile slopes where men have defied the volcano again and again after each rampage. In sections not threatened by the lava streams, but under a hail of red cinders, the peasants wore metal pots as helmets for protection.

* * *

In May, the big offensive on Rome was launched. Our armies, equipment, and supplies had been built up to a big superiority over the enemy, the assault was carefully planned, and the troops knew that this time they were going to take Rome. It was the old story—waiting until we had the stuff and then going places. It had been hoped that a large part of the German army would be trapped between the troops breaking out of the Anzio beachhead and our main force. Most of the Germans escaped, but the way to Rome was opened. On a noisy weekend in early June several units pushed patrols inside Rome, but it wasn't official until General Clark had been photographed standing before the sign of the Royal Italian Automobile Club at the city limits, bearing the white letters "ROMA" on a blue background.

Our press camp was a few miles outside the city. A field radio had been set up for the transmission of our dispatches to Naples, where they could be relayed to New York. DeLuce had entered Rome and dashed off a dispatch telling of the fall of the capital and bearing a Rome dateline. At that second we were told the story was released. I thrust Dan's bulletin into the censors' basket. We scored a beat due to enemy action. The moment DeLuce's dispatch was cleared, a German strafing plane shot out the aerial and delayed the transmission of all others for two hours. The last German remnants pulled out of Rome that night. Shortly before dawn, Price Day of the *Baltimore Sun* and Carleton (Bill) Kent of the *Chicago Sun* and I drove into the capital. One by one the old familiar streets and buildings came into view as our jeep progressed and the sky brightened. Rome was intact and never looked more beautiful. We made a quick survey of the city and its dozen bridges over the Tiber—all of them were standing. We went to the old AP office in the Stefani Building and found it occupied by a dentist. Then to my old apartment on the Via Frattina, where the same *portiere*'s wife greeted me. We looked up a Swiss friend of my former days in Rome, Rudi Bolliger. As we sat around his bed, he gave us a rapid-fire account of the last days of the city under the Germans.

Rome arose early to welcome the conquerors and celebrate the liberation. A few hundred Resistance fighters, mostly Communists, had turned on the Germans in their withdrawal. Now tens of thousands sported the Resistance insignia. A GI got into Palazzo Venezia, emerged on Mussolini's balcony, and convulsed the crowd in the square with a comic impersonation of the Duce. At the gates of St. Peter's was my old friend Monsignor Pucci, who had not fared badly through the war and occupation. "Changing of the guard," he said philosophically as he viewed the sea of khaki uniforms in the square, which so often had been filled with black ones and later with green ones. Within a few hours the whole Italian office force of our prewar Rome bureau had found me. They were well and somehow had kept out of the army—Carletti, photographer; Bossi, secretary; Alberto Blassetti, day office boy; and Dante Brancher, night office boy. (Blassetti was about twenty-five years old, Brancher, thirty-five.) Each one kissed me. They wanted their jobs back.

One by one almost all of our staff came into Rome with the units to which they were attached. George Tucker arrived fresh from an Army hospital. After his injury in Algiers, George had been wounded by a bomb at Anzio and on recovery had suffered a kidney injury while jouncing over rough terrain in a jeep. This last injury had required long hospitalization, during which he was chafing for action. Our staff at the front was inadequate due to the quota limit set by the Army, so I had arranged that George might do some work while officially a patient in a field hospital. Under this set-up he wrote excellent accounts of medical and surgical developments of the war and some notable stories obtained by talking to the wounded. As he improved, doctors permitted him to go in ambulances to the front area. As the tented hospitals leapfrogged ahead with the advance, George always managed to get in the foremost one—by this time he was the Medical Corps' favorite patient. There was a joke among the correspondents that we carried a wounded man on our staff to beat the quota system. When Rome fell, George couldn't bear being hospitalized any longer. He left his bed and hitchhiked into the capital.

As General Clark was posing for photographers before Rome's City Hall and voicing his classic remark on the conquest—"It's a great day for the Fifth Army"—press communications with the outside world were bad and getting worse. Although the main reason for the drive on Rome had been one of psychological warfare, the Army had neglected to provide adequate means for getting out the great story which the Allies wanted spread through the world. Field radios had been set up in the city for us, but they were functioning badly. Only a small part of the copy written was transmitted on that first day in Rome.

In the afternoon, word spread that the Pope would appear on the balcony of St. Peter's to give thanks to God that Rome had been spared. Several hundred thousand people went there. I had difficulty in hearing all of his words, carried through the square by loudspeakers, and as I left for press headquarters to write a story, I suggested to the indefatigable Dan DeLuce that he might try to get the text of the Pope's talk. He was off in a flash, elbowing his way through the crowd. He had never been inside the Vatican before and knew nothing of its intricacies. But a half-hour later he showed up at the press room with the text. The fact that he spoke *Schweizer Deutsch* helped him with a Swiss Guardsman, who piloted him to the proper functionary. After that he talked himself into possession of the only available copy.

Early the next day I was rushing to press headquarters with a dispatch, hoping that communications would be better. Rudi Bolliger stopped me in the street. "Don't bother to send it," he said. "Nobody will ever read it. The radio just announced the Channel invasion has begun." We had expected that once the Normandy invasion took place, dispatches from the Italian Theater would be swept from the front pages and almost entirely out of the newspapers. We were resigned to our relegation and looking forward to a rest. But Italy produced a lot of news that summer, and our stories held their own and kept us as busy as ever.

As DeLuce and Feder continued with the Fifth Army in its pursuit of the Germans as far as Pisa, we moved our office from Naples to Rome. Public relations officers installed themselves and the correspondents in the De La Ville, a hotel on the Via Sistina well-known to American tourists. The chaos there was remarkable, even for a public relations operation. British and American PR officers quarreled over rations, the

Americans charging the British with a plot to make the American Army furnish more than its share. The messes were split, the British eating British meals on one side of the dining room, the Americans eating American meals on the other. There were three other messes in the building, those of the American enlisted men, the British sergeants, and the British "other ranks." Each had its own dining space, its own staff, its own larders—but all the meals were prepared in the same kitchen and on the same stove, amidst wrangling and confusion.

The quality of the cuisine can be imagined. But rescue was not long in coming, for Major General Harry Hubbard Johnson, a big, effusive Texas oil man, had become military governor of Rome. He was proud of his job as Julius Caesar's successor and desired a good press. On learning that correspondents were grumbling about Public Relations cooking, Johnson charged down to the hotel. "Nothing is too good for the correspondents," he said. "I am going to see that you boys get what you deserve." He sent a shipment of hams and an Army band to serenade us from the courtyard. The next evening the band was busy elsewhere, but a seven-piece Italian girl orchestra appeared. The food slipped back to its former standard.

Stephen Barber showed up in Rome on crutches. He had accompanied the French invasion of Elba. This operation had been scheduled for two weeks earlier. Delays in mounting it had rendered it unnecessary, since the Fifth Army was by that time sweeping up the mainland opposite the island. But the French went ahead anyway. Barber, hit in an arm and leg by mortar-shell fragments, locked his body against that of a Senegalese soldier similarly nipped. They crawled out of danger together, each using his good arm and leg. Barber soon recovered from his wounds.

We had compiled a list of persons who had spent the war in Rome and who might have interesting stories. The day after our entry we started tracing them. I found George Santayana[4] in the Monte Celio Convent of the Blue Sisters, a small congregation of English and Irish nuns. During my previous stay in Rome, Santayana had lived a hermit's life in a downtown hotel, especially avoiding newspapermen. Now, I correctly guessed, he would be glad to see anyone with news from America. A talkative Irish

---

4. Spanish American philosopher, cultural critic, novelist, and poet (d. 1952). In 1912 Santayana resigned his professorship at Harvard and went to Europe, where he lived for the rest of his life, primarily in Rome.

sister took my message to him and said he would see me in fifteen minutes. "He really isn't ill, but only old," she said. "He came here to live two
years ago. The Germans and the Fascists never bothered him. They never
came here. Now I really shouldn't tell you this, but we hid an English general here for a while after his escape from a prison camp. Mr. Santayana
is a Catholic, but he is not what I would call a very religious man. He is
very kind and a fine gentleman, though. I understand he is a great writer.
Now I think a man with such talent should devote it to writing religious
books. . . ."

Santayana, eighty and wizened, but with flashing black eyes full of
life, looked like an undersized schoolboy in his black jersey. He held up a
book with the joy of a child showing a new toy. An Air Force officer had
called a few hours earlier with a copy of his new book, *The Middle Span*,
from his publishers. He had completed the work in his cubicle in the convent and sent it out, uncensored, through the Vatican. "I did not see the
proofs, but there are only two errors, and very small ones," he said.

Santayana had not paid much attention to the war until he saw the
Americans enter Rome from his window. He still thought Fascism had
something worthwhile to offer; at least it had given him tranquility in retirement. Apparently he had not paid much attention to its more sordid
aspects. He said he was writing a book on Jesus Christ and the Gospels.
"I don't know whether I shall finish it," he said. "I haven't much longer
to live, you know." He chuckled over his residence in the convent and the
worries of the good sisters for his soul. "I often go to church," he said,
"but never to mass. When I go to church I like to be alone."

A few days later, George Tucker and I found Pietro Mascagni in a
second-rate hotel which the French had taken over as a billet. All guests
had been ordered to leave at once, but on learning Mascagni's identity the
officer in charge had permitted the composer and his wife to retain the
two rooms they had. He had also sent meals up from the mess. Mascagni,
also eighty, was a broken man, pouring out his woes. "I am penniless," he
said. "I have been defrauded of my money and my property. They have
taken everything." I asked him if he were still receiving royalties from
Cavalleria Rusticana. He threw up his hands and motioned to his secretary
to answer. The secretary, a painter apparently as impractical as the composer about money matters, explained sadly: "The Maestro's affairs are

in a most tangled state. In fact, I doubt that they can ever be untangled. Yes, there are royalties due. But the Maestro has always been cheated, all his life. Cheated by everyone. *Cavalleria Rusticana* was once performed simultaneously in ninety-eight different cities over the world. That can be said of no other opera. But did the maestro receive all the royalties due him? No." Signora Mascagni, as gloomy as her husband, came into the room with a new misfortune. She had broken her spectacles.

I could get no clear explanation of Mascagni's troubles. He was not in good grace with the new regime; he had basked in Fascist favor and conducted operas in Blackshirt uniform. His home was held in the name of his son, an ardent Fascist, and it had apparently been confiscated. Modern music was as bad as the state of the world, the composer said. No melody, no harmony in it. But he would show the world by writing a new opera. First he must find a suitable libretto—there were no good librettos anymore. As we departed, he dropped his gloom to give us a theatrical farewell: "Tell my many friends in America that I am alive and well. I send them my greetings. Tell them I have not forgotten the kindnesses and the honors which they showered upon me."

Beniamino Gigli was billed to sing at a British army concert a few days after the fall of Rome. Italians, regarding him as a Fascist, defaced the posters. A British general, as a public safety precaution, forbade his appearance. We found him practicing for the concert when we went to his villa to break the news. "This ignominy after my glorious career!" he said. "It is true that I sang for the Germans, but that is only because they were in Rome when I sang at the opera. I have devoted my life to art and have never had any interest in politics. I was not a collaborationist. The opposition to me is not political—it is from people at the opera, who have always been jealous of my success. Oh, I don't blame the Americans or the English for this. It is the Italians. I shall never sing for Italians again in my life!" Gigli, as lacking in political sense as he was gifted in voice, had been ostentatiously Fascist in earlier days. On his return from a successful season at the Metropolitan Opera in New York in 1939 he had been baited by the Fascist press into a bitterly anti-American interview. Like other artists under the stigma of collaborationism, he had grave difficulties in reestablishing himself.

The baritone Giuseppe De Luca had cautiously refrained from sing-ing for the Germans—even when offered a high price, he said. Signor De Luca opined that if Gigli was in hot water, it was what he deserved. I took it there was little love between the tenor and baritone. De Luca was living on scanty fare in his stately marble home. A British captain had been bil-leted in the house. "I was a king today," De Luca told us. "For lunch I had a marvelous new meat which the captain gave me—spahm, it is called."

The fall of Rome disclosed that corruption under Fascism had been greater than any of us had imagined in the old days. The Duce himself had been deceived by this fruit of his system. The Italian air force, far below its listed strength, had resorted to the Potemkin Village[5] trick in moving planes from field to field as Mussolini inspected air bases. He did not know that many of them were the same aircraft that he had seen at other bases. The Fascist Social Republic, organized after Badoglio's ca-pitulation and the defection of the Monarchy, was a mournful affair. The Germans exercised the real authority; Mussolini owed his life to Hitler after his delivery from the Badoglio forces by German parachutists. Only Fascist fanatics and criminals rallied to the Republic; others knew the game was up and wanted out.

5. During the Crimean War, according to historical myth, the Russian minister Grig-ory Potemkin had fake villages built in advance of Empress Catherine II's tour of the region to fool her into believing that her army had captured them. The term now is used to mean a respectable facade covering up something shabby or undesirable.

Chapter 9

RETURN TO FRANCE

"SO YOU'RE GOING TO FRANCE," SAID STEVEDORES, STREET HAWKERS, shopkeepers, and janitresses in Naples when correspondents showed up there for the "secret" embarkment for the invasion of the French Riviera. Everyone seemed fully informed on the impending operation. Yet when the landings were made, the Germans apparently were taken by surprise.

During the last days at Algiers a new general had arrived to take command of public relations in the Mediterranean Theater. He was the mouse-like Brigadier General Tristram Tupper from Hollywood, a scenario-writing brother-in-law of General George Marshall. Although his job naturally called for contact with correspondents, he went into concealment. Efforts to seek him out failed. When months went by without a sight of him, word spread that there *was no General Tupper*. After we were established in Italy he made a few furtive appearances. He excused his absence by saying he could be of more help to us by staying far away. He was right, for when he assumed personal supervision—as press arrangements for the invasion of southern France were made—the result had almost every correspondent howling. Assignments were made with the aid of charts, lists, timetables, and the drawing of straws. Tupper planned to send correspondents in on successive waves. Had not most of the correspondents scheduled to wait for the later waves found means to circumvent his program, they might not have gotten into France until the campaign was over.

We decided to split up our staff, half remaining in Italy under Boots Norgaard, the other half, including me, going into France. Sid Feder landed with the American troops, Ken Dixon went in with the Air Force, Joe Dynan with the French. George Tucker covered the operation from a warship. I remained in Italy for the headquarters story of assault, then proceeded to France by plane. We made out well; our dispatches were spread over the front pages of almost every paper in America.

I was deeply moved to be back in France again. Immediately I sensed a certain freshness and freedom that seems to pervade France; there is nothing exactly like it anywhere else. The operation had been well planned and executed, but more than that, our soldiers had a new buoyancy, absorbed from their new environment. For the first time in the Mediterranean Theater, all of them appeared both to like and respect the civilian population. One reason for this was the genuine and effective military cooperation of the French Resistance fighters. "We don't really need infantry in this country," said a colonel commanding an American regiment. "If we supply the armor and artillery, they'll do the infantry work."

I had expected the Maquisards to turn in fury upon Vichy officials.[1] I was surprised at their comparative mildness. In the town of Tourves, the Resistance movement was mostly Communist. The mayor had been an ardent Pétainist. I asked them what they had done about him. "We have the old fool in jail," they said. "We'll let him out in a few weeks. You couldn't have expected him to be anything but a Pétainist. He hasn't had a new idea in forty years."

I was happy to find that despite privations, the French had not lost their magic touch in cooking. We took some Army rations to a woman who ran a small country inn. She converted them into a meal in the best tradition of the cuisine of the region.

The obstructions of Public Relations led to the establishment of an Underground Public Relations to take care of correspondents banished, for one reason or another, from participation in the largesse of General Tupper's press camp. Major Jay Vessels, a former AP sportswriter in Minneapolis, was a highly unorthodox Air Force public relations officer. In Naples he had run an establishment for correspondents which functioned more or less in opposition to the main Public Relations set-up. The main branch tried to crack down on him, but Vessels usually had placed himself under the patronage of some Air Force general, who protected him. "Violent Villa," the Vessels ménage in Naples, was a big apartment which served as living and working quarters for those correspondents

---

1. The Maquisards were guerrilla fighters in the French Resistance.

who preferred his establishment when they were in the city. A diligent scrounger, he drew superior rations and provided a good table, had assembled a congenial and capable staff of enlisted men, and had sufficient vehicles for adequate transportation. He charged board to cover extras, such as the services of a singing waitress and delicacies bought on the black market. He did not deluge the correspondents with handouts but had a good nose for news and each night invited combat flyers in to tell their stories. A good deal of Air Force news came out of the conversations between these guests and correspondents over glasses of Italian brandy. Ernie Pyle, Bill Mauldin, and Ken Dixon frequently lived there. They liked the free and easy air of the house and its lively happenings, such as the blowing up of the bathroom by a playful correspondent with a captured German booby trap.

Several correspondents wrangled air transport to France from obliging Army pilots in advance of General Tupper's schedule. On their arrival at his press camp, they were ordered to go back to Italy. His charts showed they had no right to be in France. Other correspondents were in disfavor at the press camp for other reasons. Vessels came to the rescue. Within a few hours he had taken over a hotel, established a mess, obtained jeeps, and arranged a rapid air service to Italy for dispatches.

After the initial success of the offensive, most of the German forces in southwestern France were ordered to pull out before the trap closed on them by junction of the Allied armies in southern France with those which had crossed the Channel. Philip Jordan of the London *News-Chronicle,* Philip Wynter, an Australian correspondent, and I got a jeep and trailer from Public Relations. We first went into the Rhone Valley, where a part of the withdrawing Germans were captured after a complicated nip-and-tuck engagement in which they almost broke through. At Crest, in this region, we encountered Graham Hovey of the International News Service and Bill Kent, immobilized by lack of transport. We took them into our party. We set off for Grenoble, which we heard was about to fall. The route took us through the Vercors, the heart of the Resistance country, where organized Maquisards had been holding out for more than two years, at one time engaging as many as two and a half divisions of Germans. Many of the villages had been bombed by the Luftwaffe in reprisal.

The Germans had abandoned Grenoble after a skirmish. We arrived as American tanks were rumbling into the city and the population was beside itself with cheers. After nightfall in marched the Maquisards from the hills, singing the "Marseillaise" and bringing with them hundreds of German prisoners. The commander of the regiment that took Grenoble told us that he had been ordered not to go farther northward, but to turn east toward Lyon. He had heard that the Germans were still holding Lyon strongly to enable more of their units to escape from the Rhone Valley. There would probably be a lull for reorganization before an attempt was made to take the city.

We decided to go northward from Grenoble, into the interesting alpine foothill country. No Allied troops had yet entered the region, but in each town the Resistance leaders assured us that the Germans had pulled out and that the road was clear to the next town. We visited Chambery, Aix-les-Bains, and Annecy; each had its own proud story of Resistance and wanted the world to know it. The Resistance forces had taken over, and the whole region was orderly. Our arrival was the same everywhere— the first startled expression as they saw our jeep and uniforms, then a burst of joy. This was their first contact with the outside world since 1940. Much as we explained that we were merely newspapermen come to report the story of their liberation, they were sure we were the vanguard of an American army and prepared for a great celebration. Their happiness seemed as natural and sincere as it was boisterous.

We had intended to visit only a few towns, but with the withdrawal of the Germans from the area we made such rapid progress that day that Philip Jordan, looking at a map, said: "You know, we could make the Swiss frontier before sundown." It seemed incredible. That morning we had thought of Switzerland as a remote, German-locked *îlot*. Now it was only a pleasant drive, over beautiful roads and amidst the friendliest of people. We decided to try for it. We reached the frontier town of Annemasse in the late afternoon. Its population was lined up along the main street, looking somber. This puzzled us, but we learned the cause when we caught that awful odor of death that is much worse than its sight. The last of the Resistance fighters slain by the Germans were being borne to the cemetery; their bodies had lain in the woods for two days before they were found. As soon as the funeral procession passed, the townsfolk turned to us with embraces—what was the latest news, how big an army was coming, would it pursue the Germans right into Germany? The mayor invited us to a reception at the Hotel de Ville. We told him we'd like to go to the frontier post first. He gave us a police escort.

The frontier at that point is on the outskirts of Geneva. Several thousand Genevans had massed on the Swiss side of the gate hoping for a glimpse of the first of the Allied Army to arrive. A thundering cheer went up—we were it. We talked over the fence to the Swiss, who acted as happy as the French. When we remarked that we had run out of cigarettes, we were showered with dozens of packs, and one man struggled through the crowd to hand me a bottle of Scotch. "I have been saving it for four years for this occasion," he said. Tom Hawkins, head of the Associated Press staff in Switzerland, appeared. He wanted to take down my story and file it without delay from Geneva. "I can't give it to you," I said, "because we are under censorship. We'll have to go back to press camp and file, even though that means a delay of two days. But since you see us here, it's obvious that the road is clear of Germans all the way from the Mediterranean to Switzerland." Back at the Annemasse City Hall, the mayor, council, and Resistance leaders had the champagne corks popping. The mayor extolled the profound friendship of Americans, Britons, and French, and Philip responded in our behalf—and possibly on behalf of the British and American governments and peoples. In the jail across the street were girls who had consorted with the Germans, their heads shaven.

On our return to press headquarters, we learned that Public Relations had suspended all five of us. As a result of the story which Hawkins had written of our arrival at the Swiss frontier, General Tupper had jumped to the conclusion that we had entered Switzerland, filed dispatches there in evasion of censorship, and probably had been interned by the Swiss. His greatest anxiety was over the supposed loss of his jeep and driver for the duration. When we set him right on what had happened, we were reinstated.

After a few days, we decided to go into the vast territory west of the Rhone and south of the Loire. No correspondent had yet entered this region, about one-third of all France. From what we heard, it was liberating itself. The First French Army, which had landed with the American Seventh Army, had gone as far westward as Nimes. After that we were in

Maquis territory. We drove through Montpellier, Lodève, Millau, Lodez, Figeac, St. Céré, Brive, and Uzerche to Limoges. Some German units were still pulling out of the area. Their route was northeastward and crossed ours. In each village the local Resistance leaders had excellent intelligence of all movements, at least as far as the next village. They told us which towns to avoid and which roads were blocked. They replenished our gasoline and oil—they had supplies of both, captured from the Germans. They gave us a heartfelt welcome, all the credentials we wanted, and were helpful in every way. They had no organized public relations corps to make our trip unpleasant. The roads were strewn with knocked-out German vehicles and some bodies. The Maquisards did most of their work at night, hurling home-made bombs at the departing columns from behind hedges, sniping from trees, felling trees across roads, placing charges under bridges. The toll they exacted was high.

Some of the towns, like Lodève, were almost bare of food. Others, like Brive, in the center of a rich agricultural district, bulged with good things to eat, for there was no transport to ship them to markets elsewhere. In each town, we were joyously mobbed, our jeep and trailer covered with flowers, bottles of wine and brandy slipped into our hands. After leaving every village, we had to stop, divest the jeep of its bouquets to make room for the ones we knew we would get in the next one. We were all embarrassed by the demonstrations; we knew that they were not intended for us, but for soldiers who were liberating France. It happened that we were the first that these people had seen in British and American uniforms. Explaining was no use. We gave up trying.

At St. Céré we met two American officers. They took us to their little encampment in the woods, from which their score of GIs, mostly French-Canadians from New England, had been making sorties for months at the side of the Maquisards. One soldier rushed up and kissed our jeep. "I never thought I'd be so glad to see a jeep," he said. "We parachuted in and couldn't bring any." At Limoges we set about investigating the main story which we had come into southwestern France to get—the massacre of the population of the village of Oradour-sur-Glane.[2] Although this was perhaps the most bestial and tragic atrocity of World War II, only the

2. On June 10, 1944.

sketchiest details, and these not confirmed, had been reported to the outside world. After talking with Resistance leaders in Limoges, we drove to the village, fourteen miles distant and linked to the city by a narrow-gauge inter-urban trolley line.

It would be difficult to imagine a lovelier village than Oradour, set in the midst of rolling, fertile fields of green and gold. The River Glane is scarcely more than a brook. It is lined with pleasant trees, and its clear water ripples merrily along to the Vienne, which in turn flows into the Loire. But we found Oradour a ghost town, and it remains a ghost town, for it has been decided that it will not be repopulated; it will be kept as it is as a national memorial. Nobody knew the exact number of victims. The best guess was that there were about 1,600 men, women, and children in Oradour that Saturday afternoon of the massacre and only seventeen persons survived, two of them mad and several others horribly burned. Oradour's permanent population was about 800, but a number of refugee families had settled there during the war and many city children had been placed to board with Oradour families, since food in the village was plentiful. The tobacconists of the region were holding a meeting in Oradour that day, and people from Limoges had come out on the trolley for a jaunt in the country or to gather a little extra food.

When German troops arrived in trucks and blocked the roads leading in and out of the village, the people were not alarmed. They assumed it was a routine check-up of identity cards. There had been no Underground activity in Oradour; because it was a refugee center, the Maquisards had kept clear of it. The women and children were ordered into the church; the men to the school. The Germans, a unit with a preponderance of very young and fanatical Nazis just brought up from service in the Pyrenees, suddenly became fiends—on orders from their officers. The men were marched to barns and mowed down by submachine gun fire. The barns were then set afire. In the church, screaming children clung to their terrified mothers as they heard the shots. Germans moved a chest of explosives into the nave, set fuses, and went out. Many of the children were killed as the explosion hurled them against the walls. Others were suffocated by the choking, black fumes. The Germans threw grenades and firebrands through the church windows. Then they pointed their guns through them and finished those still alive. They covered the corpses with straw and burned them. A woman and child who hid in a little toilet in the yard were pounded to death with rifle butts; we saw their blood on the toilet door. There was dried blood on the church walls too, and splotches on the altar and on the crucifix over the altar. Although the ashes had been removed and the church cleaned, we found bits of flesh, bone, and gristle, locks of children's hair, pieces of the toys they had held in their hands, and little metal pieces from baby carriages. The victims were buried in a great common grave. The bodies could not be counted. Of the handful that escaped, one man hid in the belfry, just above the carnage in the church. Others concealed themselves in the cornfields on the edge of town.

A few days later the Germans said the massacre had been a mistake. The troops had been ordered to punish Oradour-sur-Vayres, fifteen miles away, where one German soldier had been killed by the Underground. The error in confusing two towns of names so like is understandable, but even if the Germans had wiped out the right village, it would be difficult to explain such an outburst of organized savagery, such mass sadism, and the glee with which survivors said the soldiers performed it. The event took place shortly after the Allied landings in Normandy. Perhaps that penetration of Fortress Europe had so shaken the nerves of the commander responsible for the Oradour massacre that he went berserk. Even that conjecture is hard to accept; the spectacle of several hundred soldiers going berserk with him surpasses understanding.

At Oradour we were closer to the territory occupied by the Channel forces than to the region of the southern invasion which we had left. We decided to proceed ahead as the quickest means of getting our dispatches out. At Angoulême we found American flyers walking the streets in uniform. They had lived in the woods with the Maquisards after being shot down but now had come out of hiding. All hotels were filled, but Resistance leaders found us rooms in a brothel. Alert soldiers of the Resistance at Ruffec first mistook our jeep for a German vehicle and were within a split second of firing on us when they understood our signal. As the town welcomed us, a helpful woman presented us with an American flag to prevent a recurrence of the episode. She had made it herself. It bore thirty-four stars and seventeen stripes.

On our arrival at Niort, two rival reception committees hastily

formed, one headed by the mayor, the other composed of Communists.
The two groups were equally zealous in the cause of Resistance and
equally hospitable toward us, but not on speaking terms with each other.
We attended the mayor's ceremony in one room of the Hotel de Ville,
then walked across the hall to the Communist function. The Communists took us on an inspection of their prisoners, a group of twenty men
and women charged with collaborationism, whom they were holding under guard in the garden of the City Hall. They had been rounded up that
morning. A pretty girl prisoner with big blue eyes turned to me and said:
"Monsieur, if you only knew the real truth. . . ." The guards silenced her.
Later I wondered what her story was.

We reached the banks of the Loire, opposite Nantes, late at night. All
bridges over the wide river had been destroyed. We left our jeep with a
Resistance group, and one of them rowed us across the river. We stum-
bled through the pitch-black streets of the badly bombed city seeking
some sign of the American Army. At length we encountered an ambulance
and stopped it. We explained we were from the south and asked the way
to the nearest American unit. "I don't know much about this place," the
driver said. "I was just bringing a couple of the boys back from the cat-
house." Thus was effected the first junction of personnel from the landings in the south of France with those who had come across the English
Channel, five days before combat troops of the two forces made contact.

The next morning our task was to get our jeep and trailer across the
Loire. The United States Navy had an establishment at Nantes, but we
could get no help there. We recrossed the river to see what the Underground could do for us. Resistance men directed us to a place where there
was a small barge. We placed the vehicles onto it. One small French tug
was operating in the river. A Maquisard rowed to it and induced its captain to tow us across. During our long swing through southwest France
we had amassed considerable information on the situation there and on
the positions of withdrawing German units. This we turned over to Army
intelligence.

Because of the delay in getting over the Loire, it was late afternoon
before we left Nantes, but we decided to try to make Paris, three hundred
miles away, that night. As we sped over the roads, a sharp and unmarked
curve almost proved our undoing. Our driver, Private Douglas Hooey of

Sussex, N.J., who had shared all our experiences since we set out for the Swiss frontier, saw it in time to keep from running off the embankment, but he turned so abruptly and at such a speed that all of us except Hooey were thrown out on the road. The trailer turned upside down, but two men sitting on it were thrown clear. We picked ourselves up, righted the trailer, repacked our baggage in it, and resumed the trip. Only one bone was broken in the spill, and that was in my thumb.

We reached Paris at 3 a.m., dead tired, and got a night's sleep. On arising, I had my thumb put in splints. Then the five of us faced the wrath of Public Relations, SHAEF—Supreme Headquarters, Allied Expeditionary Forces—for having entered its domain without authorization. That our trip had been approved by existing French authority and that we had come to Paris to use commercial radio facilities did not count with the public relations officers, who fancied themselves in authority over the French government and commercial radio-telegraphy as well as correspondents. We were first told that we would be sent back without being permitted to file our dispatches from Paris. After a little arguing, we were allowed to send the stories we had gathered on the trip but warned that we could write nothing about Paris. The decision to permit us to send our dispatches may have been due to the fact that Public Relations had just experienced an extremely unfavorable reaction at home to the expulsion from France of several correspondents because they had written about the liberation of Paris instead of publicizing the Air Force. The Ninth Air Force had arranged for their transportation and billeting in France and therefore expected them to give their full attention to that organization, even though the liberation of Paris, and not the Air Force, was the story in which readers were interested at the time.

We were instructed to wait for the junction of the two armies before making the return trip. When General Tupper heard of our arrival in Paris, he suspended all five of us again and ordered other correspondents not to "go ahead of the Army." This meant that they were prohibited from investigating and reporting the liberation of all those vast areas which were not in the path of the Allied armies. Tupper later reinstated us, but our driver, Private Hooey, was sent back to Italy.

Paris had been liberated for more than a fortnight when we reached it, but the celebration was still on, spirits were high, American soldiers still were being kissed and showered with flowers. The city was a little thread-bare, its taxis, buses, and night lights were missing, but it still was Paris and still beautiful. Its trees seemed greener, perhaps because the air was freer of gasoline fumes during the Occupation. I visited my old haunts, found some of my old friends. There seemed to be a rebirth in France, a new virility and a promise of something better than the corruption and stagnation of the last years of the Third Republic. The struggle of the Underground had established a model of unselfishness and patriotism. Widely divergent elements within it, from Communists to old-line Army officers, had united in a common struggle. Unfortunately, disunity and most of the old faults reappeared as soon as the struggle was over. Liberation was followed by disillusionment and new hardships. Within a few months the high hopes of late August were mostly gone.

When the junction of the two armies was formally achieved, the American Seventh and French First Armies, which had landed in the south, were placed under SHAEF. The two groups of Associated Press correspondents in France likewise were combined into a single staff, and I was asked to head it, with headquarters in Paris. Before assuming my new post, I returned to Italy to wind up office matters. Boots Norgaard succeeded me as head of the staff there. Sid Feder, Lynn Heinzerling, and George Bria remained with him.

I left Rome on a transport plane. There was one other passenger, a sergeant. We were to put down at another airfield in the Rome area, take on a load of nurses, and proceed to France. It was a morning of treacherous cross-winds. As we came down for the nurses, the plane hit the ground with three great jolts. Gasoline poured across the floor. "Get out quickly," came a voice from the pilot's compartment. The sergeant and I had been a little shaken in the rough landing, but not greatly concerned. As we jumped from the aircraft, we saw an ambulance and fire truck rushing toward us. We then turned and looked at our plane. The undercarriage was smashed away, one wing was buried three inches in the ground, a propeller had been broken off. Only then did we realize how rough the landing had really been. "Lucky you weren't smoking, or that high octane gas would have gone up and it would have been goodbye for all of us," the pilot said.

* * *

The reestablished Paris bureau of the Associated Press had a big job cut out for it. Our staff had to cover seven armies and three air forces in combat, the SHAEF headquarters story, military government and rear-area activities, and the French political and civil situation. At the same time, we were assembling a new staff for Germany and were introducing the Associated Press service to French newspapers in accordance with the AP's decision to distribute news on a worldwide basis rather than only in the Americas. The little bureau which started in Cairo and moved with the war had grown to large proportions. Several Mediterranean veterans were on the staff which had crossed into France with the Channel forces. These included Wes Gallagher, Don Whitehead, Hal Boyle, and Toby Wiant. Pat Morin and Dan DeLuce showed up later, the former having been in India for a period, the latter in Moscow. William F. Frye, with whom I had worked in bygone years in Washington and who earlier in the war had covered the War Department for the AP, arrived to do a brilliant job with the British Second Army.

Men on the staff new to me included Robert Eunson, Ed Ball, Howard Cowan, A. I. Goldberg, Ned Nordness, Austin Bealmear, Robert C. Wilson, James M. Long, Lew Hawkins, William Boni, and Tom Yarbrough. George Tucker, Ken Dixon, and Joe Dynan had, like myself, come into France by the southern invasion. We also had half a dozen photographers. We took back most of our tipsters and part-time French correspondents in the provinces. These, with clerical help, brought our complement to about 100. Reporting the war was no longer the chummy little business it was in the Middle East; endless bookkeeping now seemed to take most of my time.

We had taken a floor of the *Herald-Tribune* building off the Champs Élysées, but we were unable to operate there except for our incoming service. All censorship was at the Scribe Hotel, and cable and radio-heads were there under the thumb of the Army. One room served as our office; we slept in others and ate in the correspondents' mess in the basement and drank at the bar there. Sometimes I was so occupied that I did not stir out of the Scribe for days at a time. A six-day stretch was the longest, I think, and when I ventured out after that the fresh air seemed strange. I was now completely a Headquarters *wallah*, as far removed from the front as though I had been in Chicago. The SHAEF briefings took place three times daily in the hotel's stuffy ballroom. Here the overall picture of developments along the vast front was handed out at 10 a.m., 3 p.m., and 10 p.m. These briefings lacked the breath of life, usually lacked the essence of good reporting, and not infrequently lacked the whole truth. They represented SHAEF's official line.

Press communications from the armies in the field had greatly improved. In most cases there was direct radio transmission from Army headquarters to New York, operated by commercial companies under Army authorization. This meant that dispatches from the front areas, based on more first-hand knowledge and closer to the facts, also were in advance of those from Paris. But each one usually covered only a small segment of the war, and they did not fill the need for a general story. The United Press met this situation by combining front dispatches, SHAEF dispatches, and other material into a story written in New York but bearing the dateline "SHAEF, Paris." By this means that rival organization was able to produce better "SHAEF stories" than we could. For a period we fared badly, most newspapers naturally preferring the UP's superior round-ups, not knowing—or not caring—that they were being written in New York rather than where their dateline indicated.

Disheartening as it was to see the opposition's dispatches favored, I strongly urged that the AP not adopt the same system, and it is to the credit of Glenn Babb, cable editor, that it did not. Instead, we worked out a system whereby we in Paris would get brief summaries of the dispatches which members of our front staffs were filing. In some cases fast transmission directly to us was available, in others the summaries were sent to New York and immediately relayed back to us. It was costly in cable tolls, but it worked. From that time on, we based our round-ups not so much on the information given out at the SHAEF briefings as on the far more reliable and interesting reports from our own correspondents. We regained all we had lost and more—a survey made by the Army showed that in papers having both the AP and UP services, we were preferred to the end of the war—about 80 percent to 20 percent.

Only the Public Relations Division of SHAEF was in Paris. The main seat of the vast and ever-increasing Supreme Headquarters staff was at Versailles, where several buildings, including the palace stables, were packed with functionaries. Even Eisenhower avoided this great nest of bureaucracy. As soon as he could, he moved his personal headquarters, SHAEF Forward, to Reims.

* * *

Shortly after I arrived in Paris, Brigadier General Frank A. Allen, Jr., florid-faced and heavisome, assumed command of SHAEF Public Relations. He had been attached to an armored division in the field; before that he had been in charge of the photographic branch of the War Department's Public Relations in Washington. He was assigned to the post in an effort to improve the Public Relations set-up of SHAEF, which had been under considerable criticism. He attempted to weed out some of the deadwood that cluttered up the organization. He had little success; the incompetents and misfits had the tenacity of barnacles. More arrived. The headquarters branch of Public Relations alone needed all of the Chatham Hotel to house its officers. The first two floors of the Scribe were inadequate for its office space; it took over the whole American Express Company building, except for the ground floor. But this was as nothing alongside the full Public Relations strength of the Theater, which Allen headed. Almost every activity of every service had its public relations officers. I was never able to find out the total of public relations personnel in the European Theater; I know it ran into thousands. Public Relations, charged with supplying information, either would not or could not make known the figure. There were many highly capable and conscientious men in this great complement. Most of these, I noted, complained about their frustrations under "the bureaucracy" almost as much as correspondents did.

A few months after I took over in Paris, two colonels of General Allen's cabinet came to our office in the Scribe and said mysteriously that they wanted to talk to me about something confidential. I led them to my bedroom. Lew Hawkins and Ed Ball were at that time covering Third Army for the AP. In charge of Public Relations there was an officer who was not only unhelpful to correspondents, but who took pleasure in being discourteous and abusive to them to an extreme degree. He was that type of civilian who becomes overbearing when vested with the arbitrary authority that goes with an Army commission—a bully for the duration. The correspondents at Third Army had complained to Allen, who took no action. When conditions at the press camp became intolerable, they appealed to General Patton, who removed the officer. The two colonels explained that the correspondents had gone "outside of channels." General Allen was not trying to "get" them for it, they said, but he believed it would be better to start over again at the press camp with a fresh slate. He wanted all the correspondents who had complained to Patton transferred from Third Army. "In other words, General Allen doesn't want to 'get' them himself, he merely wants me to 'get' them for him," I said. "We are only following our orders in asking you to do this," the colonels said. I refused to move Hawkins and Ball and heard nothing more of the case.

* * *

Smoot's law—that the cost of government always goes up, never down—is as true of war as of government. The cost of killing an enemy in Julius Caesar's time is estimated at 75¢. With some temporary deviations due to exceptional circumstances, the figure has gone steadily upward since then. In World War II it was calculated in thousands of dollars. Supporting the combat troops was a vast system of service, supply, maintenance, and bookkeeping. It was as necessary as the fighting units. The Service of Supply sometimes performed stupendous feats in getting the materials of war where they were needed and in the countless other tasks for which it was responsible. Many officers—especially high officers—of this branch of warfare seemed to be gnawed by an incontinent jealousy of the combat forces. Their rancor manifested itself in many ways and often against bewildered innocent victims.

The supply organization in the Mediterranean was under the command of Major General Arthur Wilson, whose headquarters was successively in Casablanca, Oran, Naples, and southern France. He was unflagging in prodding his organization. He kept supplies moving. In the rear areas he controlled, he was a martinet. At times officers under him were required to turn in the names of a certain number of enlisted men weekly for failure to salute them. The offenders they listed were punished. His military police were, by his orders, zealous in arresting GIs for petty offenses. On one occasion they lined trucks up in front of a movie in Algiers operated by the Red Cross for the troops and carted the whole GI audience off to cells as it emerged. There was an 11 o'clock curfew at the time, and the show did not end until 11:05.

The Algiers edition of *Stars and Stripes,* unable to attack Wilson or his methods openly, got at him indirectly by publicizing some of his disciplinary measures in its letters column. Letters describing such incidents as the movie arrests appeared over the signature of a mythical GI, T-4 Archibald MacGonigle. Far from complaining, MacGonigle praised General Wilson's measures as necessary to "make better soldiers of us all." In this manner the Army newspaper was able to expose some of the more oppressive actions and have them remedied. Eventually the ghostly MacGonigle was a feared figure in the Theater, for his praise was a kiss of death.

Combat troops back from the front on brief leave passes suffered the worst under Wilson's regime. Some of his MPs seemed to take a special delight in rounding them up, and their zeal seemed to be inspired from above. For taking a drink too many, or even being slightly "out of uniform," GIs bent on a few days of pleasure after months at the front might spend most of their leave in jail. The ill-feeling of the combat troops toward the discipline imposed on them in rear areas was the subject of many of Bill Mauldin's cartoons.

Wilson enjoyed fine living, which seems to be another characteristic of supply generals. Stories of the luxury of his personal accommodations, his table, and his gay parties were rife throughout the Theater. In the eyes of most combat troops he was an oriental despot, wallowing in pleasures and begrudging them a good time after their hardships in foxholes. While we were still in Italy, Ken Dixon wrote a story on what the combat troops thought of General Wilson. It created a stir at home, was reprinted in the *Congressional Record,* and brought Wilson a rebuke from the War Department which curbed some of the more drastic actions of his military police. Wilson summoned Dixon and in a two-hour session attempted to browbeat him into an admission that statements in his story were false and written maliciously. Dixon held his ground, pointing out that his dispatch described a common sentiment among combat troops and was mild in comparison with what they said regularly about Wilson. Dixon noticed a sergeant with a stenographic typewriter concealed behind a screen. Wilson wanted something to counteract the rebuke on his Army record. I sent word to Wilson that we would gladly publish his side in the controversy but could not retract any of Dixon's statements unless he could show they were incorrect. He was not interested in having a say; he wanted a retraction or nothing.

Months passed, and we considered the matter closed. After we were in France we received a copy of a letter which Charles Honce, one of the assistant general managers of the Associated Press, had written to Wilson. It repudiated Dixon's story and tendered Wilson the apologies of the Associated Press. We learned that Wilson, determined to get a retraction for his record, had sent an aide to the office of the Associated Press in New York. The result was Honce's letter. Dixon and I were naturally dismayed at this surrender of the Associated Press to officialdom on a question involving the integrity of one of its reporters. Wilson had been unable to show us that there was anything wrong in Dixon's story. New York had not consulted us before branding Dixon a liar. Dixon submitted his resignation, which I held up. We got word back not to worry over the matter. Kent Cooper had full confidence in Dixon, Honce said. Giving the letter to Wilson was an easy way to handle the situation. What if it did compromise the AP on a matter of principle? It wouldn't be published. As an appeasement, Dixon was given a substantial increase in pay.

* * *

The élan which the summer victories had given the Allied forces in France diminished through the autumn as it became apparent that the Germans had regained their equilibrium and intended to defend the Reich bitterly. If there had been a possibility of sweeping into Germany against a disorganized foe, it was gone now. In August, almost everyone expected the war's end by the close of the year. By October, few saw victory before springtime. The Command had misjudged the situation. The victory in France was all that it had hoped for. But it had underestimated the fanatical power of the Nazis to stave off collapse after such a defeat. If the July 20, 1944, attempt on Hitler's life had succeeded, the Command would have been right—the end unquestionably would have come that autumn. Not only would many military casualties have been avoided but also the terrible deterioration of the fabric of western Europe which marked the last six months of the conflict and had such an effect on the postwar situation.

Montgomery's prescription for a speedy termination of the war was the diversion of men and supplies to him for a powerful thrust through Holland into the Ruhr and the plains of North Germany before his armies slowed down their pace in Belgium. Generals Bradley and Patton likewise thought they could inflict a quick death blow by sending the Third Army into the Saar and through the Frankfurt Gap. By late August the armies had advanced so far that the supply problem, especially for gasoline, was critical. Eisenhower delayed actions, partly because of supplies, partly because of the wrangling going on among generals. Montgomery thought he should be field commander of the whole Theater. Many American officers did not hold his generalship in high esteem after the Battle of Normandy.

Eisenhower's decision, when it was made, was to try in both places, but Montgomery was favored in supplies and given two elite American airborne divisions. The units won their objectives, but he failed to establish a bridgehead across the Rhine at Arnhem. This time the Dutch Underground was blamed—a traitor within it had given the plan to the Germans. For Montgomery's attempt, enough was diverted from the Americans to rob them of the possibility of breaking through and ending the war—or so many of them believed. Whether Bradley and Patton could have ended the war that fall if they had been given a chance—and even whether Montgomery might have ended it if he had been given the go-ahead a little earlier—will long be debated. The feeling in the various armies that they had not been supported by the Supreme Command led to growing contempt for SHAEF. Had a hastily improvised attempt to invade Germany been launched in late August or early September, the prize of its success would have been great enough to change history. The price of failure might have been disastrous. Eisenhower followed the standard Allied practice of waiting for overwhelming superiority before attacking. He may have been wise in not letting any army stick its neck out too far. There is no way of proving or disproving this, since such an invasion was not attempted.

Fierce fighting and small gains marked the next few months. In mid-December the Germans let loose with a last great punch, their brilliantly planned and executed Ardennes thrust, which drove a wedge forty-two miles deep into a weakly held part of the Allied line. It was a stupendous gamble aimed at Antwerp and designed to cut the Allied front in two. Against the vastly superior Allied strength, it had only an outside chance of success. If it had succeeded, it might have delayed the invasion of Germany until the Germans had new and deadlier weapons on which they were working—even the atomic bomb. The surprise was complete and exposed grave faults in Allied intelligence. The strategists at SHAEF had given virtually no attention to the possibility of such an attack. Again the Command had underestimated the almost superhuman strength of dying Nazism.

One of SHAEF's reactions to the counter-offensive was the imposition of an almost complete news blackout on German gains, ordered by General Bedell Smith. The inane dispatches which this censorship compelled us to write naturally caused grave alarm at home, where the suppression of information was widely regarded as an attempt by SHAEF to cover up its shortcomings. The answer of SHAEF spokesmen was that the blackout had been imposed on the basis of opinions of generals directing the fight and that the situation was so fluid that German Command did not know the whereabouts of its own troops. Eisenhower was later quoted by his chronicler, Captain Harry C. Butcher, as saying at the time that he did not share that view. Patton likewise did not believe such censorship necessary, we learned afterwards.

As the clampdown continued for days, strong protests were voiced in Britain and America. At a stormy SHAEF briefing, George H. Lyon, Office of War Information representative at SHAEF, joined in the complaints of correspondents. "The Army is making a bigger mistake than it did in the Patton case," Lyon said. "It is following a head-in-the-sand policy. It could tell a great deal more without giving any information to the Germans. Everybody in the world knows this story and is going to print it. You say we can't tell the Germans this because they may not know it. The German record in this war is that they have shown themselves pretty good soldiers, and I think they know what went on Sunday afternoon. If you continue this, you make people think things are worse than they are. Everyone else in the world except SHAEF correspondents are permitted to tell this story." As a result of the protests, SHAEF agreed to divulge details of the fighting after a time-lag to ensure against the Germans getting any benefit from the information.

An official postwar examination of the Battle of the Bulge brought out the interesting fact that while SHAEF was gagging correspondents for fear the German Command might learn where its own troops were, the Army itself was obligingly supplying the German Command with the vastly more important information of where *our* troops were. Robert E. Merriam, chief of the Ardennes Section of the Army's Historical Division, who spent eight months investigating the operation, has disclosed that the Army was guilty of the grave negligence of broadcasting in clear, rather than in code, radio traffic messages which told the Germans the approximate speed and strength of our reinforcing movements—the most vital of all information about an enemy force in such a battle. Captured German generals twitted interrogators mercilessly about this blunder, which must have cost many lives.

In all of World War II, I know of no authenticated case in which the disclosure of information in a correspondent's dispatch cost the life of a single soldier. On the other hand, the history of the war is filled with apparently inexcusable errors by Army intelligence and Army security which took a heavy toll in human lives. The Ardennes thrust was repelled by the valor of our soldiers at the front and the field generalship of Patton in his lightning switch of a large part of his army to that sector. The fighting men redeemed the errors of Army intelligence and of SHAEF with their blood. American casualties totaled 72,000. The fact that the Germans suffered much greater losses was scant consolation and certainly did not warrant the statement of spokesmen that the Battle of the Bulge was "just what the doctor ordered" to ensure the final collapse of the Reich. SHAEF's alarm at one point was so great that Eisenhower decided to abandon Strasbourg and a large part of Alsace and Lorraine and withdraw the American Seventh and French First Armies back to the more easily defended line of the Vosges. De Gaulle, fearing that such a move would cause a bad reaction in France and the fall of his government, blocked it by issuing direct orders to the French army not to withdraw without a fight.

After the battle was over, Bedell Smith came to the Scribe to present SHAEF's side in the controversy over the Bulge. He parried questions about the Command's failure to foresee its possibility with airy answers addressed to "you strategically minded gentlemen" and by the end of his discourse had pictured the events in the Ardennes as almost a brilliantly laid trap into which the Germans had been enticed. This line may have been all right for correspondents, but it did not satisfy the Joint Chiefs of Staff, who after the Battle of the Bulge stepped in with much closer supervision of SHAEF. The Joint Chiefs, whom Smith bitingly referred to as "our masters" at his next press conference, may be said to have directed the war on the Western Front from that point on.

Eisenhower also made occasional visits to our press room, his talks usually resulting in more solid information, if less mental gymnastics, than Smith's. The imposed rule was that the Commander-in-Chief was not to be quoted directly on all that he said but that after his discourse Public Relations would select a few "appropriate quotes" which might be worked into our stories. One of his appearances was followed by a discussion between General Allen and the correspondents on what might be quoted. Allen concocted a sentence which he believed expressed what the Commander had wanted to say, and several correspondents approved it enthusiastically. "But instead of making up a quote, why not let us write exactly what the Commander said on that point?" asked Helen Kirkpatrick of the *Chicago Daily News*. Allen looked startled, then conceded that was a good idea.

* * *

Louis Lochner, Wade Werner, and Alvin Steinkopf of the prewar staff of the Associated Press joined us now that the armies were advancing into Germany. Their background enabled them to write excellent stories of the Germany which Nazism left in its wake. In the final push into Germany in the spring, Bob Wilson, reporting the crossing of the Rhine at Wesel from a plane, was shot down at 600 feet. His escapade brought the casualties of our staff, from the early days in the Mideast, to thirteen. Only one was a fatality, Harry Crockett. Toward the end of the war we learned that Joe Morton, who had been with us in North Africa and Italy, had been shot by the Germans after capture in Slovakia, where he had gone with an American group operating with the Underground.

Chapter 10

OPERATION JACKPLANE

EARLY IN APRIL 1945 GERMAN RESISTANCE ON THE WESTERN FRONT was crumbling fast. Patton's Third Army was encountering opposition in Bavaria, where the Nazis had dreamed of a prolonged stand in a "national redoubt," but the Ninth Army, farther north, reached the Elbe, a bare sixty miles from Berlin, on April 11. Apparently there was little to block it from continuing on to the capital, but it was ordered not to cross the Elbe River. In the weeks that followed, the war was to all effects over in that sector—there was even fraternization between the Americans on one side of the river and German soldiers on the other. Meanwhile, the Russians began to edge into Berlin. It was a secondary effort, their main drive being farther south, where they had been pushing toward a junction with Patton's army. SHAEF had announced that the entry into Berlin would be "on an Allied basis," and elaborate plans had been made for flying a group of headquarters correspondents there to report the story.

Our government has never given the American people full information on how and why the decision was made to immobilize our troops on the Elbe and let the Russians take Berlin. It might have been justified on the grounds that it was pointless to risk even a single American life for such a venture, since the Russians were only too willing to do the job. It might have been justified on the point that any clash between the American and Russian armies, accidental or otherwise, was to be avoided at any cost. But these, apparently, were not the reasons for the decision, at least not the main reasons. The specter of Russian distrust of us already hovered over relations between Washington and Moscow, though the people were not aware of it. We have since learned that in March, Stalin had baselessly accused Roosevelt of attempting to negotiate a virtual separate peace—a deal in which Kesselring would open up the German front with the Western Allies in return for Anglo-American support of easier peace terms. There is good reason to believe that the reason for the halt at the Elbe was that Washington felt that no matter how faithfully the Western Allies discharged their obligations toward the Russians, any action of the Germans in not strongly opposing our entry into Berlin, while holding off the Russians, would fan Russian distrust and rivalry into flames, possibly with disastrous consequences. Eisenhower said that he expected no formal unconditional surrender of Germany. The plan agreed upon by the American, British, and Russian governments was to issue a proclamation of the end of organized German resistance after the two commanders-in-chief, Western and Russian, had concurred that such was the case.

In the first days of May, organized resistance seemed ended on all of the Western Front. From the night of Friday, May 4, on, no reports of fighting were received at SHAEF. Patton's army was speeding into Czechoslovakia but was forbidden to take Prague. The Russians and Americans had met on the Elbe. Several American correspondents got in their jeeps, crossed the Elbe, and drove into Berlin without difficulty. (They were, of course, penalized by SHAEF Public Relations; two were disaccredited, others suspended.) Whole German armies were surrendering, and Allied field generals were authorized to accept their capitulations as battlefield surrenders. On May 4, two German officers, Admiral Hans Georg von Friedeburg and Colonel Fritz Poleck, came to Montgomery's headquarters. He received them expecting the surrender of some of the German forces facing his armies. But they indicated that they had been sent by the government of Admiral Karl Doenitz, who had succeeded to power on Hitler's death, to discuss the surrender of all that was left of the Third Reich. This was beyond Montgomery's authority. He telephoned Eisenhower at Reims, who instructed him to send the emissaries to his headquarters. Von Friedeburg and Poleck arrived at SHAEF Forward by airplane the next day, Saturday, May 5. Eisenhower decided not to receive them personally, since there was nothing to discuss except whether they were authorized and ready to sign on the dotted line. He assigned to Bedell Smith, his chief of staff, the job of talking with them to find this out.

The Doenitz government had fled Berlin and established itself at Flensburg, on the German-Danish frontier, where there was a powerful radio station. British troops entered Flensburg. The Doenitz regime became a captive government but apparently was permitted to function. What went on during those few days in Flensburg has never been very well explained, but the British Ministry of Information announced that the Flensburg radio was being operated by the Germans under Allied censorship.

Friedeburg informed Smith that he was not authorized to sign a surrender, but merely to obtain the terms on which the required "unconditional surrender" would be signed and to learn precisely how the Doenitz government would be required to put it into effect. Smith replied that the new German government would have to send the authorization for an unconditional surrender promptly or be held responsible by the Allies for the continuance of hostilities. In accordance with our obligations to the Russians, he told him that the surrender would have to be made to the Russians and the Western Allies on the same basis. Friedeburg sent this message to Doenitz. German communications were so disrupted that the Allies had to undertake its delivery. It was sent by wireless in code to Second British Army Headquarters, then carried by courier to the Doenitz government in Flensburg.

SHAEF had decided that no war correspondents would be permitted to witness the surrender. Although the occasion would be one of the greatest news stories of the generation, and one for which all the Allied world was waiting avidly, Bedell Smith ruled that the event would be covered by "official reporters" under complete control of the Army and who, in turn, would supply their observations to the correspondents, who would have to be satisfied with second-hand accounts of what had happened. It was the kind of press coverage which the Nazis probably would have ordered had they won the war. Captain Harry C. Butcher, whose function was to promote good relations between the Command and the press—a sort of public relations man for Public Relations—admits he was concerned over this arrangement. "I was, however, worried about the press, radio, and movie coverage of the event, but the Supreme Commander had all in his mind he ought to bear and damned if I was going to bother him with this problem at this late hour," Butcher writes in the May 4, 1945, entry of *My Three Years with Eisenhower*. General Allen mapped the plans for covering the story on this basis. To report it, he selected two public relations officers, Lieutenant Colonel Burrows Matthews, editor of the *Buffalo Courier Express,* and Lieutenant Colonel S. R. Pawley, who had been news editor of the *Daily Telegraph* of London; and Sergeant Charles Kiley of *Stars and Stripes.* There was no question of their capability; all three were good newspapermen.

There was a rule against correspondents going to Reims without special authorization. Charles Christian Wertenbaker, head of the Paris staff of *Time,* showed up there in this period. Everyone knew surrender was coming, and it did not take much imagination to guess that if any formal event took place, Eisenhower's headquarters would be a likely place to watch for it. As the arrival of Friedeburg and Poleck was awaited, Matthews spied Wertenbaker lurking in a doorway of the big, red-brick school building which housed SHAEF Forward. He told him that correspondents were not permitted in Reims and that he would have to take steps to see that he left the vicinity. Wertenbaker agreed to return to Paris at once, according to Matthews. Matthews accepted Wertenbaker's word and took no further action on his unauthorized presence there. But a few hours later, as the Germans entered the building, Matthews saw Wertenbaker again. He had not returned to Paris but had remained and seen something which gave away the whole story—two German uniforms.

Wertenbaker pleaded that he be permitted to join the party of official reporters. He offered to write an account, not for *Time,* but for distribution to all correspondents, all news services, all newspapers, and all radio networks. Matthews and Pawley told him that the official reporters had been sent there for that purpose. Wertenbaker argued that the event was of such magnitude as to merit the talents of "a great writer" and nominated himself to fill that capacity. Matthews and Pawley were distressed. Wertenbaker's proposal was out of the question. If he were the sole correspondent permitted to see the surrender, SHAEF Public Relations would face angry charges of favoritism. They felt that SHAEF's plan to have official reporters cover the signing had already been damaged by Wertenbaker's presence at Reims. Even though he had only obtained a glimpse of German uniforms, he could still write an on-the-scene story which would arouse the fury of other correspondents and their organizations.

Matthews was applying himself conscientiously to the job he had been assigned. As a believer in the free press, he had never been too enthusiastic about the "official reporter" plan and had some misgivings about the reaction at home to SHAEF's proposed method of handling the reporting of the surrender. When the Wertenbaker incident occurred, he telephoned Allen and urged him to let correspondents cover the story. When told that SHAEF's plans of keeping the surrender secret from newspapermen until after it was over had already been compromised by the fact that one correspondent knew what was going on, Smith agreed to permit a limited number of correspondents to be present at the signing. He didn't want too many.

General Allen went through the dusty archives of Public Relations and exhumed a plan entitled "Operation Jackplane." It had been drawn up in London, long before SHAEF Public Relations had crossed the Channel, and had been intended to serve as a list of the first planeload of correspondents to be flown to Berlin on that city's fall. Allen said the correspondents in London at the time had agreed to the plan. Some of them denied this, but in any case it had originally been a plan for going into Berlin and not for witnessing the surrender.

On Sunday morning, May 6, one of Allen's aides called on me while I was still in bed and said the Associated Press was entitled to send one correspondent to report an event the nature of which could not be disclosed. There was no doubt in my mind that this was the surrender. I said I'd go myself. Those selected for the assignment were taken to a small airfield outside of Paris, where we met General Allen. There were seventeen of us on the Jackplane list. The others represented UP, the INS, Reuters, Exchange Telegraph, and the French and Russian news agencies; all the American, British, Canadian, and Australian radio networks; and two official army papers, *Stars and Stripes* and the Canadian publication the *Maple Leaf*. No individual newspapers were represented, not even journals of the importance of the *Times* of New York and London. General Allen felt that his list was an air-tight one, for the correspondents chosen represented, indirectly, practically every newspaper and radio station in the Allied world.

As the airplane winged northeastward, Allen told us that the trip concerned the impending surrender of Germany. Then, in the big Army transport craft, followed the "pledge on the plane," which was to be so frequently cited in ensuing weeks. Because it suited their purposes, Allen and some of the correspondents later vested this talk with the solemnity of an initiation ceremony of one of the more mystically inclined fraternal lodges. In actuality it was a rather long and rambling talk by Allen, made against the din of the propellers. He first mentioned the possibility that the negotiations might fall through, that the German delegates might not sign. In such event, he said, premature word of surrender might have disastrous effects. He pledged us to discuss the purpose of our journey with no one outside our group during the delicate period of negotiations, to take no action which would give anyone even an inkling of what was expected to happen. This injunction seemed quite reasonable. An obvious thought flashed into my mind—and I suppose into the minds of the other correspondents present. The Army was taking precautions against a repetition of the premature announcement of the signing of the Armistice which ended World War I. That report, cabled from France by Roy Howard, was distributed throughout the world by the United Press four days before the signing.

Some historians have held that the Allies might have occupied Germany and possibly changed history had not the premature announcement of the end of the war produced an emotional state in the Allied world that made it impossible to get soldiers on the march again. Howard and the United Press long insisted on the accuracy of the report—that a secret armistice was really signed before November 11, 1918—and the argument had led to great bitterness between the AP and UP. The most credible theory, and the one generally accepted, is that the story was planted with American naval authorities in Paris by a German agent and that Howard dispatched the news to America in good faith and in performance of his duty as a correspondent when it was given to him by the American admiral in command at Brest. That had for years been my own appraisal, and my only criticism of Howard and the UP was their insistence for so long that the story was, or might have been, correct. The unctuous self-righteousness with which Associated Press officials of that period had condemned Howard had, however, always seemed to me as objectionable as Howard's refusal to admit that he had made an honest mistake.

Allen continued that if the surrender was signed, a time would be set for the release of the news, but that he did not know when it would be. He said he would be informed in due time. In a statement issued several days afterward, when his words in the plane had been made an important issue, he insisted that he had told us that "the respective heads of the Allied governments" would announce the news and had concluded his remarks with the phrase, "I therefore pledge each and every one of you, on your honor, not to communicate the result of this conference or the fact of its existence until it is released by SHAEF." I do not recall this language, although I would not dispute the point. My recollection is that his last phrase was something much less formal, like "Now does everyone here understand that this story is to be held up for SHAEF release?" To which everyone present, including myself, said yes. I did not attach special significance to the "pledge" regarding the release, and the other correspondents gave no indication that they did. For good reason: it was pure surplusage. All war correspondents were pledged to observe such rules and not to attempt to evade censorship and had signed statements to that effect on being accredited. I had always scrupulously observed this pledge, as had every member of the Associated Press staff. Apart from the question of wartime censorship, I had never violated a release time set on news, nor have I to this day.

The imposition of release time on news was an everyday practice at SHAEF. In some cases, it was enforced by censors as a matter of military security. We always had several dispatches in censorship, awaiting the time when it was considered safe to reveal their contents. In other cases, information was given to correspondents in advance, as a matter of convenience, with a set time for its release. The procedure which Allen outlined in the airplane was not unusual. I naturally and automatically registered my acceptance of the arrangements, as I had in hundreds of other cases. There was no indication at that time of the unwarranted turn of events which was to follow.

The airplane landed at Reims, and we were taken to SHAEF Forward. A few moments later, Colonel General Gustav Jodl, the new chief of staff of the German army, and his aide, Major Wilhelm Oxenius, arrived. Jodl had been sent by Doenitz in response to Friedeburg's message and had full authority to surrender. SHAEF Forward occupied the red-brick building of a French public technical school, a two-story quadrangle covering a block and enclosing a large court. The seventeen correspondents were placed in a classroom on the ground floor while General Allen and his aides went upstairs to learn what was happening. We had a nine-hour

wait. Allen paid us several visits during this period, making varying statements as plans apparently were changed upstairs. On one visit he said
that our sending of the news would be held up until the surrender was
announced by the heads of the Allied governments. After further discussions with members of Eisenhower's staff, he told us that the importance
of announcing the surrender immediately after the signing was so urgent
that he expected that the news would be given out in Paris before we
could return there.

Several of the correspondents protested this. They pointed out that
we were members of a pool especially selected to report the surrender
and asked why correspondents left behind in Paris should be allowed to
report it first. "But the correspondents in Paris will have only the bare
announcement and you'll have the descriptive, eyewitness story," Allen
said. "And you won't be much behind them. We'll get you back to Paris in
short time." A correspondent asked whether telegraphic facilities could
be arranged in Reims which would enable us to file our stories at the
same time as the correspondents in Paris. Allen called in communications
officers. They said a telegraphic wire might be opened between Reims and
Paris for our dispatches but that they could not provide facilities for the
radio correspondents who wanted to report the event by voice. The radio
correspondents objected to this as discriminatory, and Allen ruled out
the setting up of the wire. He gave instructions that our plane be held
in readiness so the return trip could be made without delay once we had
witnessed the surrender.

Colonels Matthews and Pawley filled us in on the developments leading up to Jodl's arrival. They described the rooms assigned to Jodl and
Friedeburg, reported that Friedeburg had asked for whiskey, said the
signing was being held up pending the working out of details of how all
German units were to be informed, and let us handle the pens to be used
in the signing. Meanwhile, several groups of correspondents who had
not been invited to the surrender arrived in Reims by jeep. Despite all
the secrecy imposed, they had learned what was going on and where it
was happening—presumably through leaks in Allen's public relations organization. They could not have gotten their information from any of
the seventeen Jackplane correspondents, for we were not even told our
destination until after we were in the plane.

The "illegal" correspondents arrived full of indignation and loud in their denunciations of Allen's arbitrary selection which had left them out in the cold. General Allen was deaf to their pleas. He ordered military police to bar them from the building. At sundown they were standing on the sidewalk in groups, talking angrily. Several came to the window of our classroom. In accordance with the secrecy imposed on us pending the signing, we could give them no information. They had taunts for us as well as for Allen. The noisy complaint of such notables among the "illegals" as Raymond Daniell of the *New York Times* and Helen Kirkpatrick of the *Chicago Daily News* was that they represented newspapers which maintained complete foreign staffs of their own. It was unjust, they said, that such newspapers should be barred from reporting one of the great news stories of history. They condemned Allen's selection as grotesque, since not a single American newspaper was represented, while American radio stations had four men in the pool. Allen replied that he had to draw the line somewhere for lack of accommodations. He defended his exclusion of individual newspapers.

The "illegals" found a flaw in his Jackplane plan in that one American newspaper *was* represented. Price Day of the *Baltimore Sun* had been pressed into service by the British news agency Exchange Telegraph, which had been assigned one of the seventeen places. Allen ruled that Day might write his story for Extel but might not send the same account to his own paper. (This ruling was later rescinded, and Day was permitted to file to the *Sun*, which in any case could have picked up the story from Extel in London.) The outcasts appealed to the British lieutenant general Frederick E. Morgan as he arrived at the headquarters. He sympathized with them and said he'd intercede in their behalf. He went to Allen and said he thought something ought to be done about those correspondents outside the building. Allen interpreted this as a complaint about the correspondents, instead of an intercession, and sent military police out to chase them away under threat of arrest. This did not assuage their indignation.

At 2:41 a.m., Monday, May 7, we Jackplane correspondents saw the signing of the unconditional surrender by the two crestfallen Nazi warlords. The other correspondents still chafed on the sidewalks of Reims in the chill early-morning air, although various headquarters officers managed to slip WAC and Red Cross girlfriends into the room to see the historic event.

The surrender took place in the L-shaped war room, its walls covered with maps and casualty charts. The correspondents and other witnesses were roped off in one corner, but photographers buzzed around the table and mounted a nearby stepladder for angle shots. The Allied signers—Bedell Smith for the Supreme Command, General François Sevez for France, General Ivan Susloparov for the Soviet Union, and Admiral Sir Harold Burrough, RN, for a separate naval disarmament order—were seated at the table. The Germans entered the room a little uncertainly and blinking in the glare of the lights. Jodl was solemn, Friedeburg seemed to have lessened his chagrin with whiskey. (Friedeburg committed suicide a few days later.) The Allied signers arose, and Smith beckoned the Germans to two vacant chairs on the opposite side of the table, remarking dryly: "There are four copies to be signed." After the signatures of all were affixed—the documents and pens were passed from one to another around the table—Jodl made a brief plea for such generosity as the Allies might be able to show to the German people, and the two walked slowly out of the room. They were led to Eisenhower's office. The Supreme Commander, flanked by his deputy, Air Chief Marshal Sir Arthur W. Tedder, asked them sternly if they understood the terms and if they would be carried out, and they said yes. We were allowed to witness this scene through a doorway.

In a delayed-action burst of generosity, Allen permitted the outcast correspondents to enter the headquarters after the surrender and to look at the room in which it had been signed so they might describe it in their stories. With the fury of a woman scorned, Helen Kirkpatrick obtained a tape measure and took measurements of the war room—to prove that there had been space for more than seventeen correspondents. We, the Lucky Seventeen, were led back to our classroom, while Allen talked with high SHAEF officers to get a final decision on the time of the release of the news. While waiting, I wrote my dispatch. I handed it to a censor who had accompanied us. He read it and stamped it approved. (Later, he asked me for the dispatch back and crossed out his okay, not because of objection to any information in it but because the release, which had been expected to be almost immediate, was by that time uncertain.)

At about 4 a.m. Allen appeared and said: "Gentlemen, I had anticipated that the news would be released at once, but it appears that this is

not to be the case. General Eisenhower is desirous of having the news announced immediately for its possible effect in saving lives, but his hands
are tied at a high political level and we can do nothing about it. The release has been set for 3 p.m., Tuesday, Paris time." Exclamations of dis-
gust went up from the correspondents. The bland admission that political censorship was being imposed—contrary to the demands of military
security—set off bitter recriminations. General Allen's seventeen trained
seals became almost as unruly as those he had left off his list. "I appreci-
ate your point of view, gentlemen," he said. "I personally think this story
ought to be released without delay. I will try my best to get it released
before the time set, but I don't know how effective I will be. In any case,
there is nothing for us to do now but return to Paris."

I was exasperated by the delay so far but confident that the news
would be released during the morning. The absurdity of attempting to
bottle up news of such magnitude was too apparent. I knew from experience that one might as well try to censor the rising of the sun. The war
in Europe ended after six years and the Allied governments deciding to
keep it a secret for thirty-six hours—it was as though the heads of the
governments had jointly lost their minds at the last moment as a result
of the strain. I was certain that a flash of sanity would soon come. We
flew back to Paris in the pale gold sunshine of an early May morning. I
have never seen the city, crowned by the gleaming white dome of Sacre
Coeur, so beautiful as it was from the air that day. Already the traffic of
workers to their jobs had begun; the streets were full of little black dots.
They would not work this day through. What news we had for them, and
for workers everywhere else! News that would make them throw down
their tools and celebrate the peace after years of hardship and worry.

At 10 a.m. General Allen held a press conference at the Hotel Scribe.
It was an angry meeting. The correspondents barred from the signing
were still complaining, and now the holding up of the news brought more
criticism. Allen again made clear that he agreed with the correspondents
that the news should be released. He said he was doing his best to get it
released that day. He tried to mollify the ill-feeling by having Matthews
and Pawley give all the correspondents descriptive details so they might
write stories as complete as those who had seen the event.

I took a short walk through Paris. Everyone was talking about the surrender. German uniforms had been seen in Reims, seventy-five miles away, and news like that travels fast. No great brain was required to conclude that this time the Germans hadn't come as conquerors. There was puzzlement that no official announcement had come and suspicion that the governments, for some inexplicable reason, were holding back the information. I returned to the Hotel Scribe in low spirits. To have such a story to tell and not be able to tell it—I found that depressing. This postwar world, which had already begun in Europe as of 2:41 that morning, was an eerie place; nothing like the happy world that we had hoped for. I made inquiries of public relations officers as to the reason for the delay and was told that it had been ordered "by Washington and London" at the request of the Russians, who wanted another "and more formal" ceremony in Berlin. This sounded strange. The Reims ceremony involved unconditional surrender, and nothing could be more formal that that, since it fulfilled the proclaimed objective of the Allies. The Germans had surrendered to the Soviet Union on the identical basis of their surrender to the United States, Great Britain, and France. Susloparov, as plenipotentiary for Stalin, had accepted the surrender. It was apparent that any second surrender in Berlin would be wholly meaningless and staged for Soviet propaganda purposes.

In the Scribe lobby, correspondents were standing about in bunches, muttering their displeasure and drawing up resolutions against SHAEF Public Relations. I could see little to gain in joining them, so I went up to our AP office on the fourth floor and took stock of the reports which came swiftly one upon the other. De Gaulle's office said he was writing his V-Day address. General Sevez, who signed the surrender instrument for France, had sent his own eyewitness account to the newspaper *Figaro*. Paris noon newspapers published dispatches from London saying that loudspeakers were being erected at 10 Downing Street and that Britain awaited only the formal announcement. Official word had been sent to Allied soldiers at the front. The British War Ministry made known the details to its personnel, including civilian employees. People in the know were reputed to be making large sums of money in the markets.

I was convinced that if the formal release did not come soon, the news would inevitably break through the barrier some other way. At 2:03 p.m., Paris time, the break which I had anticipated came. Count Johann

Ludwig von Krosigk, foreign minister of the Doenitz government, announced the unconditional surrender in a broadcast to the world from
Flensburg addressed to "German Men and Women." "After a heroic fight
of almost six years of incomparable hardness, Germany has succumbed
to the overwhelming power of her enemies," von Krosigk said. "A government which has a feeling of responsibility for the future of its nation was
compelled to act on the collapse of all physical and material forces and
to demand of the enemy the cessation of hostilities." I did not hear the
von Krosigk broadcast. But it was monitored by the British Ministry of
Information and immediately distributed by the Ministry for publication.
We had the office radio tuned to the British Broadcasting Corporation
for news broadcasts, and I heard a translation of it from the BBC a few
minutes later. In succeeding minutes, urgent telegrams arrived from the
Associated Press in New York and in London relaying the von Krosigk
announcement.

   I knew that Flensburg had been occupied by Allied troops. I knew
that the Doenitz government could not have broadcast its announcement
from Flensburg without the consent of SHAEF. It was evident that SHAEF
itself had authorized the Germans to announce the news while still gagging us. It was equally evident why SHAEF had done so—as a means
of saving lives. German army communications were so disrupted that a
public broadcast was the only means of making sure that isolated units
knew that the war was over. I tried to reach General Allen by telephone
to tell him that the news of the surrender had been released but was
told that he was too busy to talk with me. Accompanied by Relman (Pat)
Morin of my staff, I went to the office of Lieutenant Colonel Richard H.
Merrick, the chief American censor, and showed him the telegrams that
I had received from the Associated Press giving the text of the Flensburg
announcement. "I can't help it, no matter who is announcing the surrender and when," he said. "I have orders to follow and there is nothing
I can do about it."

   In the discussion which followed, I told Merrick that since SHAEF
itself had plainly authorized the release of the story, I considered myself
under no further obligation to observe the censorship. I pointed out that
I was in the same position of an editor at home who, while holding a
story for release, learns that the release has been violated, deliberately

or accidentally, by some other publication. It is the universal practice in such cases to regard the news as released generally and to proceed with its publication, after going through the formality of informing the person or organization which had imposed the release time. I continued with the fact that the Germans had been permitted to announce the surrender was additional evidence that no military security was involved. I said that the silence imposed on us was therefore in violation of the cardinal point of American censorship—as announced from the White House down— that censorship would be limited to matters of military security and that there would be no political censorship. I pointed out that we had also been assured that censorship—except on military matters which might be of value to the Japanese—would be terminated in Europe with the end of the war. This promise too was being violated. "I give you warning now that I am going to release the story," I said. "Do as you please," he replied, shrugging his shoulders. Merrick, of course, regarded my statement simply as tall talk. He could not conceive of any correspondent getting an unauthorized dispatch through the iron curtain that censorship thought it had thrown around the European Theater.

I went to my bedroom and considered the matter carefully. I knew that sending the story would cause a terrific storm and bring down upon me the wrath of Public Relations and other correspondents. I weighed the possible consequences. At the end of fifteen minutes I decided to send the news. Among the charges made against me later was that I was a man who would resort to anything for the sake of a scoop. Actually, I considered that aspect of the situation hardly at all. I did not need to make a scoop to solidify my position with the Associated Press or establish my reputation as a newspaperman. I had already made more scoops than any other war correspondent. That statement may seem boastful and may be challenged, but I think an examination of newspaper files would bear it out. Much more important than these scoops in my estimation was my conviction that the staff which I headed had done the best all-round job of reporting the war. My files bulged with cablegrams and letters from Kent Cooper and other AP officials attesting to this. My deliberations hinged mainly on the moral aspects of the question: Which course did my duty as a reporter dictate—subservience to a political censorship which was contrary to the principle of a free press and in violation of the word of the government and the Army or action which I believed right and which I knew would bring plenty of trouble upon my head?

Some of my critics have insisted that in addition to informing SHAEF of my intention, I had also an obligation to inform my fellow correspondents. I had made no commitment requiring this. Our relations with other correspondents were friendly, and we had often filled them in with information, but I had always opposed pack reporting, a system sometimes employed by lazy and unenterprising newspapermen under which no member of the combination sends his office a story without first informing the others. To do the job properly, it would have been necessary to have informed every correspondent in Paris—there were 100 or so—and I had no facilities for reaching them all immediately. SHAEF had such a facility—a Klaxon system in the Scribe which sounded when an important arrangement was made. My old friend of Spanish days Larry Fernsworth wrote on this point, "I don't see how Kennedy could have been expected to act as any correspondent's nursemaid. In my experience, things simply do not work out that way."

I knew that I could reach our London office through the military telephone. I had used the military telephone countless times, with the knowledge of public relations officers and sometimes at their suggestion. I had talked over it to members of our staff in front areas and to our London bureau on routine matters concerning our service. In accordance with my obligations, I had never used it to evade censorship. Anyone could call "Paris Military" from the Scribe and at the other end be connected with any telephone in London. The fact that SHAEF had left this gaping loophole in its security arrangements is its own comment on the military mind. Had my motive been simply one of violating censorship, I would not have waited until 3 p.m. to send the story. I could have done it just as easily on our return from Reims, several hours earlier. Before learning of the Flensburg broadcast, no idea of breaking the news before the official release time had entered my head.

Once having made up my mind, I began writing a shortened version of my account of the surrender and asked Morton Gudebrod of our staff to put in a call for London. He acted on my instructions, and from the start I accepted full responsibility for his action, but SHAEF Public Relations later imposed a penalty on him as well as myself. I dictated the story on the telephone until the connection went bad. I got through all the essential details of the event at Reims—enough to make it clear that this was no rumor, but an authentic account by an eyewitness; that this was the real thing, the news for which the world was waiting. "Well, now let's see what happens," I said to members of my staff. "I may not be around here much longer." They laughed nervously.

The storm broke quickly. General Allen suspended the operations of the Associated Press in the entire European Theater. Even our room telephones were ordered cut off, though the French operators at the Scribe, who were our friends, continued to put calls through. Correspondents dashed madly about the Scribe. Their chagrin and rage knew no bounds. Messages poured in from their home offices—the biggest newspaper story in history and they had been beaten on it! General Allen, by this time an expert at rubbing salt into open wounds, ruled that the official release time of 3 p.m. the following day was still in effect. He ruled that the other correspondents might quote from my story, since it was already out, but might not send their own dispatches. The effect of such a ruling on the already shattered nerves of the correspondents may be imagined. While crowds outside the Scribe were shouting themselves hoarse over the war's end, correspondents inside the hotel were losing their voices in denunciations of me, Allen, and the general situation. My dispatch was published and broadcast the world over. No news story ever had so big an audience. Even ABSIE, the Army radio station in Europe, under SHAEF control, broadcast it in some twenty languages. Allen sent an officer to investigate me. I admitted full responsibility. So far as I could determine, no action was to be taken against me immediately, but I was not allowed to work. The most practical course seemed to be to go out and join in the celebration. I did.

Allen's choleric action in suspending the operations of the Associated Press brought a bombardment of protests from all parts of the country. In the most high-handed blow ever struck at the American press, SHAEF had placed itself in a position of penalizing not only the Associated Press but every newspaper and radio station receiving AP news and their readers and listeners—at a time when they were vitally interested in information from the European Theater. The War Department, heeding public indignation, sent a strong recommendation to SHAEF to cool down. The ban was lifted, but the suspension of Gudebrod and myself as war correspondents remained in effect. Due to the time difference, my dispatch reached the United States about 9 a.m. and set off a gigantic celebration. The official—and phony—V-E Day, the day afterward, was a flat anticlimax. A distiller friend has told me that far more whiskey was consumed on the day of my story.

At noon on May 8 the correspondents met in the briefing room at the Scribe. They were angry over the lifting of the AP's suspension and wanted it reimposed to deny the AP the possibility of reporting the official announcement of the end of the war. Their motive was revenge—they said so. By this time they must all have been punch-drunk, for they talked as though the world did not yet know of the surrender and as though the official announcement would be a great news story. In truth, the world had passed by them and the official announcement and now wanted other news, such as how soon the troops would be home from Europe. As hysteria mounted, it was touch and go as to whether Allen or I would be the main target of the wrath and venom about to be loosed. Once the meeting got underway, Allen could breathe more easily, for it was going my way. The keynote was sounded by Drew Middleton of the *New York Times,* who said: "You realize, gentlemen, that you have taken the worst beating of your lives. The question is, what are you going to do about it?"

A letter was drafted to Eisenhower condemning me in language of an extravagance worthy of the frenzied mood of the assemblage and asking for a reimposition of the suspension. Several correspondents, including Andre Glarner of the Exchange Telegraph, Mark Watson of the *Baltimore Sun,* Larry Rue of the *Chicago Tribune,* and John O'Connel of the *Bangor (Me.) News,* spoke against the sending of such a letter while the investigation of the incident was in progress and the facts not yet determined. They were shouted down. "If we're going to shoot somebody, let's see first who we're going to shoot and what we're shooting him for," Watson said. But the majority of correspondents were in no mood for such nonsense as that. There were among them some who prided themselves on their liberalism and love of justice and who had written long tirades against such processes as they themselves were now engaged in. "Do the correspondents here really want to cut off the news from 1,400 newspapers and still take the position they do not believe in the suppression of news?" Rue asked. O'Connel pointed out that most of them represented newspapers which made full use of the AP story. But the minds of the correspondents were made up. The letter was adopted by an overwhelming majority. Eisenhower promptly rejected the petition. Being an affected party, my judgment of the conduct of the correspondents on May 8 is perhaps not worth much. But I do not see how anyone could rate the performance highly. That the list of fifty-four signatures affixed to the letter will ever be regarded as an honor roll of the press, I doubt.

The rancor against Public Relations then burst out. Wertenbaker, who had seen his ambitious plan to be the *only* correspondent at the surrender dwindle to the point where he wasn't even included in the Jackplane Party, offered a motion that it was the sense of the meeting that "Public Relations of SHAEF and its director no longer have the confidence of correspondents." Middleton seconded it. No action was taken on it; so far as I know, it is still pending. Much of the venom let loose at the meeting was injected into correspondents' dispatches, which embodied distortions and misstatements. My sending of the story was described as "a self-admitted breach of confidence." I had from the start admitted to breaking the news, but certainly to no breach of confidence. The text of the letter and the array of signatures were emphasized; most dispatches did not mention that it had been adopted without the slightest examination of the facts or that Eisenhower had rejected it. During this period, no harsh word was exchanged between any of the signers and myself. The white heat of the occasion was beyond person-to-person recrimination. The encounters which I had with them were remarkably pleasant. Several told me quite blandly that I had put them on the spot and that they intended to do the same to me. The only way they could explain a beating of such magnitude to their home offices, and permit their organizations to save face, was to brand my action as an outrageous offense against decency.

Before the meeting, no correspondent made any attempt to learn what reasons or justifications I might have had for sending the story. After the meeting, Gladwin Hill of the *New York Times,* who had formerly been a member of our staff, came to see me. He conceded that the gathering had been "pretty much a lynch meeting." "In view of the way the head of our bureau felt, what could I do but sign the letter?" he said. Hill wrote a dispatch outlining my side of the story in part, which the *Times* published under a miniscule headline.

The correspondents also had plenty to say in their dispatches about General Allen and SHAEF Public Relations. Middleton wrote that all the correspondents (except me) had been caught "in the most colossal 'snafu' in the history of the war." "The manner in which the last big story of this war was covered for the American people under the direction of Brigadier General Frank Allen," said a dispatch from Daniell in the *Times*, "can only be described as one of the greatest fiascos yet in the long history of blundering bureaucracy."

In their excitement over the affair, the correspondents overlooked one of the biggest stories of the war—one almost as important as the German surrender. It was placed under their noses by no less august an official spokesman than General Allen himself, but not one of them, apparently, recognized it as news. At the May 8 meeting, Allen remarked that the official announcement might be delayed even beyond the time set for it—3 p.m., Paris time. He revealed that the Russians, having induced Washington and London to hold up the announcement until the hour set for their own ceremony in Berlin, now were asking that news of the real surrender at Reims be suppressed until some hours *after* the phony surrender of Berlin. His disclosure was "off the record" at the moment but could legitimately have been reported the following day. It never was.

The sole purpose of the Soviet request, it later was established—and even then obvious—was to convince a large part of the world that the Russians had obtained the surrender of Germany, with but contributory help from the Western Allies, whom they had generously invited to share in the final honor. The Berlin ceremony was staged purely for Soviet propaganda purposes. Although a Russian correspondent was one of those whom General Allen had invited to Reims to the exclusion of any reporter of an American newspaper, no word of the Reims surrender appeared in the Russian press. So far as I know, none has to this day. The Russian action was the inauguration of the propaganda build-up for the course of expansion on which the Soviet Union was shortly to embark in Europe. Its importance as news was that it was the first clue to Moscow's postwar policy. But it went unreported at the time.

The "high political level" from which emanated the order to Eisenhower to delay the announcement has never been officially identified. The order came from the Joint Chiefs of Staff in Washington, but since it was political in character and involved top policy, it seems safe to assume that it was made, or at least approved, on a still higher level. My best information is that the decision was taken by President Truman and accepted reluctantly by Prime Minister Churchill. There were reasons to impel President Truman toward yielding to the Soviet request, even though it meant breaking faith with the American people, who had been assured that they would be subjected to no political censorship. As we know now, the late President Roosevelt was disillusioned at Yalta over the prospects of postwar cooperation from the Russians and convinced that the time for firmness had come. Truman shared this view but had succeeded to the presidency at a time when he could not very well display firmness without appearing to break sharply from the Roosevelt policy. In the public mind, the Russians were still our gallant allies. The agreement to delay the news of the surrender was an appeasement on a par with the concessions made at Potsdam.

* * *

On May 10 General Allen announced his findings in a document which should be of value to future students of the military jurisprudence of World War II. He endeavored to pin the statement closely to General Eisenhower, but according to the most reliable information I could obtain, Eisenhower had no part in drawing it up and did not personally see it; I was told that it was a collaborative effort of Allen and Bedell Smith. It was issued over Allen's signature. The surrender story, the statement said, "was not one obtained by press representatives in the ordinary course of their activities with this theater; it was obtained through the courtesy of SHAEF." This assertion was a reflection of the Public Relations attitude toward correspondents—a lack of comprehension that the job of a reporter is to report news and a belief that news was the property of SHAEF, to be bestowed, or not bestowed, on correspondents and the public as it chose.

Allen said publication of the news had placed Eisenhower "in the position of having broken an understanding with our Russian allies and because of which he feared that the entire chain of negotiations involving an agreed-upon later meeting between German, Russian, and Allied High Commands might break down and therefore prolong the war." I have yet to meet anyone who can make sense of this assertion. The "chain of ne-

gotiations" was completed when the Germans surrendered unconditionally. The only apparent way in which the war could have been prolonged
would have been for Russia or the Western Allies to have violated their
acceptance of the surrender and continued fighting Germans.

Allen concluded that my action was a violation of "security definitely
involving possible loss of American and Allied lives." Lives are not lost
by announcing the end of a war; they may be lost by withholding announcement of it. Not a scintilla of evidence has ever been presented to
show that the AP story caused the loss of any life, or how it could have
caused the loss of any life. The decision of Washington and London to
keep the surrender secret for thirty-six hours might have cost lives. As it
turns out, I do not believe it did, since all fighting appears to have ended
before the surrender. The danger of delaying such announcements was
illustrated a week after the Reims surrender in northern Italy, where an
American division—the Eighty-eighth—continued to fight for hours after the German surrender there because it had not received the news. At
least ten casualties were suffered in this period. Correspondents on that
front have attested that American lives were lost because of a delay in
announcing the surrender there.

General Allen's charges, if true, would have applied with much greater
force to the Flensburg and ABSIE announcements, both of which were
made before the agreed-upon time and were authorized by SHAEF. He
did not mention them in his statement. Allen's statement that military
security was involved was, of course, refuted by his own previous asser-
tions to the contrary. Captain Butcher has since disclosed that SHAEF,
immediately after the signing, had decided to send even the "cease fire"
orders to the Allied troops in the clear and switched to code only when
he pointed out that they would be intercepted by monitoring services
serving the press. There was no fear that the former enemy would get the
news, but only that the newspapers might get it. The "cease fire" order to
Allied troops was not formally effective until one minute after midnight
May 8/9. But that no security was involved in breaking the news before
this time is evidenced by the fact that even the official announcement
was scheduled in advance of it.

Having convicted me of an offense serious enough to warrant a possible death sentence, General Allen then decided to accord me a hearing.
He designated three of his subordinate officers for this purpose. Their

proceedings consisted of telling me that they'd be glad to take any statement I cared to make. Since Allen was one of the principals in the case, any decision in my favor would virtually have amounted to insubordination on their part toward their commanding officer. I was not much concerned over the actions of Public Relations or the correspondents, none of which had risen above a level of hysteria and farce. There was no precedent in my case; the means by which a war correspondent might obtain a dispassionate hearing were not well-defined. The seriousness of the charges against me and the wide interest in the case, however, certainly warranted such a hearing. I was confident that I could obtain it and not worried about the outcome if all the facts were presented.

While I was deliberating on what step to take in this direction, something upon which I had not counted happened. It was a statement by Robert McLean, publisher of the *Philadelphia Bulletin* and president of the Associated Press, that "the Associated Press profoundly regrets the distribution on Monday of the report of the total surrender in Europe which investigation now clearly discloses was distributed in advance of authorization by Supreme Allied Headquarters." McLean's statement was accompanied by a message from Kent Cooper that he was "reserving judgment" until talking to me. He instructed me to take no further action there, but to proceed home for a conference. To Allen and the correspondents, the McLean statement was a windfall. They seized upon it. They needed to argue the case no longer now—the Associated Press itself had repudiated my action. My position in the Theater was indeed untenable. The only practical course was to return to the United States and resume the fight there.

Chapter 11

HOMECOMING

GENERAL ALLEN ARRANGED A SUITABLE CEREMONY FOR MY DIS-
accreditation as a war correspondent and my expulsion from France. It was
held in his office. The order was read by an assistant adjutant general
while Allen looked on sternly and his cabinet stood at attention. A
stranger happening into the office at that moment might have thought
Allen was accepting the surrender of the German General Staff. It was a
good show and one of the general's final acts as commander of SHAEF
Public Relations, for he was removed from that post by Eisenhower a few
days later. The attacks on his handling of the surrender story had been so
general and so widely publicized that keeping him in the post would have
been an embarrassment to the Army. But in the Army's manner of taking
care of its own, especially when under attack from outside, he was given
a medal—the Legion of Merit—before his transfer.

My expulsion from France by the Army was of questionable legality.
Unlike most war correspondents, who traveled solely on Army credentials, I had kept my civilian passport in order throughout the war. French
officials, never pleased over what they considered SHAEF's infringements
on French sovereignty, issued me a French visa and French ration cards
and told me that I was welcome to stay in France. I had, however, decided
to leave. I boarded a fast Army transport at Le Havre. The vessel carried
a big load of American airmen just released from German prison camps
and an Air Transport contingent bound for Trinidad to handle homecom-
ing air traffic through there. In mid-Atlantic, the captain received instructions to make the Trinidad call before putting into New York. The trip
was long and crowded but extremely pleasant. Every one of the liberated
flyers had an interesting story to tell. For one being sent home in disgrace, I was the recipient of quite a few courtesies. I was flustered when

these men—all of whom had been shot down in combat—asked me to autograph their scrapbooks. Six months or a year in a prison camp would make anyone detest red tape, I suppose, and they looked with favor on anyone who had balked at it. The captain, an old Coast Guard officer, also expressed himself on my side. He invited me to lunch one day, kept me talking in his quarters all afternoon, and asked me to stay for dinner. I was finding life in the doghouse which General Allen and my fellow correspondents had built for me rather enjoyable and wondering how long it would last.

I knew from the start that sending the surrender story would bring fireworks, but it was not until we docked in New York that I realized how big the reaction really was. It had not only set off one of the hottest controversies the newspaper world ever had but was the subject of a debate which had swept the country. Everybody, down to the last office boy, it seemed, had an opinion of me, and nobody was neutral. They were either for me or against me. I was astonished to find thirty reporters and photographers waiting for me at the gangplank and no little abashed that with the arrival of a shipload of war heroes, each with a genuinely thrilling story, they were singling out me, no hero, but only a reporter who had done his job as he saw it. I held my first press conference in a room on the pier. It was a new and unusual experience; I had been at hundreds of press conferences, but always facing in the other direction. Before I met the ladies and gentlemen of the press who had come to see me, I received another visitor, an emissary of Kent Cooper, who had succeeded in getting aboard the ship and who proceeded to coach me on how to handle myself at the press conference. Mr. Cooper was not attempting to gag me— perish the thought!—but it probably would be better to say nothing before seeing him.

Since I was not aware of what developments might have taken place while I was at sea and my whole purpose of returning home was to confer with Cooper, I had no intention of shooting off my mouth before seeing him. I resented his solicitous advice, which his minion said he had transmitted entirely in my own interest. Having spent years fighting against the coached interviews of Army Public Relations and against censorship of ideas in general, I was in no mood to accept either from the head of the Associated Press, an organization dedicated, I believe, to the free flow of information. But I swallowed my anger and decided to act as though I had not received Cooper's message. I told the reporters that I did not want to appear to be dodging the situation but that I had come home to see my boss and naturally couldn't be expected to say much before I had seen him. Several questions were thrown at me, and I parried them. A girl reporter asked me if I'd "do it again" under the same circumstances. I replied that since I had already stated that I believed myself to have acted rightly, that conclusion might be logically drawn.

I went to the Associated Press headquarters in Rockefeller Center and found Cooper awaiting me. Our meeting was cordial. While we were talking, his secretary brought in a report of the gangplank interview, and I gathered that he didn't like it. I learned later that his objection to it was that it sounded too much like Roy Howard's "I'd do it again" assertion after his premature announcement of the World War I armistice. I told Cooper that I could regard the McLean statement only as a complete repudiation of me and that if it represented the attitude of the Associated Press, I did not see how I could take any course but submit my resignation. He seemed alarmed at this and strongly urged me to take no hasty action. "You have worked very hard and haven't had a vacation in years," he said. "You have one due you. I suggest that you take it, and we'll see how we can work this thing out. Time is a great healer, you know, and we don't know what the situation may be a month or two from now."

I spent that evening with two assistant general managers of the Associated Press, Alan Gould and Claude Jagger. I told them that I did not believe I had any future in the Associated Press after the McLean statement and was preparing to make plans accordingly. Taking Cooper's cue, they seemed alarmed and counseled me against taking any action of any kind— their prescription was to lie low and hope the thing would blow over.

The Associated Press had amassed hundreds of editorials and thousands of letters on the case—such a volume that I could not hope to read it all. I was amazed by the tremendous interest in the affair, by the intensity and extent of the debate which had raged over it. The letters came from every state and many foreign countries. Some were addressed to the AP, some to individual newspapers which had passed them on, and some to me personally. Despite the accusations of Army Public Relations, the distorted dispatches of the griped correspondents, and McLean's repudiation, the editorials and letters were overwhelmingly favorable to me—I would say in the proportion of about 80–20. I was told that the War Department had made its own survey of comment in the case, which had, to its distress, shown about the same result. The comment was as extreme on one side as on the other. The favorable letters lavished extravagant praise on me, proposed medals and monuments and in some cases included money gifts, which I returned. The attacking letters included the crudest abuse, profanity, and obscenity and compared me to Judas Iscariot and Benedict Arnold.

In New York, the *Times* and *Herald-Tribune* had published editorials condemning my action, and a number of other large papers throughout the country had taken a similarly dim view of it. The *Times,* which had made the fullest use of my story, carrying it under a boxcar byline in two columns on the right-hand side of the front page, in twelve-point type, reading out of a four-line streamer head across the page, was the most severe, branding my sending of the news as a "grave disservice to the newspaper profession." The United Press and International News Service had dropped all pretense of impartial reporting in the case, and the Scripps-Howard papers, owned by the same interests as the UP, had denounced the AP.

Some rather incontinent boasting on the part of AP officials in New York had added to the anger of newspapers and news services whose correspondents had missed the story. The AP had touted my story as a "news beat acclaimed by editors throughout the United States as one of the greatest in newspaper history." An analysis of the editorial attacks showed that almost all of them could be traced, directly or indirectly, to the correspondents who were beaten on the story. The service messages they had sent their home organizations on "the biggest double-cross in history" went far beyond what they had written in their dispatches about me. This was their only way out in explaining why they had been beaten on the biggest news story in history.

As a matter of record, practically every other big story of the war which officials had attempted to bottle up for reasons other than military security was broken before the official release time. The Russians insisted on a seventy-two-hour delay after the end of the Tehran Conference before the announcement of it, then released the news in the Soviet press before the expiration of that time. At the Cairo Conference,[1] the control of correspondents was so rigid that they complained they were treated like cattle. A Reuters correspondent who stopped off for a day in Cairo en route from China to England by air broke the news of the conference when he reached Lisbon. He was technically in the clear, since there was no censorship in Portugal and he was not subject to the commitments imposed on the correspondents in Cairo, though he had obtained his information from other Reuters correspondents there who were bound by the commitments. Throughout the war, the British Broadcasting Corporation, a branch of the British government, repeatedly disclosed news "prematurely," while correspondents in the field were prevented from sending it, allegedly on security grounds. With the liberation of Paris, a group of correspondents, including James F. McGlincy of the United Press, made uncensored broadcasts on a Paris station taken over by Resistance forces. As the Germans knew that Paris had fallen, these broadcasts obviously did no harm, but they constituted a serious violation of censorship rules, since they disclosed a military position before it had been announced by the Army. The correspondents were suspended for a month.

* * *

I took a short vacation. On my return to New York, my first step was to investigate the circumstances under which McLean had issued his repudiation of me. Under the AP set-up, Cooper, as executive director, was the operating head. McLean, as president, was merely the presiding officer of the Board of Directors, charged with policy and not with operations. His action in issuing the statement was, as far as I know, the only instance in

---

1. The Cairo Conference, November 22–26, 1943, addressed Allied war strategy toward Japan. It was attended by U.S. President Franklin D. Roosevelt, British Prime Minister Winston Churchill, and Generalissimo Chiang Kai-shek of China. The Soviet Union's Joseph Stalin refused to attend on the grounds that Chiang Kai-shek's presence would cause tensions between the Soviet Union and Japan, who had signed a five-year neutrality agreement. Stalin did, however, attend the Tehran Conference, from November 28 to December 1, 1943, along with Roosevelt and Churchill, to design the final Allied strategy against Germany.

which a president of the AP had acted in an operational matter. I learned that after the War Department had been bombarded with protests over SHAEF's ill-considered and intemperate action in suspending operations of the AP throughout the European Theater—and had advised SHAEF to end the suspension—the business of dealing with the AP was placed in the hands of Arthur W. Page, vice president of the American Telegraph and Telephone Company, then acting as a special advisor to Secretary of War Henry L. Stimson on public relations. Page engaged in a series of telephone conversations with McLean.

There was still widespread criticism throughout the country over the holding up of the news, and the War Department was not too happy about the affair and preferred to see it ended as soon as possible. Page told McLean that in reinstating the AP in the European Theater the Army had shown that it was not fighting the AP, and suggested that it would be a good thing for the AP to make a similarly conciliatory move toward the Army. He said he was sure that the AP did not favor the violation of news releases, and he suggested a statement to that effect. Such a statement would, of course, put the onus on me. McLean replied that since he had not heard my side of the story, he was disinclined to take any action which would abandon me to whatever penalties the Army might care to impose on me. He pointed out that the sanctions might be grave for a violation of security, possibly even a death sentence. "Oh, you needn't worry about that," Page replied. "We're not going to do anything very serious to Kennedy."

Whereupon McLean, admittedly not knowing all the facts in the case, was neatly taken in by Page and issued his statement in which the AP washed its hands of my action on the say-so of the Army that I had violated a confidence. McLean, before acting, conferred by telephone with at least some members of the Board of Directors, especially Arthur H. Sulzberger of the *New York Times,* who was being prodded to "get" me by his Paris correspondents. I know that Col. Robert R. McCormick and some other directors were on my side. As far as I know, no formal vote of the board was taken. Once McLean had issued the statement, neither the board nor Cooper could very well have taken any different stand without repudiating McLean. Cooper, nevertheless, was playing safe. In case sentiment veered too sharply in my direction, he was still "reserving judgment." I called on both Page and McLean, and they confirmed the details of the telephone conversations.

Robert McLean and his brother inherited the *Philadelphia Bulletin.* It is one of the most profitable newspapers in the country, and like its publisher, it exudes a prim respectability and a high integrity of mercantile flavor. Outside of its own territory it has practically no influence; it is little short of a marvel how a newspaper of such size and wealth can be so devoid of national journalistic standing. McLean received me in his office in a friendly—almost fatherly—manner. He assured me that he had not intended his statement to be a repudiation of me or a reflection on my honor. He said it merely represented his disapproval of an action of mine, his disagreement with my judgment in a single instance. He said that I had acted improperly in sending the story and urged me to purge myself by admitting my wrong. If I would do that, he said, he could see no reason why I should not continue to work for the Associated Press. Or if I would like a job on the *Bulletin,* that was possible. But only if I purged myself.

He admitted that he had been under some criticism for his statement from people who were on my side. But all the "more thoughtful people" believed he had done right, he added quickly. It was plain that the criticism nettled him. If I "purged myself," his own position in the matter would be unassailable—my admission of "guilt" would end any support I might have. I told him that I was convinced that I had done right and did not intend to confess to a "guilt" in which I did not honestly believe. He discussed world affairs at some length and impressed me as a man who got most of his ideas out of the *Reader's Digest.* Our chat ended with his reading to me a passage from a moral tract. But I went away unreformed.

McLean, certain of his rectitude in the affair, apparently had no realization that in his pronouncement he had placed the Associated Press on record as adopting one of the very Nazi ideas which the war had been fought to destroy. He expressed regret for the distribution of news before it had been "authorized." To me, news is a report of something of importance that has happened, not a report "authorized" by officials. In my view, the precise difference between the Associated Press and the Nazi press was that the AP published news and the Nazi press published "authorized news." But that difference ended with the McLean statement—if it is to be taken at its face value.

* * *

I had two or three more conferences with Kent Cooper in succeeding weeks. I offered my resignation; he refused to accept it. I suggested that unless he was prepared to support me he ought to fire me, but he hurriedly said no, he wasn't going to do anything like that. At one point he suggested, like McLean, that I purge myself. At length he relayed to me a job offer from Joe Patterson, publisher of the *New York Daily News,* who wanted me for his Washington bureau, presumably to be an understudy to John O'Donnell. Cooper suggested that I take that job or one of the other jobs which had been offered me. His plan was for me to leave the AP, not because of the storm which followed the V-E Day story but to take a better job elsewhere. "And I'll be just as generous with you as I possibly can," he said with a knowing glance. I told him that if I resigned from the AP, I would give the real reason for my resignation and not a phony reason and that I wasn't interested in a payoff to go quietly.

Three magazines made me handsome offers for my "inside story" of the V-E Day scoop. One of them was Hearst's *Cosmopolitan.* Although Hearst's International News Service regarded me as a monster unfit to be at large, Hearst's *Cosmopolitan* wasn't letting that stand in the way of what it considered a good article. Cooper and his satellites seemed deathly afraid that I might succumb to one of the offers. Their one big solution of the case was the soft pedal. I realized that Cooper himself was on the spot. The newspaper world was watching closely to see how my case would end. *Time* and *Newsweek* were harassing poor Jagger weekly to find out what would be done. Some newspapers had threatened to quit the AP unless I was fired, others had threatened to quit *if* I was fired. None would have quit, of course; their threats were just a form of expression.

I did not desire to embarrass Cooper or the Associated Press. I had worked there for thirteen years and always had been treated fairly. I had been entrusted with positions of responsibility. Within the AP there is a loyalty of a strange type; I shall discuss it later in this book. Much as I disapproved of the attitude of the AP toward my case, I had no intention of doing anything which would add to Cooper's difficulties. I naturally disliked his suggestion that the promise of gold was necessary to keep me that way. I appraised the situation as follows: from Cooper's point of view, I was a hot potato. The sensible thing to do with a hot potato is to drop it, preferably when nobody is looking. Too many people were looking just now, so he wanted time. A really nice potato, mindful of past favors and anticipating possible future rewards, would lie lightly until the dropping time, not burning his hands too much.

Some of my friends told me that I was a fool. "Whether you like it or not, you are typed for the rest of your life," they said. "You are the smash-through-it-all type of newspaperman—Get the story at no matter what cost, but get the story, wrap it up, and deliver it to the public. That's what people expect of you. If you don't take advantage of the publicity and the excitement now, you'll be sorry later. You'll end up on the rim of some copydesk. You have to take the rub from those you beat on the story, you have to take all the disadvantages of your position; you're a fool if you don't capitalize on its possibilities."

In this tone came a job offer from an agency specializing in "packaged" radio shows. "We can get you a sponsor at the very start for a Sunday night broadcast," the head of the firm told me in the agency's plush Fifth Avenue headquarters. "Our idea is for you to go on *late* Sunday night—say about 10 o'clock—after Drew Pearson and Walter Winchell. It will be a program for adults. We would suggest that you build up your own system of tipsters. We'll supply you with $400 a week for that. You ought to have some red-hot exclusive stories. But besides that, we suggest that you criticize all the other commentators. They've been getting away with murder. Whenever they go wrong on a prediction, expose them. That would give you an audience right away. Everybody has a favorite commentator, and they would never know when his name was coming up in your program. You're just the man for it because you're a reporter that other reporters don't like and you don't like them. You get the idea? It's a natural. We expect you to out-Winchell Winchell. If we don't get at least 100 letters a week demanding that you be taken off the air, we'll consider you a flop." Then a glossy-haired assistant chirped: "You don't know what a future there is in radio for an unethical newspaperman."

* * *

I turned down all the job offers and all the magazine article and book propositions. On August 18, 1945, I submitted my resignation to the Associated Press in writing. In the politest of terms, I wrote that I had done what I regarded as right in sending the surrender story and that since McLean had expressed another view, I desired to quit. Even this was too hot. Jagger thrust the letter back into my hands and told me to take another vacation. I still have the letter. I lost interest in the AP from that day on. I considered myself out of the organization for good and went about living my own life. I had just turned forty, and I had always heard that that is a good time for introspection. I lived quietly at the Hotel Bedford and read many of the books I had always wanted to read but had never got around to. I was fortunate in knowing a lot of people connected with the theater; I went to about thirty premieres on passes. I had spent practically nothing during the war and had about five years of salary accumulated, so I had no worries over money. I did a couple of special jobs which paid well, but I was determined to take no newspaper job as long as any question of my professional integrity was at issue.

Although I had told Cooper that I did not want money for not working, my AP paychecks arrived regularly. Then, on October 20 the sum of $4,986.80 was deposited in my bank account by the AP, and my paychecks stopped. Presumably this was the amount of severance pay due me on being dismissed under the AP's contract with the Newspaper Guild. I was not a member of the Guild, as it did not function in the foreign service, but the contract covered all employees. I never could get a word of explanation from the AP about the mysterious deposit. I never was informed that I was fired. My status, if I want to be fatuous about it, is that of an employee who submitted his resignation, had it refused, and is awaiting further instructions. A good lawyer has advised me to wait twenty years and then sue for all back pay. Inquiries from outside sources as to my status with the AP were referred to me. I had nothing to say, since I didn't officially know, and I took the view that it was up to the AP to say whether or not I was still working there. I left the $4,986.80 untouched in the account for more than a year as I tried unsuccessfully to find out from the AP what it was for. Then I decided it was probably mine, so I switched it to a savings bank to get some interest on it.

* * *

Meanwhile, I had set out on my own account to obtain a fair hearing on what had actually happened on May 7. I never lost confidence that if I could get that, only one result was possible: complete vindication. I knew that SHAEF itself had broken the release by authorizing the Germans to announce the surrender. But proving this was another matter. The only way I could do so was by getting the Army to admit that it was true. That entailed difficulties.

Major General Floyd L. Parks had succeeded Alexander Day Surles as the head of Army Public Relations in Washington, and it was reported that there was going to be a new deal: the Army was going to play squarer with the public on information. I wrote to Parks, pointing out that the British, who had been occupying Flensburg at the time and were in control of the radio station there, had said that the decision to permit the Doenitz government to announce the surrender was not made by the field commander but came from higher authority—presumably SHAEF. I asked him for specific information as to just how the announcement was authorized and by whom. He conceded that the question was a legitimate one and that I was entitled to an answer. He agreed to try to get the information for me. He followed up with statement with a letter saying that "I suspect that it will take some time in view of the fact that it involves the British authorities. It is quite probable that the matter will have to be referred to Europe." (As a matter of fact, the information was available in the Pentagon, where Parks had his office.) I heard nothing further from him.

Representative Albert Gore of Tennessee, who had become interested in my case, requested the same information of the War Department. His first letter was not answered. On a second request, he received a letter from Brigadier General Joseph F. Battley, Parks' deputy, conceding that the Flensburg announcement had been made prior to the publication of the AP story and adding: "I have been unable to find any indication that Allied military authorities authorized the broadcast. Although it is the impression here that the broadcast was made without the consent of the Allies, I have queried the theater for further information on this point. It may be quite difficult, if not impossible, to obtain accurate information from German military authorities." Gore likewise heard nothing further.

Thomas Vail Motter, who was retained by the War Department as an official historian and entitled to access practically all records of historical interest, agreed to inquire into the matter for me. The most he could get from higher authorities was a memorandum which read: "1. The area was under British control. 2. Americans exercised no control over the radio there. 3. General SHAEF policy permitted freedom of action to the German staff officers there. 4. From the above it can be inferred a) that the Germans broadcast on their own responsibility, but b) within the limits imposed by whatever local British authority there was. In other words, on the basis of information now available, the question of precise responsibility for that particular broadcast is still unsolved." That memorandum was nonsensical. One does not grant "freedom of action" to an enemy who has just surrendered unconditionally—at least that was not the policy at the close of World War II. I don't know how much of the taxpayers' money War Department Public Relations spent in its efforts not to answer my question, but a good deal of time must have been devoted to thinking up reasons why the information couldn't be obtained.

A friend of war days, J. R. "Tex" McCrary, who had headed Air Force Public Relations in Italy and was now editor of the *American Mercury,* offered to see what he could do. The Air Force posed the question to Bedell Smith and got from him a memorandum that SHAEF had not only authorized but *ordered* the Flensburg announcement. "Ludwig Schwerin von Krosigk did officially announce the unconditional surrender of Germany in a broadcast to the German people and to the world from Flensburg," Smith said in his memorandum. "I believe that this announcement was made on 7 May. The so-called Doenitz Government had not at this time been taken into custody and this announcement was made pursuant to orders from Supreme Headquarters that the German troops were to be informed by every possible means of the surrender and directed to cease resistance." That was all I needed. My case at last was complete.

* * *

Several members of Congress familiar with the high-handed methods sometimes employed by the Army had expressed an interest in my case. Shortly after my arrival home, Senator Styles Bridges of New Hampshire had sent word to me that if I believed that I had not received a square deal, he was willing to take the matter up in the Senate Military Affairs Committee. In deference to the AP's desire to soft-pedal the case, I declined his offer. In the meantime, I had come to know Senator Sheridan

Downey of California, who said he considered me justified in sending the story. After I obtained the Smith memorandum, Downey agreed to reopen the matter of my disaccreditation. He offered me either a formal hearing before the Military Affairs Committee or to take the case up informally with Eisenhower. I said that if the result could be obtained informally, I saw no reason for taking up the committee's time.

Eisenhower agreed to review the case personally. When Downey submitted documents showing that my action followed the release of the news by his own command through the Germans, he said he had not been aware of all the facts in the case. He restored my credentials as a war correspondent, ordering the Public Relations Division to "remove any bar that may prohibit Mr. Kennedy from working with the War Department and the Army in the future in following his profession as a writer." He added his personal wishes of success to me. His order did not rescind SHAEF's action in disaccrediting me. Although he reversed the effect of the original revocation, he held it "fully justified." In his curious stand, I had to admire one thing—he was backing up his subordinates in SHAEF; he did not formally repudiate their action. On this score, General Allen triumphed over me, for McLean had apparently harbored no such notions of loyalty. If Allen's famous communiqué on the reasons for my disaccreditation were to be taken seriously, Eisenhower's action meant that he conceded Allen's point that I had imperiled both lives and the peace of the world but was nevertheless willing to have me with the Army in the next war. Once again, Eisenhower had demonstrated his basic decency and sense of justice; also his inability to escape from the stereotype of Army thinking or the straitjacket of a West Point education. These traits have always marked the man; they always will.

I was not interested in quibbling over the vagaries and compromises of the military mind. Senator Downey asked me if I was satisfied or wanted the matter carried further. I told him that I thought that the restoration of my credentials spoke for itself. That, together with the documents on which Eisenhower's action was based, would be satisfactory. On July 22, 1946, more than fourteen months after SHAEF's action, Downey arose in the Senate and announced Eisenhower's restoration of my credentials. He also put into the record the documents which I had obtained in a year of digging—proof that SHAEF itself had ordered the release of the news through the Germans and that after this release I had informed SHAEF censorship that since the news had been officially released, I intended to send it. These documents were complete refutation of the charge of breach of confidence which had been made against me and constituted a full vindication.

There was a stir in the press gallery as Senator Downey brought my name up and a hurried consultation with New York over Associated Press wires as to how the story should be handled. After a brief delay, the AP carried the text of Downey's remarks but no amplification or background. The vindication story was fairly widely published but probably did not receive one-tenth the publicity accorded my disaccreditation. This was natural; the story had grown cold. It is only fair to say that the *New York Times* and *Herald-Tribune* devoted almost a column to it, and almost every paper that had attacked me in 1945 at least printed the fact of the restoration.

Army Public Relations begrudgingly put into effect Eisenhower's restoration order, emphasizing that it did not reverse SHAEF's original action—the Army was still right, as always. General Parks attempted to induce Senator Downey merely to place in the record Eisenhower's letter and not the documents on which the restoration was based and which were so damning to the statements made by General Allen in Paris. Downey presented the whole case. I wrote to Parks asking that the restoration of credentials be extended also to Gudebrod but did not get the courtesy of a reply. This was a logical but purely perfunctory request; Gudebrod had acted only in carrying out my instructions and had never been under any personal attack. The AP had continued to permit him to work for them but had done nothing to clear his name.

The story naturally brought queries to the AP as to what my status there was. Cooper decided to follow the head-in-sand policy which he had pursued from the start. Finally, the *Des Moines Register* and *Tribune*, which had been partial to me, demanded sharply whether or not I still worked for the AP. As member papers, they certainly had the right to such information, but the AP was silent—it had clamped a censorship of its own upon itself. I was in New York that night, and the harassed editor in charge of the desk pleaded with me by telephone to issue a statement which would satisfy the Des Moines papers and spare the AP from answering this query. I told him that since I hadn't been officially informed by the AP about my status, I couldn't answer the question. I felt sorry for the editor personally, and if I showed insufficient sympathy for his predicament, I hope he has forgiven me.

My vindication was evidence, of course, that if the AP had supported me instead of allowing itself to be panicked into a cowardly retreat, it would have come through with flying colors. Had McLean not turned tail, an honest examination of the facts could have been obtained at once; vindication would not have been a matter of fourteen months, but of a few weeks at most. Instead, the AP now found itself in an embarrassing position and was making itself all the more ridiculous by still refusing to face the facts. The case offered a new evidence that any compromise of principle for expediency may have had long-range effects.

I felt much better after the development in Washington; I was ready to take a job again. The year which followed V-E Day had broken into my career like a great cross-current, but far from being an unhappy year, it was one of the most satisfactory of my life. I was buoyed, of course, by the conviction that I had done right and by confidence in the eventual outcome. Had I yielded to the pressure of McLean and Cooper to plead guilty and beg forgiveness as the most expedient course, I know that I could never have forgiven myself. In the voluminous commentaries on my case a great deal has been written, especially by those favorable to me, to the effect that the V-E Day scoop brought only grief to me. This view is due partly, perhaps, to the fact that I did not seize such opportunities as I had to capitalize on the publicity at the time. I regret to destroy a myth that I came to a bad end as a result of the story, but the fact is that the whole affair, while altering the course of my life, did not bring me one minute of grief. I was disappointed, of course, that the AP did not support me, but I had previously seen enough of the ways of the world—and of the AP— not to be too shaken. I tried not to become embittered or imagine myself a martyr. I think I succeeded.

Chapter 12

WESTWARD HO!

ONCE THE RECORD HAD BEEN CLEARED, I WAS READY TO TAKE A new job. I found two opportunities to return to Europe, various offers of posts on newspapers in this country, and a chance to be a Hollywood press agent. I decided to remain in this country; after an absence of ten years it was a new and fascinating land to me. It has often been said that newspapermen spending long periods abroad readjust themselves to living and working at home only with difficulty. I had no great trouble, although for months I was startled from time to time on hearing English spoken by civilians in the streets.

The biggest news of the period which I spent in New York was President Truman's announcement of the atom bomb. Like everyone else, I was a little terrified on reading the story. I turned to a friend and said, "What do you think about it?" He replied, quite seriously, "It looks like a second term for Truman. No opponent can stand up against a man who's got one of those things." For a day or two I thought so frightening a development might scare mankind into a different way of life. Then I noticed that although everyone was proclaiming that the A-bomb and its possible consequences demanded an entirely new outlook, each one was clinging to his old outlook—and offering the situation brought about by the invention of the bomb as a new reason in support of his stand. It was the same old human race, A-bomb or no A-bomb.

As I sorted over the job possibilities, the one which appealed most to me was a chance to become managing editor of the *News-Press* in Santa Barbara, California. I had never seen the West, and I was curious about it. I have not been disappointed. On first sight Santa Barbara, nestled in mountains rising from a sparkling blue sea, reminded me of some of the more beautiful Mediterranean towns I had seen. Even more so did Monterey, where I eventually went to become assistant editor and publisher of the *Monterey Peninsula Herald*. Both cities had something in addition to their beauty: they were friendly communities of my own people with rich cultural lives and spirited, influential, liberal newspapers.

There was another reason which impelled me toward a small-city editorship rather than back into the field or reporting world affairs: I was uneasy and perplexed over the course of postwar events. There seemed no standards to judge them by. During the war, I had tried to convince myself that World War I had failed to produce a satisfactory peace because it never really ended, that World War II was its conclusion and that this time things would be different. But with the passing of scarcely a few years, as world time goes, since the end of the carnage of World War II, victors are suspicious and quarreling, apparently divided by a chasm as unbridgeable as that which divided the nations in World Wars I and II. I have no prescription to cure the world's tension and the people's sense of frustration. But I can assuage my own by throwing all my efforts into trying to put out the best and most honest newspaper I can.

I don't think there is much that an individual can do about the appalling uncertainties of the future of the human race except to pursue his own work conscientiously and give unflinching support to the conceptions of freedom and the dignity of man, which spell the difference between life that is worth living and abject slavery. I believe that such conceptions represent the most important of all human progress and am confident that their appeal to almost all men is so great that they are ultimately bound to prevail. But should a third world conflict come in our generation, as many persons fear, I am convinced that our best defense lies in the jealous preservation of our liberties over all other considerations, for it has usually been the judgment of history that when free peoples and slave peoples come to grips, it is the free men who triumph.

Epilogue
JULIA KENNEDY COCHRAN

I DON'T KNOW MUCH ABOUT HOW MY PARENTS FIRST MET, BUT Ernest Hemingway had something to do with it.

My mother, Lyn Crost, was working as a reporter for the AP in Washington when the United States entered World War II. She begged for an assignment as a war correspondent but was turned down. Among her Capitol Hill assignments were the offices of West Coast congressmen, and Hawaii's delegate to Congress was Joseph R. Farrington, publisher of the *Honolulu Star-Bulletin.* Farrington agreed to send her to Europe for his newspaper to cover the 100th Battalion/442nd Regimental Combat Team, which was made up of Japanese Americans from Hawaii and the West Coast.

Before she shipped over to Europe to start her assignment, she stopped in New York to obtain her press credentials and uniforms. War correspondents were required to have a shoulder patch with a large *C* sewn on their jackets. The Army was out of the patches but told my mother she could find them at the Abercrombie and Fitch store in midtown Manhattan. She went to the store and asked a clerk whether they had the patches in stock. "No," he said, "but you can probably get some from that gentleman standing over there." He pointed to a tall man in front of another counter. My mother walked over and introduced herself to the man, whom she immediately recognized as Hemingway.

"I'm looking for some war correspondent patches, and the clerk over there told me you might be able to help me," she explained.

"I think I can," he replied. He reached into his pocket, drew out a large wad of the patches, and peeled off a few for her. Hemingway had them, of course, because he was also a war correspondent at that time.

During 1944 and 1945 my mother accompanied the Nisei[1] troops and reported on their heroic fighting at Monte Cassino and Anzio, as well as in southern France, the Rhineland, and the Vosges Mountains of France. In early 1945 she landed in Paris for a few days. She stayed at the Hotel Scribe, a few blocks from the Place de la Concorde and the Champs Élysées. The Scribe was where most American correspondents were billeted and where the AP and other news organizations had their offices. One evening she spied Hemingway and another man chatting at the Scribe's bar. "They were dead drunk," she recalled, "and could hardly stand up." She asked someone the identity of Hemingway's companion and was told it was Ed Kennedy, head of the AP's Paris bureau. My parents never spoke to me of their first meeting, but it must have been in Paris at that time, because my mother did a few assignments for the AP while she was there. I imagine my father, as the busy chief of the AP's overloaded and understaffed Paris bureau, was relieved when an extra reporter turned up, if only for a short time. They did not meet again until after the war, when they had both returned to New York. They married in 1946, during the period when he was trying to exonerate himself.

After clearing his shattered professional reputation, my father began looking for a permanent job. In 1947 he and my mother moved to California, where he spent two years as managing editor of the *Santa Barbara News-Press*. In 1949 he accepted an offer to become associate editor and publisher of the *Monterey Peninsula Herald* (now called the *Monterey County Herald*). At that time the *Herald* was a fourteen-page daily that sold for seven cents a copy. It was so parochial that locals often bought the San Francisco papers in order to get any real national or international news. Monterey itself was a sleepy fishing town whose economy depended largely on the sardine industry. While the charms of Carmel-by-the-Sea were becoming recognized by tourists, the settlement of Pacific Grove, founded in 1875 as a Methodist summer-camp retreat, was still best known for its numerous churches. Although the famous Pebble Beach Golf Links were built in the first decade of the twentieth century, Pebble Beach itself was relatively undeveloped. It would be several years before the Monterey Peninsula's main industry became tourism and it

1. Japanese-language term for children of Japanese immigrants to the United States.

gained fame for such annual events as the Monterey Jazz Festival, Raceway Laguna Seca, the Carmel Bach Festival, the Monterey Wine Festival, and the many world-class golf and equestrian competitions that take place in Pebble Beach.

The *Herald*'s owner, Colonel Allen Griffin, was a white-haired patrician with a posh Pebble Beach estate who preferred to concentrate on business matters and leave management of the staff and editorial writing to someone else. When my father accepted the job, he vowed to drive out the San Francisco papers and make the *Herald* an award-winning publication. With his extensive background in world affairs and politics, my father wrote knowledgeably and lucidly about topics of the times in his daily front-page editorials: the Cold War, nuclear-weapons testing, the beginning of the U.S. space program, the McCarthy anti-Communist hearings, and civil rights, signing each editorial "E.K." He attended city council meetings, wrote about protecting the area's watershed and wildlife, became heavily involved in efforts to push through a new freeway (Highway 1's rerouting around Monterey), and followed local and regional political races. He got to know every important person on the peninsula and a lot more who were not important. He initiated poetry and essay contests for kids and showed up to meet people of all types at local events. He was an unabashed booster of events such as the Monterey County Fair and the California State Rodeo. The latter, which took place in Salinas every year, was, he wrote, "one of the finest displays of Western horsemanship in the world." As "E.K." he became the face of the newspaper to his readers.

Within a few years of his taking over at the *Herald,* hardly anyone bought the San Francisco papers anymore. Under my father the *Herald* became a quality publication. During the period he worked on the paper, from 1949 to 1963, it won thirteen awards from the California Newspaper Publishers Association. These included first places for best front page, best special edition, best typography, best editorial page, and general excellence. A photo of the 1950 CPNA prize winners shows my father lined up with fourteen other California newspaper executives, each clutching a tall brass award statue. He is the only one holding two of them, for best front page and best special edition. In 1960 he wrote an editorial that included a proud announcement: a Chicago auditing firm had surveyed twenty-five papers of comparable size and found that the *Herald* was number one in value for the amount of money spent on newsgathering. The paper, it said, provided the best available columns, comics, and wire services, augmented by a dedicated staff that covered the news of six municipalities.

* * *

After my parents divorced about 1951, I lived for a time with my mother in Los Angeles, where she worked for *Time* magazine. In 1953 she accepted an offer to work for President Eisenhower in the White House, and we moved to Washington, D.C. My parents agreed that I would spend the school year with my mother on the East Coast and the summer with my father in Monterey.

After picking me up from summer camp in midafternoon, my father often took me to the *Herald,* where I waited while he finished work. Like many newspaper offices, my father's had a glass door through which he could look out into the open newsroom at the writers working away on their assignments. With the jacket of his tweed suit slung over the back of his creaky brown leather chair, he talked on the phone or did paperwork at a large, glass-topped wooden desk, his thick glasses sometimes sliding down his nose. A huge ceramic ashtray overflowed with butts of the unfiltered Camels he chain-smoked. His trusty old Underwood typewriter sat on a small portable table behind the desk, its keys tinged brownish from his nicotine-stained fingers.

The walls were hung with photos of him accepting awards for the newspaper from the California Newspaper Publishers Association. There was also an old cartoon of him from a Bucharest newspaper during World War II. "Ziaristi strain in capitala," it read, which translates as "Foreign journalist in the capital." The cartoon showed him as unsmiling with thick wavy black hair, large round eyes, and eyebrows raised in an expression of skepticism, perhaps a reflection of how he felt about what he had learned while in Rumania. Behind his desk was the framed front page of the *New York Times* with his bylined V-E Day story.

I spent many hours in the little conference room next to his office, doodling and drawing pictures of horses (my passion at the time) while I waited for him. The room had a large library table with several chairs. I always sat in a chair facing a glass door through which I could watch him.

His office door into the newsroom was always open, and through it flowed a stream of reporters and editors carrying galley sheets for his approval or posing questions about how to handle some news event. He would look up from his typewriter, where he was writing his latest editorial, and bestow his opinion on them. Often, laughter would erupt as he entertained them with his wonderful sense of humor. I had the feeling that while his colleagues respected and perhaps feared him a little, they also felt real affection for him.

Sometimes he would stride into the newsroom to check the Associated Press or United Press International wire-service machines as they clacked away, delivering the latest national and international news. He would tear off a section of the paper spewing out of one of them and carry it back to his office. Maybe he needed the story for an editorial he planned to write, or if it concerned regional news, he would assign a reporter to give it a local slant. These were the same machines that had delivered his stories to thousands of newspapers all over the United States during the war. He must have chuckled when he read stories by his former AP colleagues, such as Pulitzer Prize winners Hal Boyle and Relman Morin. Perhaps he also pondered whether he might still be working for the AP had not the story of the German surrender changed his career.

* * *

In 1956 President Eisenhower vacationed on the Monterey Peninsula, golfing at the fabled links of Pebble Beach. My father was one of five reporters chosen to accompany him as he attended church on Sunday. He must have had a sense of déjà vu as he followed Eisenhower, the general—and now president—whom he had known well during the war. It was Eisenhower who had angrily stripped him of his press credentials over the German surrender fiasco and later restored them when my father exonerated himself. He never expressed to me what he felt that day, but he wrote glowingly about the visit.

As the entourage left the Cypress Point Club in Pebble Beach, "there were little knots of people along the Del Monte Forest road between there and the Carmel Hill Gate," he wrote. "A few golfers were so intent on their game that they didn't look as the President was driven by. But most of them did. I saw one man stop in the middle of a stroke to look at the President."

People lined up along Highway 1 to wave, and some 3,000 were waiting for the president outside of the Carmel Mission. Later, another 3,000 gathered in front of the Carmel Presbyterian Church, where Eisenhower and his wife attended a service.

"Perhaps 15,000 people in all saw him and we may be sure that all of them will remember it for the rest of their lives," he wrote. "We may be sure that long after most of us are gone, some of the small children who were thrilled to have the President wave to them will be telling their grandchildren about the great day. And indeed it was a great day for the Monterey Peninsula."

Three years later, in 1959, Eisenhower invited my father to accompany him on a trip to Pakistan and Afghanistan. Reporting from Kabul, my father wrote that Afghanistan was "a country that has gone almost directly from the camel to the jet airplane. Not that Afghanistan has given up camels. A caravan of seven of them, with two calves walking beside their burdened moms, was slowly moving across the terrain only a mile away as Ike's big plane, which travels at least 200 times as fast, descended at the airport."

I know my father was thrilled to be invited to accompany the president on his trip. Was Eisenhower's inclusion of my father in his entourage meant to show forgiveness for the past? I imagined them encountering one another and shaking hands. Locking eyes, each of them must have had some inexpressible thoughts, perhaps even emotions, tied to their meetings in years past.

Was my father bitter about the outcome of his fateful decision to defy the Army censors in 1945? He probably was, although he could not have expected a young child like me to understand the story, so he never spoke of it. But I knew there was something in his past that bothered him. Sometimes he sat at the kitchen table late at night and drank heavily, muttering softly to himself words that I could not catch.

* * *

Although we always went to see the July 4 fireworks over Monterey Bay, the most important summer holiday for my father was July 14, Bastille

Day. He always took me to the annual Bastille Day celebration put on by the large community of French expatriates who lived on the Monterey Peninsula. It usually took place at Ring's, a restaurant with a large patio where pink bougainvillea cascaded down the stucco walls and ceramic tubs overflowed with summer flowers. The patio was transformed into a replica of a Parisian sidewalk café. The buffet table groaned with Gallic cuisine: patés, cheeses, ratatouilles, sweetbreads, French bread, wine, and delectable petits fours. An accordionist played "La Marseillaise" and other French songs, and everyone sang along and danced. My father and his many friends spoke French all evening. He had learned the language, of course, during the years he spent in France before and during World War II.

* * *

In 1997 Kurt Hartmann, a writer for the *Herald,* wrote about a special experience he had with my father in 1960, when Hartmann was the editor of a small weekly newspaper in Seaside:

> The year was 1960, and on the phone in my darkroom I heard a gravelly voice: "This is Ed Kennedy at the Herald."
>
> Edward Kennedy, associate editor and publisher of the *Monterey Peninsula Herald,* as it then was called, and I had known each other ever since I had become publisher, editor, and linotype operator of the weekly paper in Seaside. Under my stewardship it was the area's lone liberal voice and Kennedy, almost 20 years my senior, seldom missed a chance to twit me about what he saw as my idealistic views. But it always was with a wry smile, and I knew he meant it in good humor.
>
> I liked Ed, all the more because he was a lonely man—divorced, with a little daughter far away, whom he missed.
>
> During World War II he was at the apex of his profession as Associated Press bureau chief at Supreme Headquarters Allied Expeditionary Forces (SHAEF), Gen. Eisenhower's command post.
>
> The very idea that, on occasion, I found myself in the company of a man who had attended news conferences with Eisenhower, Roosevelt, and Churchill was no minor boost to a small-town editor.
>
> On one of these I got him to talk about the most memorable event of

his career—when he achieved the scoop of the war and simultaneously plummeted into disgrace.

Hartmann then recounted the story of the German surrender and my father's disaccreditation by SHAEF for violating the embargo.

The AP story unleashed a violent controversy within the news corps, and Kennedy quickly became a pariah among his peers, among them Walter Cronkite, then his counterpart at United Press International.

"Yes, Mr. Kennedy," I responded. "How are you?"

Small talk was not Kennedy's way, and he immediately came to the point.

"Your liberal presidential candidate (John F. Kennedy) is going to be in San Francisco on Friday, first to appear before some fat cat Democrats at the St. Francis Hotel, and then he'll speak to a rally at the Cow Palace. I'm going up to cover it. Would you like to come?"

Would I!

En route to San Francisco several days later, Ed tried to persuade me that Nixon was a knowledgeable candidate and that Kennedy was callow and untested—a man who became his party's nominee through the machinations and money of his father.

At the St. Francis we made our way to the ballroom, already beginning to fill, where we were told that John Kennedy's speech would precede the banquet and that the press corps would be served dinner, albeit in a screened-off section at the rear of the hall. We took seats at one of the two long tables facing each other, and soon became aware of the august company surrounding us.

There they were—the media titans of that era: James Reston of the *New York Times*, Marquis Childs of the *St. Louis Post-Dispatch*, Edward P. Morgan, a radio network commentator, Carl Levin of the *New York Herald-Tribune*—and Walter Cronkite, now of CBS News.

I could only guess what Ed felt as he found himself amidst his former colleagues, some of whom had disavowed him after the Reims episode. But such imaginings vanished as a roar suddenly rose from the main section of the ballroom.

As one, scribes and broadcasters rushed from behind our screen to see men in tuxedos and their bejeweled ladies in formal gowns climb onto tables, whistle, rhythmically clap their hands and stomp their well-shod feet—all in tumultuous greeting to the appealingly youthful man making his way through the room.

A hand extended over and over to his well-wishers, John F. Kennedy slowly drew nearer the platform erected against the wall.

Batteries of klieg lights suddenly engulfed the large room, cameras whirred, flashbulbs exploded, and a nearby orchestra burst into "Happy Days Are Here Again."

Waves of applause and cheers rolled through the ballroom, the women, many still atop their tables, responding as though in the presence of a film star. Nor was the news corps immune. Seasoned journalists had stopped scribbling—they seemed as enthralled as the party faithful. Out of the corner of my eye I noted that even Ed Kennedy was not unaffected.

The charismatic young candidate began his speech—promising a "New Frontier," "Let's Get America Moving Again"—a preview of the cadence and Boston accent which were to become so familiar.

And then the words were finished. Once again the thunder of applause, the quick-time sounds of the band, hands reaching out to touch the new idol, as John F. Kennedy took his leave.

The well-heeled diners began to address their plates and glasses, and the fourth estate retreated to its confinement, there to face charred filet mignon on paper plates and domestic champagne in Styrofoam cups.

Ed and I were finishing our meal when a tall, distinguished looking man, perhaps in his early 50s, approached, shook Kennedy's hand, and greeted him: "Hello Ed. It's been a long time." It was Edward P. Morgan, the ABC network commentator and a wartime colleague. They exchanged awkward pleasantries; Ed introduced me, and shortly Morgan returned to his table.

Several minutes later Marquis Childs, debonair, elegant, stopped by. The words were different, but the undertone of embarrassment was there again.

Neither Kennedy's face nor his throaty voice betrayed emotion as several others exchanged greetings with him. But no smile graced his mouth.

I excused myself, re-entered the dining room, and shot the remaining film in my ancient Nikon.

When I returned I spotted Ed in quiet conversation with another man, about his own age. As they talked the man's arm lightly embraced Ed's shoulder, and when they parted, his hand affectionately patted Ed's back. It was James Reston.

On our way out we passed Walter Cronkite. Kennedy hesitated and said, "Hello, Walter." Removing his pipe from his lips and speaking in little more than a whisper, Cronkite responded with "Hello Ed, good to see you." He remained seated. There was no handshake and no more passed between them.

Speeding through the night, barely a word was spoken in the car, though at one point Ed predicted that it would be a close election. "Kennedy," he said. "You have to admit he has charm."

And then, as he left my car near his Monterey apartment, Ed turned to me and said: "Scotty Reston is the best newspaperman I've ever known. Not only that, he's also a gentleman."

Three years later in Dallas, on Friday, Nov. 22, 1963, President Kennedy was felled by an assassin's bullet.

A week later, on Nov. 29, 1963, Edward Kennedy in Monterey was dead as well, struck by a car as he was walking home.

All three networks that evening reported his passing. Both NBC and ABC mentioned the Reims incident but the overall tenor was one of respect for a departed colleague. Only Cronkite, in his clipped voice, still sounded unforgiving in reporting Ed Kennedy's death.

* * *

The summer of 1963, I had just turned sixteen. My father, who always had a bad cigarette cough from chain smoking, was trying to stop. It was futile. He bummed cigarettes off everyone he could. There were a few times during that summer when he felt too ill to get out of bed. I began to worry about his health and begged him to see a doctor. A few days later, he told me he had visited a doctor and that he was fine. He resumed his two-packs-a-day habit.

In November 1963, just a few days after President John F. Kennedy's assassination, my father was walking home from work on a rainy night. It was dark and windy as he stepped off the curb to cross the street. A sports car swerved around the corner and hit him. Although he was expected to recover from his injuries, he died a few days later. The coroner's reporter listed the cause of death as cancer of the throat complicated by the injuries he sustained in the accident. It turned out that he had not seen a doctor in more than five years.

My father's obituary was carried by hundreds of newspapers across the United States. The *Herald* reported receiving calls from some people in tears as they expressed their sorrow; many local residents sent letters of condolence to the paper. Among the expressions of sympathy from outside the Monterey area was a telegram from Richard M. Nixon (at that time the former vice president) calling my father "one of the finest newsmen in the nation" and noting that "his passing is a great loss to the paper and community he served so well."

My mother and I flew out to California for the funeral. I was so stunned by his death that I was almost catatonic. I adored my father and had always longed to live with him year round in Monterey, which was the most beautiful place I could imagine. As I looked at his waxen face in the coffin, it seemed as if I were in a nightmare. San Carlos Church was packed with my father's many friends and business colleagues. Monsignor John J. Ryan delivered a long eulogy and ended it with a tribute: "He gave the world twenty-four more hours of happiness."

* * *

In his final editorial, published while he lay in the hospital, my father expressed his lifelong dedication to journalism and the newspaper business:

> One of the problems of publishing a newspaper is that you have to sell something that is dead.
>
> It was once alive, standing high in leafy splendor in the woods, swaying, breathing and sighing. But it has not only been cut down; it is floated down rivers, soaked in water, ground up, treated with chemicals, made into a pulp, and put through rollers until it comes out as paper, shipped to San Francisco, trucked to Monterey and then run through a press.
>
> Not even the smallest bug on the bark, nor the smallest termite inside the tree, can stay alive through all this ordeal.
>
> We can sell these pieces of dead trees only by creating the illusion that they are alive. This we attempt to do, with varying success, by headlines that grip the eye and written material that clutches the heart and soul of man.